COTTON

Textiles that Changed the World

Series Editors
Linda Welters, University of Rhode Island
Ruth Barnes, Yale University Art Gallery

ISSN: 1477-6294

Textiles have had a profound impact on the world in a multitude of ways – from the global economy to the practical and aesthetic properties that subtly shape our everyday lives. This exciting new series chronicles the cultural life of individual textiles through sustained, book-length examinations. Pioneering in approach, the series will focus on historical, social and cultural issues and the myriad ways in which textiles ramify meaning. Each book will be devoted to an individual textile or to the dye, such as indigo or madder, that characterizes a particular type of cloth. Books will be handsomely illustrated with color as well as black-and-white photographs.

Titles published in this series

Tartan
Jonathan Faiers

Felt
Willow G. Mullins

COTTON

BEVERLY LEMIRE

BERG

oxford + new york

English edition
First published in 2011 by

Berg

Editorial offices:
First Floor, Angel Court, 81 St Clements Street, Oxford OX4 1AW, UK
175 Fifth Avenue, New York, NY 10010, USA

Berg is the imprint of Oxford International Publishers Ltd.

Library of Congress Cataloging-in-Publication Data

Lemire, Beverly, 1950-
    Cotton / Beverly Lemire.
        p. cm. — (Textiles that changed the world)
    Includes bibliographical references and index.
    ISBN 978-1-84520-300-9 (pbk.) — ISBN 978-1-84520-299-6 (cloth) 1. Cotton
textile industry—History. 2. Cotton trade—History. 3. Cotton—History. I. Title.
    HD9870.5.L46 2011
    338.1'7351—dc22

                                                                    2010053259

British Library Cataloguing-in-Publication Data

A catalogue record for this book is available from the British Library.

ISBN 978 1 84520 299 6 (Cloth)
        978 1 84520 300 9 (Paper)

Typeset by JS Typesetting Ltd, Porthcawl, Mid Glamorgan.
Printed in the UK by the MPG Books Group

www.bergpublishers.com

CONTENTS

ACKNOWLEDGEMENTS

The volume is a distillation of past research and more recent investigations. I can remember the occasion many years ago when I first saw an eighteenth-century Indian palampore, a painted cotton hanging, likely intended for a bedroom wall or as drapery for a poster bed. It featured a tree of life with an amazingly sinuous botanic design and still glorious colours. At that time I was working to decipher the economic and social dynamics of the Indian trade to Europe and this artefact encouraged me to combine material with documentary sources wherever possible. I returned to this topic in a very different context as a participant in the Global Economic History Network project on cotton. I am grateful for the opportunity to consult and collaborate with the colleagues involved in that venture. First, I thank Patrick O'Brien, who headed the enterprise and pulled me into this circle. I also thank Giorgio Riello who, at that time, was the research officer of the project and with whom I shared many conversations. His exceptional organizational capacities helped ensure the success of the venture. I profited immeasurably from repeated discussions with him and other participants in this global project and I thank them for their generosity: Prasannan Parthasarathi, Kaoru Sugihara, Tirthankar Roy, Harriet Zurndorfer, Suraiya Faroqhi, Colleen Kriger, Om Prakash, Bozhong Li, Robert DuPlessis, Huw Bowen, Olivier Raveux, Ian Wendt and George Souza. I have enjoyed recurring conversations in and out of the global project and benefitted from the insights of Maxine Berg, Laurence Fontaine, Negley Harte, Pat Hudson, Adrienne Hood, Peter McNeil, Lynne Milgram, Lesley Miller, Arlene Oak, Ruth Phillips, Osamu Saito, Yoshitaka Suzuki and Karen Tranberg Hansen. My debts are many and my thanks are sincere. The opportunity to discuss historical topics is invaluable in the development of ideas. I am greatly indebted to these and many other colleagues.

Many years ago Adrienne Hood, then senior curator at the Royal Ontario Museum, Toronto, gave me the opportunity to develop skills in object analysis. I am thankful for that original experience and for the subsequent years of discussion and debate on historical issues related to material culture and to this project. In recent years I have accumulated many other debts to museum curators who have been unfailingly generous with their time and their knowledge. The opportunity to study artefacts in conjunction with documentary research provides valuable insights unattainable through other means. Lesley Miller, Rosemary Crill, Clare Brown and Susan North at the Victoria and Albert Museum have been repeatedly generous in every respect and opened a treasure trove of artefacts to my scrutiny, as well as sharing ideas and listening to hypotheses with great patience. Ruth Barnes shared the exceptional Newberry Collection at the Ashmolean Museum, Oxford and I am grateful both for the opportunity to see these relics and to discuss their significance. Ebeltje Hartkamp-Jonxis and Bianca Du Mortier from the Rijksmuseum graciously provided me with opportunities to see some of their singular collections, for which I am grateful. Berit Elkvik of the Nordiska Museet and Merit Laine of the Royal Court Museum, Stockholm were both very generous with time and attention. Ana Cabrera at the Museo Nacional de Artes Decorativas, Madrid and Maria Dolores Vila shared their rich knowledge of the Iberian world with me. I thank them for their generosity. The insights they provided were invaluable, as were those of Teresa Pacheco Pereira, Museu Nacional de Arte Antiga, Lisbon and Isabel Mendonça, Escola Superior de Artes Decorativas, Lisbon. Jacqueline Jacqué of the Archives du Musée de l'Impression sur Etoffes, Mulhouse, was generous with her time and knowledge of the critical subject of textile printing. Pam Parmal, Museum of Fine Arts, Boston and Dilys Blum, Philadelphia Museum of Art, were wonderful guides to their exceptional textile collections, as was Linda Eaton at the Frances Du Pont Winterthur Museum. Alexandra Palmer was similarly kind in providing access to the Royal Ontario Museum Collection and Ryan Paveza, of the Art Institute of Chicago, was instrumental in organizing my visit to their collection. Vlada Blinova is a continuing support in my work with the Clothing and Textile Collection, Department of Human Ecology, University of Alberta. My thanks to Vlada and to Julia Petrov, former acting curator and to Anne Lambert, now retired curator of this collection, and to Anne Bissonette, curator of the Human Ecology Collection. Along with Marijke Kerkhoven, my colleagues in Human Ecology offer unfailing encouragement and access to this marvellous resource.

During my research for this project I travelled to various locations. My research assistant, Filip Ani, made a trip to Spain and Portugal more profitable and I thank him. Elysia Donald, Deanna Bullock and Margaret Luzono also assisted with this project and I thank them also, as did Nadine Lewycky and Matthew Neufeld. Eiluned Edwards provided a fascinating account of contemporary textile practice in India and as a result of her contacts, my colleagues and I had a rich introduction to the textile regions of western India. Mohmed Husain Khatri was an invaluable guide to the sites surrounding Bhuj, Gujarat, India and in this same region Ismail Mohammed Khatri revealed the exceptional skills required to perpetuate traditional wood-block printing. Both men illustrated the living and evolving textile traditions of their region. The staff at Maiwa Handprints, Vancouver, were likewise helpful, providing access to their library and collections. They work to maintain the viability of handcrafted textiles, particularly in India, and bring full circle the commercial connections that began this voyage.

Over the course of years spent working on this project, I have presented sections of this research at conferences and symposia in different parts of the world and benefitted from the comments of audiences and colleagues in attendance. Some of the ideas represented in this volume have been published in different versions in two edited volumes arising from the Global Economic History Network cotton project: Giorgio Riello and Tirthankar Roy (eds), *How India Clothed the World:*

The World of South Asian Textiles, 1500–1850 (2009) and Prasannan Parthasarathi and Giorgio Riello (eds), *The Spinning World: A Global History of Cotton Textiles, 1300–1850* (2009). Themes addressed in Chapters 2 and 5 have also been published in Japanese and Italian in the journals *Shakai-Keizaishigaku* (2006) and *Quaderni storici* (2006), and elements of Chapter 5 in *As Artes Decorativas e a Expansão Portuguesa: Imaginário e Viagem* (2010).

The Social Sciences and Humanities Research Council of Canada provided funding for some initial research. The Pasold Research Fund generously assisted with funds in support of the cost of images for this publication, for which I am grateful. In addition, I receive the ongoing support of the University of Alberta through the research chair that I hold. I am very conscious of the value of the time and resources that come with this appointment. Research is a continuing series of challenges and extended explorations. I benefit from the ongoing conversation with colleagues who contribute to the wider context of discovery. Likewise, I rely on Morris Lemire and on Shannon Lemire, who keep me moving forward.

Beverly Lemire

1.

INTRODUCTION

There are almost as many histories of the cotton trade as there are nations and, within these nations, narratives are further subdivided.[1] Communities hold this heritage dear, despite the frequent trials embedded in these pasts. The stories that survive are often the lifeblood of regions – the tales of grandparents and great aunts, and the focus of local museums.[2] The American states of North Carolina and Rhode Island are two cases in point – cotton represents exceptional periods in both their histories. From the slave labour of transplanted Africans on cotton plantations, to share cropping after the Civil War, cotton was a cruel master for many Southerners of African American heritage, even as this crop funded wealth for the building of great plantations and commercial infrastructure. The advent of cotton mills in North Carolina followed in the nineteenth century after English and then New England forerunners, and these mills employed many thousands through much of the twentieth century, with a new way of life for once-rural people. Cotton seemed a permanent feature of this state, entwined with the local culture and economy in distinct ways. Yet this tradition was not proof against the migration of manufacturing to other regions of the world in the later twentieth and twenty-first centuries. For Rhode Island, the connection with cotton took an industrial form from the outset.[3] Rhode Island's mills predated those of North Carolina by generations – indeed, the state boasts the first American water-powered machinery for carding and spinning cotton, opened in the 1790s by an English immigrant. The Rhode Island mill inaugurated an industry that flourished throughout New England, pulling in young female labour from the surrounding countryside, later drawing French Canadian migrant families with the hope of a better life.

There are common threads to the narratives in many former cotton districts. In Lancashire, the site of the world's first Industrial Revolution, there is pride in past achievements, as well as a sometimes palpable sense of a lost golden age after textile manufacturing moved offshore. Over several centuries, the cycle of economic development brought cotton, an alien fibre, to northern latitudes where it became the driving force in global change. More recently, the industrial strength of Asia has pulled production back to some of the original sites of cotton manufacture.

Long before factories were conceived, long before cotton T-shirts, dresses or jeans became the stuff of daily wear in the West, India was the largest producer of cotton cloth in the world. Indian artisans created the finest diaphanous muslins or the heaviest blue dungaree. Indian cottons were also renowned for their designs – brilliantly coloured and patterned, dyed and printed to the tastes of innumerable communities. These cloths were known and valued across much of the world from ancient times, from the South China Sea to the Mediterranean. For the Indian subcontinent, cotton represents a heritage unique among the world's nations, a heritage revived and celebrated in many regions and renewed in the contemporary production of hand-printed cottons, sold worldwide.[4] Theirs was the model of trade and production that inspired imitation in Persia, Egypt, Turkey, central Asia and Indonesia and, finally, the West. Many regions aspired to match the breadth and quality of Indian-produced fabrics, but the skills underlying these textiles remained unsurpassed for millennia, in terms of their mastery of the fibre and proficiency in spinning, weaving, dyeing and printing. Likewise, the commercial acumen of India's merchants moved the products across much of the globe. The cotton plant that proved so successful in cloth production was selected through trial and error from the various natural stocks extant on the subcontinent. The colourfast washable dyes that distinguished their fabrics came from the natural wealth of flora and mineral resources in the Gujarat, Coromandel and Bengal regions, their dexterous use honed over generations.

Chapter 2 begins with an examination of the long process of development of the Indian cotton trade and its significance in the ecumene. I explore the intersecting skills required to build this industry and the context of its growth and dominance as a global commodity before 1500. The breadth and dynamism of this trade was in place long before the arrival of Europeans in the Indian Ocean commercial circuits. Only by giving full weight to this Asian tradition of industry and commerce can we comprehend the later transformations that arose in other parts of the world, as the reverberations from this commodity moved from one region to another. This perspective necessarily readjusts the narrative of Western development in important ways, acknowledging the centrality of Indian products to later Western growth. Material evidence forms an integral part of this study. The assessment of surviving Indian fabrics from the twelfth, thirteenth and fourteenth centuries provides invaluable insights into the nature of the Indian cotton trade and its cross-cultural appeal. This chapter next considers the long process whereby Indian goods diffused through the early modern Western world following the arrival of Europeans in the Indian Ocean about 1500. One of the first responses to Indian goods in Europe can be traced in European needlework, as women interpreted Indian designs through their needles from the sixteenth century onwards. Their material translation was a key facet in the acceptance and domestication of these commodities into new venues. Women have left few written accounts of their response to these new material forms, but the renditions portrayed through their needles offer telling evidence of early globalization and reactions to this phenomenon. These features of exchange provide the foundation for the chapters to follow.

Fashion figures prominently in this volume. The role of Asian commodities in the genesis of a fashion system in Europe has been too generally ignored and is only now getting the attention deserved.[5] Chapter 3 explores the sociopolitical tensions around dress in early modern Europe, looking most particularly at the British example. I dissect the rationale behind sumptuary legislation that attempted to regulate the clothing of ordinary people, a practice that accelerated from 1500 as European economies grew, not least because of the growing trade with Asia. The forces of tradition and innovation collided repeatedly in this era, most particularly around the question of clothing. Wool cloth held a unique place in the British pantheon of goods, politically and socially. Wool was the material and cultural antithesis of Indian cotton and, thus, to understand the explosive political response to cottons we must consider its opposite. It is obvious that men and women wore clothes differently, evident in the cut of the garments and also the social politics of dress; the political climate in which men and women wore calico exemplifies this fact. Elite men wore Indian calicoes as banyans or informal robes, a mark of their intellectual affiliations with travel, scientific collection and mercantile advances. They also wore these robes in semi-private situations. Women wore calicoes in public and as such were the objects of violent retribution campaigns spanning decades. The advent of popular fashion and its articulation in women's calico gowns was a deeply contentious project with profound political and economic repercussions. This chapter uncovers the dramatic politics of fashion surrounding the gendered wearing of calico, events that rent British society. The anti-calico campaign was recorded on the bodies of women, targeted for their fashion transgressions. The eventual political acceptance of cotton textiles signified major transformations, including a broad acceptance of plebeian fashions as a driver of the economy.

The European textile environment was founded on wool and linen and those systems of production were critical to the later grafting of cotton to this industrial base. In Chapter 4, I investigate the gendered structures of manufacturing in both city guilds and rural putting-out systems. The latter was of particular importance. Both relied on a mass of female labour spinning thread in the quantities and qualities required by weavers. I take a long-run perspective on this subject, which better allows an assessment of regional developments across Europe, ultimately leading to the genesis of the cotton industry in Britain. The linen/cotton trade took root in north-west England in the seventeenth century, positioned to prosper as the geopolitics of cotton changed over the next century. Indian cottons were largely banned from British markets in the 1720s, as in most parts of Europe. Lancashire manufacturers were well aware that they could thrive by supplying facsimiles of Indian textiles, as close as possible to the originals. That became the goal of British manufacturers in Lancashire and Scotland; they began as specialists in linen textiles, evolved to produce a range of fustian[6] cloths and ultimately triumphed by creating all-cotton fabrics in a vast array of styles, from warm velvets to fine muslins. The technological leaps that ensued during the 1700s altered the foundations of British society and then reshaped the wider world. Equally important were the implications for the regions supplying raw cotton, as cotton plantations expanded in parallel with industrial production. Plantation slavery grew dramatically in nineteenth-century America to feed the insatiable appetite for raw cotton in Europe and America, illustrating the wide-ranging effects of industrial innovation. Mills, factories and plantations represent the institutional features of the first industrial age.

Indian textile products included much more than plain or printed bolts of cloth – cotton quilts were among the most significant cultural commodities to arrive at early modern European ports. Quilts are a subject of extensive popular interest in the present day. They are typically described in a Western context, as a Western craft idiom, having decorated homes and warmed beds for centuries.

The assumption is often made that these were a European invention and that their popularity flowed from European initiatives, later transported into colonial regions of the world. Quilting was known in the medieval West and employed in items such as the jackets worn under armour; some date the appearance of quilts in twelfth-century Europe to contacts by Crusaders with the more dynamic material environment of the eastern Mediterranean, the terminus of well-developed trade routes with Asia. Rare examples of fourteenth-century European silk quilts in museum collections illustrate the value assigned these singular commodities.[7] The later evolution of Western quilt culture is part of a broad global dynamic, beginning with the export of Indian quilts to Europe in the 1500s. Chapter 5 reveals the evolution and spread of quilt culture from India to Europe and beyond, from the 1500s to the twentieth century. Object study is critical to this investigation. The first generations of Indian quilts offer extraordinary evidence of cross-cultural exchange – embroidered treatises on the early years of Portuguese imperial adventures, with the figurative patterns presenting masculine celebrations of empire. India, once again, provided the template for a popular bedding that added new comfort and new cultural forms to ordinary lives. The gender and class focus of quilts shifted over the eighteenth century. And, with the industrialization of cotton production, quilts received an added boost, becoming a staple female craft across a vast range of communities. Ordinary people had more textiles to work with and could recycle and reuse in different ways, and the patchwork quilt is emblematic of these profound societal changes. This chapter traces the variable gender practices of quilting in Europe and America, creative systems animated by industrialization and mass migration in the nineteenth and early twentieth centuries.

Chapter 6 is a meditation on jeans. In this brief concluding chapter, I ask readers to consider the wider implications of the commonest, coarsest industrial fabric. In previous chapters I charted the great changes that arose with the adoption and adaptation of cotton textiles in the West, leading to exceptional industrial innovations that swept out from north-west Europe across the Atlantic world. The modern age has likewise been defined by the cultural meanings of jeans. This chapter assesses the various political connotations ascribed to hard-wearing fustian fabrics, from the radical English politics of the mid-1800s to the elaboration of jeans culture throughout nineteenth- and twentieth-century North America, Argentina and Europe. The ubiquity of jeans exemplifies the industrial age of cotton, with vast production and large-scale distribution, as well as the modern age of communication and advertising. Jeans are distinct in their democratic provenance and chameleon-like in their cultural capacities. Jeans are culturally tied to the American West, but for all that they reflect a demotic sensibility that is not constrained by the whims of advertisers or manufacturers. In my reflections on twentieth-century jeans, I consider the gendered meanings of fashion, anti-fashion and sufficiency as illustrated by this garment. The world was remade when cotton textiles spread west from India after 1500. Fashion and industrialization are exemplified in the heritage of denim jeans.

Throughout this volume I carry readers to times and places that encompass millennia and span the globe. The focus on fabrics requires careful study of surviving artefacts and wherever possible, I use museum resources to illuminate my analysis as well as illustrate these pages. This history of the cotton trade does not follow a well-worn path in all things, and this is an incomplete story. The impact of cotton extends well beyond the geographic boundaries I explore. Brazil, Russia and Japan, for example, are just three of the nations touched by the economic forces considered in this book. But they do not figure in this volume; constraints of space dictated this choice, rather than the value of their histories. One of the intentions of this book is to inspire readers to think again about the commonest cloth, to prompt questions that may be answered in part by this work, or which may require a wider search among the wealth of new research on this and related subjects. Indian cottons were one of the first global consumer commodities serving more than half the world long before Europeans arrived off the Indian coast in 1498. I call Indian cotton a catalyst commodity, whose very presence in a society inaugurated innovations. The industrialization of cotton in the West, centuries after its initial arrival, has employed a small army of historians and economists, all seeking to uncover the factors in this exceptional turn of events. The world was changed as a consequence of multiple sets of global forces, each interacting with the others. The changes, innovations and upheavals traced in this book touched generations, directly and indirectly. White shirt or print tunic, blue jeans or patchwork quilt, the everyday stuff of life that we take for granted depends for its existence on cotton. The history of this fibre has shaped our world.

2.
BOUND UP WITH COTTON
World Markets, Global Trade and Cotton Histories, c.1300–1800

The Indian Ocean teemed with sea-going traffic in the medieval era, linking the Red Sea and Persian Gulf in the west and the Straits of Malacca, Java Sea and South China Sea in the east, as craft of all sorts plied well-travelled routes. Trade by land was more physically challenging, yet here too there were seasonal circuits for great caravans and solitary travellers. Generations of pack animals and peripatetic merchants beat tracks across the face of continents, linking cities and peoples. Global trade before 1500 was complex and vibrant, even if very different in orientation than the era that followed. Most historical attention has fallen on the landmark events that came after the breaching of Europe's maritime boundaries with Columbus's arrival in America and Da Gama's landing in India, both in the 1490s. However a global trading system was in evidence even before those events and it is to this era that I turn first. The trade systems created in this era laid the foundations for global commerce in cotton, shaping the tastes and appetites that would animate this critical commodity in the centuries that followed. Looking at this earlier period demands a grasp of geography, along with a clear understanding of the connections that bound together land-based and water-borne commerce. Systems of trade, with mercantile, military and religious interactions developed over ancient times to the extent that some suggest a nascent commercial 'world system' a millennia prior to 1500.[1] Cycles of growth oscillated in waves from before the first century onwards, the ebbs and flows following a generally upward curve, building on the interactions of empires, kingdoms and regions. Ultimately this produced what has been called the Eurasian and African world system, the connections wrought by trade, religion and conquest crafting an intersecting network along which commodities and ideas flowed (see Figure 2.1). Philippe Beaujard describes the characteristics of this extended process: 'Each period of growth was accompanied by technological innovations in the domains of production, transportation, and

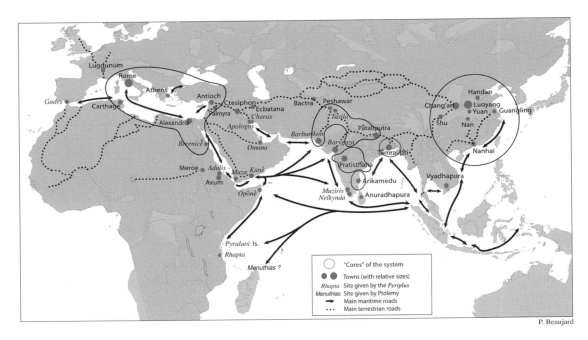

2.1 Map of the Eurasian and African world systems: reflecting economic growth and the connections wrought by trade, religious contacts and political conquest from the first to the third century.

trade, which allowed populations to overcome ecological constraints and human limitations by increasing productivity and transforming production.'[2]

Networks of trade flourished and declined over millennia. The trade in cotton was part of the cycles of commerce. At its medieval apogee this network tied together regions from the East China Sea to Western Europe, commercial and social organisms that together constituted a dynamic world system of trade, anchored by major urban centres. Cities were well established and growing, but most were not yet large even by nineteenth-century standards.[3] Trade drove the growth and expansion of these centres, intensifying the urbanization process; but again the volume of trade cannot be compared to modern or even early modern levels of exchange. Yet this commerce was decisive in societal development, as one region strived to produce what another intensely desired. The importance of commodity trade in this context cannot be overstated, supplying wants that were 'humanly assigned and culturally constructed'.[4] The collective material desires of Eurasian and African communities gradually expanded over centuries and fed all segments of the producer/consumer networks connected through this trade.

Seasoned merchants from this era often knew from personal experience only segments of busy mercantile channels, not surprising given the rigours of travel at this time. Nevertheless, evidence survives of those who travelled far and learned much about the ways to profit from trade. For example, a young Islamic trader, Allān B. Hassūn, journeyed from Cairo through the Red Sea to south-west India in the twelfth century, sending letters back to his family, marking his commercial adventures. After an absence of many months, Allān celebrated the loading of textiles, iron and pepper onboard ship, ready for his homeward journey from the south-west Malabar Coast and eventually to Cairo.[5] Commodities were produced in surprising quantities and circulated along chains where the merchant of origin rarely encountered the final retailer, where contacts were largely indirect and intermediaries were crucial actors. Travel was physically taxing, with few comforts, and routinely required months or years, a timeframe that contemporaries accepted as common and unavoidable. Balducci Pegolotti published a manual in about 1340 describing the preparations necessary for a journey along the Silk Road through central Asia. He estimated the outbound trip at over 270 days; it was a safe and well-travelled route at the time of his writing.[6] Commercial information was hard won. Yet, despite the impediments and great distances between makers and consumers, trade goods flowed across these networks, markets were cultivated and new tastes spread to distant consumers. As Andrew Sherratt observed: 'Materials and ideas moved, sometimes in quantity and often over long distances before what are conventionally thought of as markets or capitalist rationality.'[7]

The romance of the Silk Road, and the glories of Chinese silks and associated artefacts have generated innumerable studies and inspired exhibitions where silk garments and lengths of cloth are displayed as remnants of this extraordinary exchange.[8] At its height in the fourteenth century, this commerce forged routes across the steppes of Asia, linking northern China to the Black Sea, caravans and foot travellers transected the Himalayas, and all the while this commerce nurtured storied cities along its course like Samarkand, Kabul and Leh. It was the lure of silk that in the thirteenth century drew Italian adventurers along routes already peopled by Armenian, Jewish and Muslim merchants and scholars. On arriving in Georgia or Persia, they discovered that silk production had been transplanted there, the wealth-creating capacities of silk adapted for new locales.[9] The scale of the silk trade and the passions it unleashed continue to beguile acolytes, academic and amateur. Indian cottons have inspired a comparatively less celebrated public response and these textiles have perhaps filled fewer display cases in the world's museums. The low survival rate of cottons from the ancient and medieval eras, especially in regions of high humidity, might explain this phenomenon. Likewise, the technological dating of Indian cottons is only in its infancy and there might well be more ancient textiles in some parts of the world than is currently realized.[10] But whether or not historic Indian cottons survive in abundance, cottons from India were a staple of international trade; their circulation through communities from China to the Mediterranean, the Red Sea to central Asia restructured economies and material culture in profound ways. Marco Polo is the best known of the Italian adventurers to head out along the Silk Road. Yet on arriving in Persia, he thought it worth mentioning not only the silk he found but that 'Cotton grows here in abundance'.[11] Cotton was another Asian textile with unique qualities and characteristics unknown in the European textile compendium. Even at this date, Italian traders were aware of its exceptional features and sought out sources of raw and manufactured supplies for Mediterranean markets. The history of cotton textiles as a commodity is ancient, multifaceted and compelling and also culturally variable.

Cotton was grown, processed and woven for apparel in a number of locales throughout the pre-modern world. In pre-Columbian Meso-America and South America, cotton garments were worn by elites and commoners within these societies, serving as armour padding and clothing, while elaborately decorated cotton fabrics were an important facet of tribute systems. The skills of cultivation, fibre processing and production resulted in a variety of cotton textiles which were sometimes elaborately embroidered; these were of great importance to their communities. As Angela Lakwete notes, 'The people of the Amazon River Basin had cultivated G[ossypium] *barbadense* for millennia'.[12] This species of long-staple and large-seed cotton was easy to clean and diffused north to Central America and the Caribbean. Cotton fabrics from this era are associated with Mayan, Peruvian and New Mexican societies, among others.[13] Across the Atlantic, Colleen Kriger has mapped the history and extent of West African cotton textile production extant before the colonial period. Kriger suggests that local cotton was being cultivated from about 1000 CE and fourteenth-century chroniclers reported on the high quality of cottons, usually produced in narrow strips that would be sewn together for later use. Here, too, cotton was grown, processed and woven into cloth for garments, patterned in the loom to produce stripes of various colours. Timbuktu, a vibrant inland hub in western Africa, boasted a healthy trade in these goods and cotton textiles were also evident in numerous coastal centres, usually as the garb of the elites. Overall, cotton strips and fabrics were broadly available throughout this extended region.[14] The cotton plant also found its way to China by 1300 and became widely cultivated in China and other regions of East Asia. But it was India that established world standards of production and whose fabrics diffused through the widest commercial networks. The Indian subcontinent produced the largest array of textiles for customers from Java to Jidda, Canton to Cairo. Thus, the Indian subcontinent has the most powerful claim on our attention. It was the birthplace of this world trade and the place of origin of the commonest species of cotton plant.[15] Their history forms the foundation of the worldwide interactions that followed. Without a clear understanding of the origins and significance of this trade, we would have half a narrative and a lesser half at that.

Few topics have received more attention than the interaction of Asia and Europe, particularly in recent years. The contemporary dynamism of Asia's economy has stimulated some of these reassessments. Another factor has been the critical re-examination of claims for Western exceptionalism that were once ubiquitous in histories of the West and its wider interactions; this rethinking is producing new interpretations of a range of subjects where formerly other paradigms predominated. Global historians are among those academics re-evaluating cross-cultural contacts, rethinking relations and recasting Eurocentric historical narratives that were first formalized by Europeans during the professionalization of the academy in the nineteenth and twentieth centuries. That period coincided with the apex of Western imperial power and scholarly theories mirrored this political environment. The unthinking assumption of a perpetual Western dominance has long passed.[16] Jack Goody observes that: 'The superior achievements of the West can no longer be seen as permanent or even long-standing features of those cultures but as the result of one of the swings of the pendulum that has affected these societies over the millennia'.[17] It is also important to recognize that underneath the history of Western industrialization and modernization was the implicit premise of Asian backwardness as a counterpoint to Western exceptionalism, articulated by theorists from Adam Smith to Friedrich Hegel and Karl Marx, and many of their heirs in the humanities and social sciences. Indeed, Antonia Finnane reminds us, 'Hegel described China and India as lying outside the domain of history, waiting to be initiated into the process of development and change on which Europe had long embarked.'[18] It is not surprising that many older treatments of the Indian cotton trade were framed within the context of advanced, innovative European industrialization, with India cast as a passive understudy before the principal actors arrived on the world stage.[19] The history of Eurasian interaction through the Indian cotton trade is more complex and more interesting than would be supposed from this well-worn account.

In this chapter I will explore the history of Indian cottons as a decisive catalyst commodity in the development of world trade. I begin by refocusing our historical lens to give a fuller picture of the characteristics and significance of this key textile – in this regard material evidence plays a key part. Indian cottons were unique as agents of new consumer tastes, stimulating appetites for goods with diverse qualities, but also standardized forms. The global trade in cotton commodities demands a rethinking of categories and a questioning of causation as the dynamics of this mercantile venture resounded over centuries.

COTTON, COMMUNICATION AND CULTURE BEFORE 1500

Lynda Shaffer describes the advance of cotton production on the Indian subcontinent as a key feature in what she terms 'southernization'. Shaffer explains 'southernization' as a broad sequence of 'interrelated strands of development' proceeding from about the fourth century onwards. This amalgam of social, economic and technological changes came to animate and define the societies of southern Asia, with an influence that flowed from core regions to touch all parts of the world. The original components of development included 'the production and marketing of subtropical or tropical spices; the pioneering of new trade routes; the cultivation, processing, and marketing of southern crops such as sugar and cotton; and the development of various related technologies'.[20] The deft development of environmental resources, linked to mathematical and technological innovations, animated the 'southernization' process, resulting in the production of commodities intensely attractive to a heterogeneous range of societies. Shaffer's analytical framework offers an important foundation for discussion of the Indian cotton trade, for this commodity did not evolve in isolation, but was rather embedded in an environment generating a range of supporting technologies within conditions that enabled its growth.

Cotton's birthplace was the Indus Valley. The Indus River Valley borders the north-west of the Indian subcontinent, flowing for nearly 2,000 miles and emptying into the Arabian Sea. This fertile stretch of land nurtured important cities and civilizations in the ancient world and it was in this area that the earliest cotton cultivation and manufacturing developed sometime between 2300 and 1760 BCE. Advances took place incorporating local species of gossypium (cotton), one of a handful of cotton plants that flourished throughout a geographic band between 47° north and 35° south.[21] Similarly, using the mineral and botanic resources to hand, local artisans devised methods of dyeing and patterning, with evidence of their success apparent by about 1000 BCE. Medical knowledge was another of the technological systems Shaffer includes in her compendium of advances native to the 'southernizing' regions. Many of the components of dyeing also possess medicinal properties and thus it is not surprising to find dyeing as a subject in an early Indian medical treatise. This particular text listed a total of forty-five shades and more than seventy processes to achieve the desired colours. An estimated 300 individual plants afforded the basis for the exceptionally robust dyes devised in India, used in combination with mineral-based mordants and other techniques to fix clear, vibrant, colourfast shades.[22] The Indus region offered a critical proximity to other developing societies with major urban centres, along key trade routes. Products and techniques flowed through the subcontinent and cotton manufacturing took root in many parts of India, with subsequent regional specializations. Evidence of fibre preparation survives in a fifth-century Buddhist painting in the western region of Maharashtra, depicting a woman working a cotton gin, removing seeds from cotton fibres prior to spinning.[23] Trade expanded with the perfection of techniques. Roman-era archaeological findings indicate a routine traffic across the Indian Ocean through the Red Sea prefiguring the route that later residents of the eastern Mediterranean would follow. The monsoon trade winds were mastered about 300 BCE and one of the then new Red Sea ports, Berenike, developed into a major entrepôt and cosmopolitan centre, first in the service of Egyptian kings and then the insatiable Roman market where Indian textiles were noted luxuries[24] (see Figure 2.1). Recent archaeological excavations reveal that staple Indian Ocean commodities passed through this port – goods such as pearls, spices and textiles. The Red Sea route remained one of the key commercial channels to the eastern Mediterranean, its vitality linked to the wider geopolitics of the region. During early centuries of the first millennia, cotton textiles became one of the staples shipped from ports or carried by pack animals through Asia Minor out of the Indian subcontinent.

Skills in agriculture, fibre preparation, spinning and weaving coalesced in the production of many sorts of cotton cloth. Proficiency in all these sectors was critically important. But it was printing on cloth that became a truly exceptional contribution to world material culture. Printing enabled a relatively inexpensive decoration of a plain cloth surface using carved wooden blocks to apply dye components. Patterns could be developed with single or multiple cycles of block printing, producing simple or complex designs, with coarse or subtle forms. Figure 2.2 suggests some of the steps in wood-block printing, as the printer applies the main outline to the cloth. The right-hand portion of the cloth contains additional elements of the final design. Painting on cloth was another inspired procedure that offered an exceptional level of decorative possibilities at much lower cost than the alternatives. These techniques were unmatched elsewhere in the ecumene and were much more flexible and less costly than patterning in the loom or embroidery. Weaving and embroidery were the other standard methods employed to pattern or embellish cloth and both were more time-consuming and expensive than printing or painting. The production of embroidered designs can be subdivided, assigning less complex stitches to less skilled hands, and a striking effect can likewise be produced with relatively plain stitches; in that respect, embroidery could be less costly than woven techniques. But if woven designs move beyond simple twills or stripes, this demands a meticulous dressing of the loom as the warp is tied and an equally close attention to the weaving of the weft – procedures requiring skilled artisans. The resulting fabrics can be beautiful indeed. But the cost is high and the market is limited. Decoration through printing represented a fundamentally demotic process, aesthetically responsive to varying demands and accessible to the widest range of customers. Printing also enabled the production of bordered whole cloth for use as floor coverings, hangings or patterned yard-good for a myriad of dress and furnishing applications. Thus printed cotton was

2.2 Watercolour of wood-block printing, India, *c.*1820. British Library.

a singularly adaptable commodity; the quality of the cloth and variations of printing, painting or combined methods determined the price. Indian artisans were unparalleled practitioners of all these forms, with block printing more commonly employed than the somewhat more costly painted processes. In combination, these two techniques (printing and painting) represented exceptional complementary forms of design application, facilitating an immense variety of visual effects for everyday or special-use textiles. Simultaneously, as the flow of commerce brought cross-cultural contacts, the needs and expectations of various societies were translated into hybrid motifs applied to the surface of the textiles. Indian designs reflect an amalgam of aesthetic elements from Persia, Turkey and south Asia. The production and diffusion of these printed patterns enabled a material conversation across cultures, as artisans in Gujarat, the Coromandel Coast and Bengal revised, devised and invented in accordance with the tastes of their customers.

Cotton was not alone in sustaining a cross-cultural aesthetic exchange. Porcelain and printed cottons were among the most important of the manufactured commodities that flowed from

Asia. Commerce in these items lay at the heart of the Asian-based ocean-going trade system. The decorative platforms represented in these materials were key elements in their success, not least because of the aesthetic versatility characteristic of these products. Robert Finlay describes the multifarious features of porcelain: 'simultaneously functional wares, treasured possessions, and bearers of cultural significance'.[25] Like porcelain, printed cottons circulated through a complex of civilizations, each with different religious, cultural and functional priorities. Cottons, like porcelains, were treasured for their capacity to transmit 'cultural significance'. The makers of porcelains and cottons crafted surface designs suited to distinct markets, the one great difference being that cottons were accepted by Hindu communities while porcelains were not. Indian cottons flowed through all areas of eastern, southern, central and western Asia, as well as along trade routes beginning in East Africa and the eastern Mediterranean. Designs coursed along commercial channels, however distant the markets might be from the sites of production. Thus Islamic elements employing arabesques, variants of Arabic calligraphy and twinning vine and leaf motifs appeared on the surfaces of Indian cottons as well as on the sides of Chinese bowls. Decorative elements circulated across the ecumene, blending visual aspects arising from one community, adapted for another.[26] Moreover, cotton textiles were essentially more egalitarian than porcelains. Many cheap, coarse woven fabrics came from the Gujarat or the Coromandel Coast. And even India's cheapest patterned fabrics served as aesthetic conduits, bringing an exceptional assortment of coloured prints to the poorest of distant buyers. Those with more money to spend could also find the quality and design they desired. As a result, cotton textiles became essential components of religious and social practice, as well as of everyday use and wear. Mattiebelle Gittinger describes the skills of the artisans who sustained this commerce.

> The mastery of the technical aspects of this craft allowed the dyer the freedom to respond to orders for different patterns and designs with assured success. He could meet the demand – in design and, unusually, colour preferences – of virtually any market. Dark maroons, blacks and deep reds – patterned in grids with details worked with 'nervous' white resist lines – went to Thailand. To Southeast Asia went hip wrappers with large saw-toothed borders and fields worked with geometric patterns or small flowers. To Armenia went Christian altar frontals.[27]

These patterns embodied a wealth of cultural meanings and embraced a range of aesthetic styles; the fabrics also added a unique material richness to the lives and cultures they touched, augmenting the ebb and flow of design elements across seas and continents. Trade made manifest the desires of generations and of civilizations, wants both ephemeral and profound.

The significance of this commerce is immense, both in terms of the wealth created as well as the material conversation it fostered across great distances. K. N. Chaudhuri notes that 'long-distance trade subsumes an exchange of information on cultural values and interpretations, social systems, technology, and artistic sensibilities', adding that this trade 'transcends far beyond its immediate economic value and hence by association long-distance trade is instrumental in the creation of a language of signs with an immense range of significance'.[28] Cotton textiles were one of the world's great mediums of communication. Indian printed and painted fabrics facilitated iconographic interactions in a largely unlettered world, where signs and designs resonated with diverse peoples steeped in visual and symbolic literacy, even if formally unschooled. Through the diffusion of these printed patterns – incorporating flora, fauna, geometric and heraldic forms – a multi-faceted discourse enriched the visual and material resources of much of the world. This process is part of what Andrew Sherratt termed 'consumption as communication and performance'.[29] The legions of unlettered shoppers who bought and used these decorative fabrics have not recorded their motivations, yet their appetite is clear, sustaining commercial networks. S. D. Goitein documented the routine traffic linking Cairo to Indian Ocean commercial ports in the twelfth and thirteenth centuries, with examples of Jewish merchants with far-flung ties. A scattering of letters and accounts survive from this period, testimony of routine commercial travails. For example, Goitein uncovered the return to Cairo of Halfon be Nethan'el in 1134, after a lengthy journey from India via Aden; the next year this same merchant was in Spain and Morocco conducting his business affairs.[30] These were not unique or singular voyages; rather they sketch the overlapping networks that carried cargoes from distant origins to neighbouring households.

The interlocking medieval trade networks of about 1300 described by Janet Abu-Lughod, represented an important next stage of development. Along well-travelled sea lanes and over diverse terrains, merchants and sailors, caravan porters and pedlars carried goods, along with information and ideas. The focus of this commerce was not the kingdom or principality prominent in national histories, but the port or metropolis that drew necessities and luxuries from near and far. What has been called 'an archipelago of towns'[31] linked shipping routes and overland trails, which in turn funnelled Asian manufactures along mercantile channels. The hinterlands served by these metropolises showed varying levels of economic development; but the cities stood as nodes of urban dynamism, pulling in labour from the surrounding localities, a base for the development of craft skills. Merchants congregated in these centres, work was relatively plentiful for the labouring classes and those who worked in skilled or semi-skilled crafts found opportunities. These sites anchored trade routes, attracting and dispersing goods from far afield. The collective demand drove international commerce. Indian cotton textiles were more varied in quality than Chinese silks, and typically less costly; cotton textiles came in a range of qualities that included the most gossamer muslins and heavyweight cotton checks, turban cloths and tent hangings, as well as printed or painted cottons of many sorts. In medieval Old Cairo, bales of printed and plain cottons from Gujarat were routinely sold in local bazaars, while in the same period, merchants from the Coromandel Coast of India carried cottons eastward to Indonesian and Chinese markets[32] (Figures 2.3 and 2.4).

Over the centuries, demand for Indian cottons was cultivated among the island communities of what is now Indonesia, where the cloth payment for spices native to those islands cemented the ties between Indian and local merchants. Both profited from the connection. In turn, these islands absorbed Indian printed cottons into the heart of their society, culture and religion. Mattiebelle Gittinger points out the unique relationship forged in this region through the trade in Indian cottons, noting that: 'Nowhere was the effect of these cloths … more profound than in Indonesia.'[33] Ultimately, cotton textiles printed in accordance with locally preferred patterns became the sole commodity accepted in exchange for spices, whoever was negotiating the deal. Within the Indonesian archipelago, the passion for block-printed cottons brought these patterned

2.3 Ceremonial banner, block printed cotton made in Gujarat, western India, for the Indonesian market. Radiocarbon-dated 1340±40 years. Victoria and Albert Museum, London.

goods into the core of social and religious practices.[34] Indian cottons were an essential element in gift exchange in South East Asia and Gittinger has made a particular study of the importance of these textiles and their designs in the island communities. Gittinger writes that:

> The prestige of the textiles was so great that their designs or basic format were adapted in locally made textiles ... Even more telling ... than the imitation of motifs is the sacred aura attached to the textiles themselves. In Java they are esteemed as garb for weddings and the rites marking other transitions in life, and at one time certain motifs were reserved for private use by the royalty of Central Java.[35]

Indian cottons animated the monsoon trading system that fully connected the China Sea with the Red Sea, and the Persian Gulf with the western reaches of the Indian Ocean by the medieval era (Figure 2.5). However, extensive written records of this trade only appear when Europeans arrived and began to chronicle a pattern of exchange of great antiquity, in which both commercial and symbolic practices allied. The new arrivals quickly discerned that the influence of Indian textiles extended over 'the courts of Java to simple mountain villages in the outer islands', affecting 'virtually every major island in the archipelago'.[36] John Guy notes the 'non-utilitarian uses to which Indian textiles were put in Southeast Asian societies ... [where] the sheer volume of the trade ...

2.4 Cotton fragment, block-printed with band of rosettes and flowers. Made in Gujarat, western India between 1250 and 1350. Ashmolean Museum, Oxford.

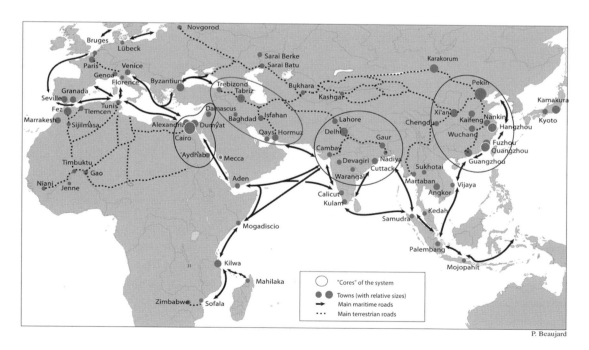

P. Beaujard

2.5 Map of the Eurasian and African world systems: reflecting economic growth and the connections wrought by trade, religious contacts and political conquest in the thirteenth and fourteenth centuries.

far exceeded the needs of the region, given that much of the clothing of the people was provided by inexpensive locally woven goods'.[37] Thus, the peoples of this region, rich in essential spices, did not depend on India for the provision of practical fabrics, having learned to make their own based on the Indian exemplars. Rather, cultural attributes integral to the cotton textiles themselves appealed to rich and poor, male and female. Indeed, Indian cottons were imbued with different meanings by different societies and peoples. Desire, not necessity, directed trade among these South East Asian customers, desire rooted in the cultural contexts of societies where the requirements of self-definition, hierarchical display and ritual gift-giving shaped the acquisition and use of patterned cottons. In whatever context, whether to sustain customary social events or to feed powerful new consumer forces, culture shaped markets.

At the western edge of the Indian trade nexus, the ports of Hormuz to the north of the Arabian Peninsula and Aden in the south were major commercial hubs. The overland route through central Asia also fed these ports and others on the eastern Mediterranean coast. Indeed, Armenian merchants in Persia and the Ottoman regions prospered through their trade in Indian cottons. Armenians cultivated their roles as intermediaries showing 'a preference for the major routes linking India and Persia to the West, either via the commercial ports of the Levant and Asia Minor, or via the Caucasus'.[38] The dynamism of Cairo, as a maritime and overland entrepôt, further connected the Mediterranean, Asia Minor, northern as well as eastern regions of Africa. Cairo was a long-standing destination for more distant Indian Ocean merchandise, a pattern that continued into the medieval period. 'By the second half of the thirteenth century,' writes Janet Abu-Lughod, 'all three [Middle East] routes were functioning – for the first time since Rome had controlled the gateways to the east.'[39] Written medieval accounts are few and scattered; however, important material evidence also endures, unique in its depiction of the wealth of textiles traded and the breadth of markets served. Textiles typically deteriorate with wear and decompose rapidly under the effects of humidity, heat, moulds and insects. Some mordants, like iron, used to fix certain dyes likewise become destructive over the life of the cloth. Ordinary fabrics produced in the greatest quantities are the most vulnerable; heavily worn and reused, they leave too few traces of their social history. However, when they survive they inject life and breath into human endeavours long past. The Newberry Collection at the Ashmolean Museum, Oxford, represents dramatic, visible testimony of the medieval traffic from the manufacturing centres of western India, across the Indian Ocean and through the Red Sea to this city at the mouth of the Nile Delta. The Newberry Collection is composed of approximately 1,200 fragments of cottons, dyed and block-printed, uncovered during excavations outside Fustat (Old Cairo) in about 1900. Cotton scraps from these excavations are held at a number of major museums and have been a focus of study in years past.[40] Figure 2.6 is another example of a printed cotton from Gujarat, uncovered in Fustat. The Ashmolean Museum holds a unique collection rich in number and quality, and rich too in the suggestive evidence of heavy use and visible mending that can be seen on various pieces. These echo the everyday life cycle of common fabrics.[41] Ruth Barnes, past curator at the Ashmolean, undertook a detailed analysis of this disparate assemblage, combining her careful visual assessment with the selective use of carbon dating. Barnes concludes that these cottons span the medieval to early modern era and are 'of outstanding historical importance'.[42] It is rare for such an extensive number of materials of this type

2.6 Cotton fragment, block-printed, made in Gujarat, western India, excavated in Fustat (Old Cairo), fourteenth century. Victoria and Albert Museum, London.

to survive, especially those previously involved in ordinary uses.[43] These cottons clothed the poor as well as wealthier merchants or officials, serving as wraps, headgear, bedding, curtains and cushions. Local Cairo shops and bazaars were renowned for their variety of wares, including substantial stocks of cotton textiles.[44] Flowered or plain-dyed, with patterned stripes or borders, the coarse and medium-quality Indian cottons served practical and aesthetic functions for a cosmopolitan community.[45] Barnes observes that: 'The considerable number of Indian cotton fragments that have survived in Egypt from the medieval Islamic time onwards give us only a relatively small and late glimpse of a much larger, continuous trade network of considerable time depth.'[46]

Cairo absorbed volumes of assorted Indian materials, over countless centuries, for local and regional needs. Following the scourge of the Black Death in the mid-1300s, this city's standing declined.[47] Yet the culture of cotton was ingrained in that society and generations of men and women bought and used these fabrics. They selected on the basis of different costs, in red, blue and cream printed designs, with many varieties of border decorations, flowered or geometric, with motifs consistent with the cultural preferences of a heterogeneous population. The 'banded ornamentation'[48] that was a feature of Islamic design had long since been integrated into Gujarati printed patterns, possibly even before Islam itself had spread to that western region of the subcontinent. Some fragments incorporated large animals, such as elephants, while others were decorated with modest repeat patterns, geometric or floral-inspired. We can only guess at the past histories of these fragments. Perhaps one of the remnants came from a cotton robe like the one worn by a visiting Tunisian merchant; possibly others were part of a trousseau, like the cotton textiles pawned by a woman named Giw in the eleventh century, who juggled family resources during the long absence of her merchant husband.[49] The random survival of these fragments speaks to the vigour of this trade and to the cargoes routinely arriving in this city. Ruth Barnes describes this collection as containing 'the foremost surviving examples of the pre-European Indian fabric'; they include examples that 'catered both for the luxury market and for general distribution and common consumption'.[50] I was privileged to be able to examine a large number of these artefacts. It was a breathtaking experience to look at the remnants laid out end to end on the table in the Ashmolean Museum study room: the vibrancy of the colours was extraordinary. Equally striking was the fact that the collection drawers were filled with still more of the Fustat cottons. The plenitude suggests the sort of voluminous factory-made diversity typical of more recent times. The variety of decoration and qualities of textiles offer tangible evidence of the scale of the Indian enterprise, far more compelling than simple written records. These fragments illustrate the areas of the world draped and covered in cloth from India. The surviving bits of cotton announce the exceptional choices available to shoppers in medieval Cairo (and elsewhere), for home or dress.[51]

Merchants and Indian manufacturers collaborated in the deft selection of patterns suitable for disparate regions. However, distinctive design elements could sometimes suit several communities. Ruth Barnes discovered proof that Indian manufacturers provided customers at great distance from one another with similarly patterned fabrics, leaving the recipients to interpret them as they saw fit. The vendors were evidently sure that similar designs could suit very different cultural contexts. Cottons patterned with a goose motif caught Ruth Barnes's eye. She then carbon dated two of the fabrics held at the Ashmolean of very similar styles – one of these was a small fragment from Fustat and the other was a large, whole piece of printed Indian cotton from an Indonesian site. Carbon dating revealed that both were manufactured around the 1400s, though sold to customers thousands of miles apart. The sacred goose (or *hamsa*) was a popular image in Indian culture and geese were plainly established motifs in other regions as well. In Cairo the fabrics were cut for household use; in Indonesia the cloth was kept whole for ceremonial purposes. Similarly patterned remnants excavated from Fustat are held in the Museum of Textiles, Washington, DC, and the Museum of Fine Arts, Boston; while a large whole cloth of similar design, sent to a market in the Indonesia Archipelago and dated to the thirteenth century, is part of the TAPI collection at the National Museum in Delhi.[52] Plate 1 is another example from this period with a similar motif, from the Victoria and Albert Museum. There can be few more telling illustrations of the scale of the Indian cotton trade and the expanse of the markets than the happenstance survival of these similarly printed cottons dispatched to different corners of the world over five centuries ago. Two were reunited by chance in a collection in Oxford.

European merchants eventually intersected these robust trade routes. As we have seen, Italian traders headed out along the Silk Road during the thirteenth and fourteenth centuries. Merchants from Italy's city states were alive to the possibilities of Eurasian commerce. Venice and Genoa competed fiercely for advantage in the medieval era and beyond, their agents yearning for a bigger slice of the cotton trade in the Mediterranean. Cairo authorities frustrated these ambitions for a time. Cottons were slow to penetrate Europe as a whole, but had well-established markets in the eastern Mediterranean as well as throughout North Africa.[53] Geopolitics ultimately proffered opportunities for these Italian merchants after the fourteenth century, as they manoeuvred to fill the void left by an Egyptian government weakened by the effects of the Black Death. Like many regions, Italy also attempted to copy Indian cottons and manufacturing began in the Italian peninsula in about the thirteenth century. (That subject is discussed in more detail in Chapter 4.) Plain narrow cloths and heavier goods they called 'fustians', named for the city of Fustat, were among the first kinds of cottons attempted in parts of Italy.[54] This was a modest beginning. The full impact of cotton textiles in Europe would come only after 1500. That date marked a milestone as a determined Portuguese fleet arrived on the coast of the subcontinent in 1498. These Europeans encountered a vibrant system of manufacture and exchange flourishing throughout the Indian Ocean. The coming interaction of Asian manufacturers and European markets would change both parts of the world now connected by sea. Lynda Shaffer observes of this event: 'The wealth we now associate with north-western Europe came about only after . . . [the European] seizure of tropical and subtropical territories and their rounding of Africa and participation in Southern Ocean trade.'[55]

CONTACT, CONNECTION AND THE POTENTIAL OF NEW COMMODITIES

Direct sea-borne trade with India was momentous for Europe and various outcomes from this event will be discussed in later sections. In this chapter, I will sketch the broad processes of the transformation. The next phase of this narrative explores several key repercussions of the cotton trade to Europe and the profound effects it wrought. The world was remade as a result of a singular voyage by a great seafaring nation of little wealth or political stature at this juncture. Portugal had sent mariners down the coast of West Africa for decades during the 1400s, looking for the sources of gold that emanated from those lands. Maritime knowledge was accumulated with each voyage and it was eventually clear by the 1490s that the African continent could be circumnavigated. Vasco da Gama captained the Portuguese fleet that set out on this venture in 1497 and he arrived on the coast of India in 1498. Contemporary European writers thereafter marvelled at this good fortune. Even 150 years later, a French author celebrated the fact that, 'After Two Years' Absence [from Lisbon, De Gama] ... brought the Newes himself of his Prosperous Voyage, and laid the Foundation of greater Hopes to Come.'[56] Portugal became renowned in the annals of later Western accounts for this achievement. For many generations, Portugal remained the vital conduit for Asian goods in Europe, maintaining this pre-eminence through the 1500s and early decades of the 1600s. The histories of Dutch and English ventures are more generally known and more celebrated, especially in the English language.[57] But Portuguese vessels arrived first in Indian ports and exerted considerable military and political muscle to carve out a place within the dynamic cross-cultural trading community in that sphere. The combative commerce they introduced to this trade zone was unfamiliar to regional states and kingdoms, with the result that the Portuguese rapidly consolidated a territorial foothold on the west coast of the subcontinent, seizing the port of Goa. Initially, Portuguese trade benefited a small group of elites most immediately tied to the venture, that is, the king and his chosen coterie of merchants. But, within a generation, opportunities were extended more widely, including to the New Christians – members of the Iberian Sephardic Jewish community forcibly converted to Christianity. They possessed extensive global mercantile ties that were already knitted into pre-existing commercial networks and they were well placed to profit. Men from this community quickly developed expertise in moving goods like 'cotton and silken cloth, precious stones, indigo, furnishings, drugs, as well as spices' that flowed from Goa.[58] Some of these items were already well known in Europe, but had been scarce and costly as a result of the tolls and time spent traversing the overland caravan routes from India. The bulk shipments that soon flowed into Lisbon brought greater quantities at somewhat lower prices. Once landed in Lisbon, dealers great and small began searching out markets; they were quickly able to cultivate outlets for Indian manufactures, even among those relatively unfamiliar with the fabric.[59]

Cotton was little known in central, northern and north-western Europe. The plant could not be grown in those climates and few if any cotton textiles had percolated into those regions, although raw cotton had been used to pad some military garments, as an adjunct to other forms of armour. Cotton did not have the value of silk or its association with luxury and, thus, it had not been a coveted marker of status in a way that ensured its diffusion through court circles in Europe. Silk was the subject of innumerable European sumptuary laws from the time it began arriving in quantities in Europe in the thirteenth and fourteenth centuries.[60] Cotton never featured in this legislation. The challenge now facing Portuguese traders was how to integrate cotton into the European textile lexicon. Jan de Vries has considered the process of reception for new consumer goods and he observes that 'New goods must be "recognizable" to the consumer and, hence, combinable with other elements of consumption practices in order to become widely and continually consumed.'[61] Linen was the closest European equivalent to cotton, although that fibre was not as malleable. However, for many functional purposes, cotton textiles were culturally recognizable as 'linen' and it was as a linen substitute that cottons were first sold. The many connections between linen and cotton production are discussed in detail in Chapter 4, along with the development of the cotton industry in Europe. Indian cotton stretched the existing material categories of early modern Europe, particularly with the introduction of printed cloth. But for the moment, Indian cotton textiles slid along existing commercial channels, with the port of Lisbon flourishing as the first Western distribution centre for this exceptional fabric and other Asian wares.

There is scant early history of the reception of this commodity in Europe. It is impossible to calculate the exact quantity of Indian textiles arriving in the first few decades of the sixteenth century as they were carried on designated Portuguese craft predominantly as private trade; but there is no doubt that the early voyagers returned with Indian fabrics. Mention of 'pintado' appears almost immediately in the public record – *pintado* being the Portuguese name given to Indian printed or painted cottons. The attention paid these goods and the esteem accorded them was immediate. In Lisbon, as early as 1508, church vestments and accessories were being made of patterned fabrics from the major Indian ports of Calicut and Cambay.[62] Portuguese merchants shipped cottons initially to locales already familiar with these goods: 'Iberian, West African, and

Mediterranean markets consumed between one-third and one-half of the *carreira* cloth shipments … [while the] American tropics consumed the finer cottons'.[63] Trade, once established, persisted for centuries across the Atlantic and later Spain sent Asian commodities across the Pacific Ocean on Manila galleons, landing in Acapulco – the significance of the Pacific circulation remains to be fully explored.[64] Within Iberia, prominent families began collecting Asian rarities. Likewise, Lisbon-based merchants carried goods to northern Spain, the great market of Antwerp, the coast of France and as far as southern England before 1550. East Indies merchandise also appeared in the myriad small ports that dotted Europe's southern coastline and, though legitimate and legal commerce was a mainstay, smuggling was also an important mechanism that brought new commodities from sellers to buyers.

The historiography of trade with Asia, especially in the English language, has been weighted towards the later seventeenth and eighteenth centuries, following the establishment of the great Dutch and English East India trading companies, both founded about 1600.[65] Thereafter there was a visible upsurge of commerce between north-west Europe and Asia. The teleological assumption was that prior to the launch of the companies, Asian goods were rare or virtually non-existent in northern Europe. With the exception of silk, spices were assumed to be the only familiar items among the Asian goods now landed in Lisbon warehouses. This supposition is patently false. The association of Asia with bottomless riches, the myths and first-person accounts that circulated in mercantile and literary circles cultivated a signal cachet for Asian manufactures of all sorts. Social and commercial elites amassed rarities from Asia, while less affluent folk tried out the new-style manufactures encouraged by their low cost. The sixteenth-century European traffic in Indian cottons represents a first phase in a process whereby these new commodities were absorbed into existing categories, even as they expanded the boundaries of these categories. In this era, Europeans from northern and western communities encountered printed, painted and embroidered cottons and reacted both to the form and qualities of these goods. Over the 1500s, Indian cottons percolated through elite and non-elite European markets, though this growing traffic left fewer traces than the latter formal ventures. While kings and queens, dukes and nobles assembled collections of exquisite luxuries from Asia, including embroidered and painted cottons,[66] more pedestrian textiles were being bought and used in plebeian circles. This was part of the 'recognition' process. These textiles carried new designs to disparate communities as new practical and aesthetic uses were devised for calico or 'pintado': as cassocks or chasubles, cupboard clothes or cushions, shirts or bedcovers. This transition has been too little documented and many elements are still to be discovered.

Pedlars were essential intermediaries, especially for those living outside major ports or large cities. They carried small luxuries and new commodities to neighbourhoods across Europe, items that common people and their wealthier neighbours could afford. Authorities typically disliked these mobile retailers and disliked the new patterns of consumerism they introduced, resulting in denunciations of these itinerant retailers and prosecutions in some precincts. A 1516 Swiss reproof is typical of official complaints. Pedlars were charged with 'hawking their cheap goods, from village to village, from farm to farm and from house to house, up hill and down dale. So much so that no house is safe'.[67] This persistent retailing undoubtedly helped introduce Indian cottons to communities well before 1600. Laurence Fontaine has revealed the extensive pedlar networks that enveloped all regions of Europe, the medieval origins of which arose in the mountain communities of the Alps, Pyrenees and Scottish Highlands. The 'family networks' she describes doubtless apply to the Portuguese enterprise that moved calicoes through parts of Iberia and beyond during the 1500s.[68] For example, the Basque region was visited early and often by Portuguese pedlars selling Indian calicoes. The Basque lands are located at the western end of the Pyrenees, abutting the Bay of Biscay, with easy sea access, as well as proximity to pedlars' trails through the mountains. The successful Portuguese trade in calicoes so alarmed the authorities that hearings were held by Basque officials on several occasions in the 1550s to consider this development. One witness from the town of Renteria confirmed that 'many Portuguese men were going in this Province selling some clothes that they called 'calicús'. By mid-century, local Basque administrators from one district instituted regulations to try to eradicate, or at least limit, the selling of calicoes because of the effect on local linen production. Other Basque officials proposed that Portuguese pedlars come before notaries who would fix the prices of calicoes sold in their region.[69] Despite these concerns, Indian cottons were introduced, accepted and embedded into the material repertoire of Basque men and women far from major urban centres and long before the period normally associated with calicoes in Europe. New fashions are typically connected with great cities where we assume taste leaders of various sorts will initiate stylistic innovations. This example confirms the more complex social politics of fashion, whereby regions with access to commodity flows played a vital part in the iteration of new styles, independent of dictates from metropoles.

The arrival of calico in the Basque country points to the early and steady percolation of Indian cottons through a range of regional markets throughout the sixteenth century – some markets have been identified; others wait to be discovered. Previously overlooked, this commerce laid the groundwork more generally for new wants and needs, transforming European material culture over generations. More evidence will doubtless be found in regional archives about the particular role of Portuguese pedlars. James Boyajian recounts that: 'At least from the 1560s one of the most common of petty merchants in Lisbon was the keeper of a shop selling Indian cloth.'[70] Shopkeepers habitually employed pedlars to extend their market reach. Thus there can be little doubt that calicoes and other cottons joined the stock of goods being carried far afield. Portugal's varied commercial sector played a crucial role in this era, refashioning consumer tastes as they marketed this exceptional product. Housewives and maidservants saw these new fabrics, marvelled at the colours and designs, and celebrated their colourfast, washable qualities. There were no equivalent European textiles. Europeans did not routinely print on fabric. Common textiles had at best a modest decorative component, through stripes or twill patterns woven on the loom. The cheapest fabrics were uniformly drab. Dyeing was an additional costly process and a number of traditional wool cloths, or even some new lighter worsted fabrics, relied on the colours of the fleece for patterning. We can imagine the word of mouth endorsements that spread from house to house and district to district when Indian textiles first appeared. Expenditures on textiles represented one of the principal expenses for labouring families. Inexpensive decorative cottons called for a modest outlay, but provided a profound change in the material environment of Europe. It was not simply the practical features of this commodity that charmed. They were sold at prices that initially undercut most comparable goods.[71] Equally importantly, cottons offered a medium of communication through their surface design of sufficient malleability that they appealed to Europeans as well as Indonesians. These fabrics were an inducement to cultural exchange and cultural change.[72]

The sea route between Lisbon and Antwerp was heavily travelled in the sixteenth century, with vessels skirting the western margins of Europe and then travelling east through the English Channel. Antwerp was the greatest northern entrepôt until the late 1500s and part of the Spanish Hapsburg Empire that, after 1580, included Portugal. Little wonder, then, that England was also visited by Portuguese sea-going traders traversing this circuit. Alvero Nonnez and Jaspar Diaz landed in Southampton in 1541 with 'Callicowte Clothe … expecting to have been as free to sell the same as formerly'.[73] This seems to have been a routine commercial venture (perhaps somewhat illegal) that in this instance caught the attention of officials. That year calicoes were also the cause of a grievance when 'On 12 March, James Crane, captain of the blockhouse next Gravesend [on the Thames River], took Calicut cloth out of a ship called the Johne Arthur'.[74] These scattered notations hint at a circulation of at least small quantities of Indian goods in these northern realms before the 1550s, sometimes eliciting bureaucratic remarks and otherwise passing without formal comment. Further evidence appears in a survey of English maritime trade prepared for one of Elizabeth I's advisors between 1575 and 1585. This summary of the sea-based traffic includes several references to commerce in 'callicowe clothe', suggesting the general knowledge of this commodity and the availability of Indian textiles through regular and irregular means. In the first instance Lisbon was cited as the source of 'callicowe clothe, all kinde of spices … and all other Indews wares whatesoever [including] … yndewes cobbard [Indies cupboard] clothes called paintohos [pintado]'.[75] But in addition to Lisbon, the French west-coast port of La Rochelle, long a thriving hub of trade with Spain, England and the Netherlands, figured as another source for Asian wares. The author observed that 'all the pirates of Fraunce doe discharge here … [and] You shall have manye thinges of the Indews [Indies] of portingall [Portugal], Better cheape then in Portingall'. This harbour had its risks, however, as it was the haunt of pirates and mariners were advised to travel in 'a goode shippe or elss youwe are like to be Robbed … either outwards or homewards'.[76]

There are obvious difficulties in tracking the history of smuggling, not least that outlets for illicit merchandise were legion. Smuggled goods leave too few official traces in their passing. However, quantities of textiles certainly travelled untaxed through European precincts, without benefit of the custom's house sanction. Anthony Disney outlined the extensive and persistent smuggling that bedevilled Portuguese officials in the Indian Ocean – Portuguese officials were themselves some of the most determined smugglers, also employing intermediaries. Smuggling was a socially tolerable vice in many communities.[77] Seventeenth-century British merchants employed some of the same techniques in European waters that Disney describes in the Indian Ocean, and a century later these traits still plagued London officials.[78] Still, enough calicoes circulated in England after the 1550s to leave a mark. The Tudor Book of Rates summarized all commodities on which duty could be charged in England for the second half of the sixteenth century. Calico was included under the category of 'linnen cloth', confirming its well-known status in mercantile circles and beyond.[79]

English consumers embraced new domestic items, leading William Harrison to observe in 1577 that 'The furniture of our houses … exceedeth and is grown in manner even to passing delicacy; and herein I do not speak of the nobility and gentry only but likewise of the lowest sort in most places of our South Country'.[80] Cottons probably arrived first in southern England, and Southampton probate inventories from the 1550s record merchants with small caches of calico stock, while Southampton's affluent commercial and middling classes also had East Indian textiles among their furnishings. Cushions, cupboard cloths, curtains and yards of coarse and fine calicoes appear before mid-century, with some goods described as old in 1566.[81] This pattern of consumption was mirrored in Somerset. In 1545, Dame Elizabeth Fitz-James, of Wells, widow of Sir John Fitz-James, Chief Justice of the King's Bench, left her son-in-law a pair of calico sheets among other things.[82] Joan Thirsk recently noted the particular role played by clergy in the introduction of new foodstuffs in English neighbourhoods in this period: carefully cultivating exotic novelties in their gardens, clerics often received seeds through their wide-ranging social networks.[83] A similar pattern for East Indian goods is suggested in probate documents. Numbers of clerics included chintzes and calicoes among their property at their death, like Henry Clarke, vicar of Stoke Gifford near Bristol. His 1620 inventory included a '*pintado*',[84] two calico sheets and four calico pillows among his house wares.[85] There was an early, steady percolation of Indian cottons through homes and shopping precincts. Overall, many regions of Europe displayed an increasing vitality, invigorated through closer contacts with the most advanced manufacturing regions of Eurasia.[86]

FASHIONING THE HOME: NEW PATTERNS OF MATERIAL CULTURE

The descriptions of Indian printed, painted or embroidered cotton goods in European homes, however abbreviated in form, mark an innovation that is more than the sum of random purchases. The examples from England's Southampton region include the widow Margaret Pyd's calico curtains (1559), John Smith's 'Cubborde clothe of Callycowe' (1559) or the merchant Thomas Goddard's 'pare of Callycowe sheets' (1555),[87] and signal the arrival of commodities that embodied a potent force. Alfred Gell insisted that we recognize 'things' as having social agency in more real ways than might at first be supposed.[88] Indeed, Gell argued that: ' "Things" with their thing-ly causal properties are as essential to the exercise of agency as [human] stages of mind.' Gell claimed that certain kinds of objects reflect a 'manifestation of agency . . . a mirror, vehicle or channel of agency'.[89] Indian cottons exhibit this agency. They carried motifs, repeat patterns and characteristic decorative forms and wherever they travelled they sparked reactions, efforts at emulation or reinterpretation. From Indonesia to Persia, central Asia to Western Europe, once Indian cottons arrived in quantity the affects resounded through those societies in one form or another. Attempts to establish locally based cotton industries constituted one of the reactions and economists might characterize these processes as 'import substitution'. However, as this commodity travelled the world, the affects extended well beyond regional economic development. Indian calicoes had agency in the cultural as well as the economic milieu, sparking powerful and sometimes unexpected responses in these encounters.[90]

London records from the sale of East India cargoes are incomplete before 1641, however it is clear that the passion for Indian wares that predated 1600 continued into the next century. The English East India Company was established in 1600 and launched its first voyage in 1601. Between the return of its first ships in 1603 and 1615, twenty ships returned safely from their voyages to their London base, each laden with cargo. In 1616 the vessel *New Year's Gift* carried freight valued at £150,000, it being among the thirteen Company vessels to return between 1616 and 1618, described as 'very rich ships … with costly merchandise'.[91] One investor reported with satisfaction in 1617 that 'England is constantly setting her feet more firmly in the East Indies'.[92] Competition among European traders would profit some nations over others. But whoever provided the Indian wares, there was no question of their significant impact on commerce and culture in Europe. During the first half of the seventeenth century the combined efforts of Portuguese, Dutch and English moved impressive quantities of Indian textiles, more and more of which remained in Europe. Whether through English trade or English plunder, the arrival of Indian textiles on English shores produced a flurry of interest among commercial and amateur buyers.[93] Cheap cottons, called *Guinée*, sold by Europeans in West African markets since the sixteenth century, were also being bought by the Netherlands in greater volumes by the 1620s, further building on the taste shift of the previous century.[94] The wealthiest buyers turned to embroidered or finely painted textiles, but the growing quantities of cheaper printed Indian cottons were a critical element of this commerce, as we have seen.[95] Interior spaces were remodelled at the same time as trade accelerated.

Why did early modern Europeans react so warmly when they first encountered Indian textiles? There is more room for speculation than there is actual evidence. We have no diaries narrating the responses of genteel ladies or common good wives. But reactions can be inferred in the reinterpretations of Indian designs produced by Europeans – these provide a gauge of consumer reaction. As elsewhere, most of Europe was untutored in letters. But ordinary men and women were not illiterate. Religious instruction and popular culture employed a complex profusion of symbols that infused the lives of common folk. They could read the signs of spring and fertility in Mayday blossoms and detect trades and social ranks in the badges or symbols displayed on bodies and buildings. The common literacy in which commoners and even some higher classes were schooled ideally suited the intricate designs impressed on cotton surfaces. Europeans responded first in the form of stitchery.

European embroiderers took to their needles almost immediately they encountered the cotton quilts, cushions, cupboard cloths, curtains and the like arriving from India. Surveys of European needlework show the power of Indian design throughout the later sixteenth and seventeenth centuries.[96] Despite the cultural distance, both societies shared a familiarity with botanic subjects at a time when the agrarian idiom was a common part of the metaphoric and visual vocabulary. Specific Asian motifs were unfamiliar to Europeans, but communication through this visual vernacular bridged distance and linked societies through the adoption and adaptation of Asia's hybrid motifs.[97] A dialogue began as the forms of one were introduced to another, a discourse visible today in surviving sixteenth- and seventeenth-century European needlework.[98] Some European examples suggest a struggle to understand and interpret the Indian designs; Indian artisans likewise toiled to replicate European patterns sent to them, often broadly reinterpreting the subjects. A number of Indian embroiderers travelled to Lisbon in the early sixteenth century to instruct local craftspeople in their techniques. Thus, over the years, a cross-cultural translation and reinterpretation of the Indian language of design took place, materialized into curtains, hangings and coverlets.[99] The Indian original was transposed into Western forms through cycles of inspiration, adaptation and recreation; sometimes there was straight copying, as illustrated in the number of surviving crewel work bed-hangings modelled on Indian palampores. As well there were untold numbers of innovations and even new idioms devised, such as the Portuguese Castelo Branco embroidered quilts, or *colcha*, a renowned Portuguese manufacture from an area bordering Spain. This style of quilt was modelled directly on Indian palampores, replicated by Portuguese embroiderers in a form that developed a characteristic charm and became a popular product of that region from at least the seventeenth century.[100] Similarly, examples of what are termed 'traditional' embroideries from the Salamanca region of Spain also show inspiration from Asia.[101] Renditions into European forms were part of a critical sequence in the development of communications between India and Europe. Thus, the *domestic* material culture of Europe was in transition long before European artisans successfully printed cottons in a systematic way beginning in the later decades of the 1600s.

European women served as cultural mediators as they plied their needles. In England, what are called Jacobean tapestries or hangings, a form of crewel work embroidery, took their inspiration from Indian palampores and other furnishings. Plate 2 is an example of a painted palampore from about 1700 and Plate 3 offers an embroidered form of this hanging, both styles of which were immensely popular in elite circles during this era. The later sixteenth-century English diarist John Evelyn describes one of Lady Mordaunt's rooms as 'hung with *pintado* full of figures'.[102] These textiles inspired local variants by professional and amateur needleworkers. Some of the women involved in these projects had connections to court or elite circles and saw early examples of Indian wares. Crafting large hangings took hundreds of hours of diligent labour by women of the household, an opportunity to meditate on the foreign patterns inspiring the project, while also adding local touches. A set of seventeenth-century English crewel work panels, held in the Art Institute of Chicago, speaks to this hybridization practice. These incorporate the standard combinations of floral and tree of life elements typical of this form, with the requisite parrot amongst the boughs as a signal of exotic provenance. But the embroiderer also added a cow and sheep to the animals gambolling among the herbage. At the same time, the European figures clustered together employ a large umbrella to indicate their standing, a device introduced to Europeans by Asian sovereigns and eminent functionaries. The panels are a testament to the power of Asian forms, in aesthetic and geopolitical terms.[103] The Philadelphia Museum of Art houses a similarly large crewel work bed-hanging, a verdant exposition of needle skills, interpreted from the Indian mode[104] (Plate 4). Through their needlework these women showed what Rosalind Jones and Peter Stallybrass describe as 'links to … the larger world of culture and politics'.[105]

Natalie Davis describes the practice of translation, observing that this 'is a movement between languages and also between cultures, as the translator seeks words that will bring about the same effect as those in the source language'.[106] In this context, Western needleworkers did not translate as much as they inferred, searching for common connections between one cultural form and the other. In this manner, the new links to India were celebrated through this stitchery and at the same time, women crafted new standards of comfort. The women who interpreted the new Indian motifs came from the middle and even labouring classes, as well as the elites. Projects large and small reflect women's engagement with the new designs, visible in items from pincushions to work bags, pockets to aprons. Museum collections across Europe and America are replete with smaller embroidered items of furnishings and clothing from this period, reflecting the reinterpretation of motifs from once rare and exotic Asian artefacts. This transformative impulse flowed across borders and oceans, occupying generations in a generative exercise. A small purse or pocketbook, possibly from Chester County, Pennsylvania reflects an Asian-inspired design element common to European domestic needlework: a central vase motif out of which flowering vines twined (Plate 5). This embroidery also embodies the early globalization process. As ideas, images and materials circulated the globe in new ways, women were called upon to reorder and re-imagine their environment. A vast range of objects survive from this period, chronicling women's responses to these new trading ties, evident in items from a 1664 pincushion to the many decorated pockets worn by women from the late 1600s (Plate 6). These domestic projects pre-date commercial attempts to replicate Asian commodities in workshops and factories in northern Europe. This stitchery was part of an essential digestion and integration of Asian forms into Western life. Unfortunately, the very intimacy of this domestic production rendered this crucial process invisible to economic historians or historians of trade, empire and industrialization. Over many decades women, young and old, articulated their understanding of global trade through their needles. Their work speaks powerfully to the transformations under way and their commitment to the practical and aesthetic components of the new commodities. This early trade in Indian textiles, the growing use of Indian cottons in home décor and the subsequent renditions of these goods by Atlantic world needleworkers represent decisive steps in the relationship between Asia and the West, and in the material culture reshaped in this era. The economic implications were profound. Cycles of trade and cycles of reception took place over many years, rippling out from the major trade routes to more remote locales. This extended process shaped the acceptance and integration of Indian cottons into Western life.

Aside from needlework, other reinterpretations soon became available with European artisans working on painted facsimiles – these artisans struggled for decades to replicate Indian colourfast dyeing techniques, until their ultimate success in the mid-1700s.[107] In the sixteenth century, a type of decorative hanging, much cheaper than those with woven or embroidered patterning, was produced by painting on coarse canvas. Called 'painted cloths', there are numerous examples noted in probate inventories from Southampton, Oxfordshire and elsewhere for the sixteenth century. Mention of painted cloths also appears in the Tudor Book of Rates, suggesting a trade in a decorative commodity heretofore understudied.[108] Of the surviving examples in the Victoria and Albert Museum, most depict stiff rudimentary images, but in one seventeenth-century example, the painter adopted the newest Asian floral motifs, including exotic birds within a sinuous herbaceous design.[109] This striking example stands out among the other rigid, naively executed subjects, suggesting previously unknown ways in which new design elements permeated existing forms. Did some of the painted cloths listed in the mid-sixteenth century Southampton probate inventories also show the influence of Asia – and what of the painted cloths traded throughout Europe? These items were imported into England from Continental sources.[110] Without a larger sample of the items themselves, we cannot know. However, material evidence in at least one case confirms the impact of Indian forms on local artisans working with a cheaply produced coarse canvas, painting images designed to appeal to the men and women of England's growing middle classes. Europe's homes were the first and most important entry point for Asian commodities and Asian-inspired design; intimate social spaces, their presence allowed daily interaction, as well as being a significant stage for plays of fashion. I will discuss the spread of quilt culture from East to West in a later chapter. It too was another manifestation of the impact of Indian cottons.

The sale of calicoes in the Basque region, the traffic in Indian wares in a western French port and the apparent routine commerce in the southern regions of England and the Low Countries all point to a sixteenth-century circulation of Indian cottons that has gone largely undetected. There can be little surprise then that a foreign hawker was fined for selling 'callacow' on the streets of London in the 1590s.[111] England's elite and even middle-ranked families, in proximity to metropolitan markets, along well-used pedlar routes and major shipping routes, could buy the newest and most desirable fabrics from India from the sixteenth through the early seventeenth centuries. The 'calico craze' is a phenomenon usually associated with the early decades of the eighteenth century.[112] However, this period of consumer conflict was preceded by a long-running calico fever, or as an opponent termed it, a 'Plague of Callicoes over-spreading the Land'.[113] Whether 'fever' or 'plague', there is no doubt about the impact of these commodities.

The Indian cotton trade exemplifies important elements in the relationship between East and West, inaugurating profound changes in the European economy, industry and material cultures of elite and commoner alike. These transformations will be explored in greater detail in the chapters that follow. The desire for Asian commodities and the depth of this demand sparked a more generalized consumerism for new categories of goods, with unexpected results. Thirty years ago Joan Thirsk identified the importance of new trades that produced small niceties, English-made, many projects employing the poor. As the poor were employed, they were also better dressed, their houses better equipped. Speaking of the late sixteenth century, Thirsk observes that, 'Elegant clothes and ornaments about the house were catching on rapidly as money circulated more freely … Worse than this was another complaint: London fashions were not confined to foolish, light-headed Londoners. The craze had spread to the provinces …'[114] Thirsk highlighted the expanding manufacture of cheap goods such as buttons, buckles, ribbons, lace, combs and pins. In recent years Jan de Vries has similarly underscored the importance of these small enterprises as collective catalysts of an 'industrious revolution'.[115] But, Asia also figured centrally in the genesis of a European consumer society. The qualities and characteristics of Asian imports set a standard to which European manufacturers aspired.[116] Moreover, the characteristics of commodities like cotton set a template for new expressions of fashion. Cottons were affordable, uniquely attractive and made in the widest range of prices, unmatched by European wares. Thus, economic and cultural dynamism in Europe arose on two fronts: through the generation of small luxuries indigenous to Europe, and as a result of Asian imports that unleashed unprecedented economic and cultural reverberations. The arrival, in north-west Europe, of one of the most important global commodities was decisive in Europe's development, essential for the stimulus of early modern consumerism and the articulation of popular fashions. Material desires take many forms. However, societal acceptance of novel, foreign or exotic artefacts was vital for new forms and formulations of fashion.[117] The innovative needlework trends that emerged over the seventeenth century highlight the ways in which new products were incorporated into existing hierarchies of goods.

CONCLUSION

The full potential of Asian manufactures, like cotton, became apparent as cotton became an ever larger component of dress and furnishings, a vehicle for stylish tastes and functional utility across social ranks. For Indian merchants, the growth of new European markets represented one more series of negotiations on the colours, patterns and textures most in demand.[118] Fernand Braudel observed that 'Fashion is also a search for a new language to discredit the old'[119] and in this respect, the merchants and manufacturers of India acted as 'linguistic' intermediaries, bringing a new visual language to Europe and helping nurture the craze for Indian textiles that ensued. The Dutch and English East India Company landed ever larger cargoes of cottons from 1660 to 1690; at the same time, local artisans laboured mightily to replicate the imports and new social and economic forces were unleashed to feed the appetite for this textile.[120]

I have argued elsewhere that Asian cottons became 'naturalized' over this time period, domesticated in much the same way that exotic flowers took root in seventeenth- and eighteenth-century European gardens.[121] Over several centuries, the complex and varied motifs of Indian textiles had been integrated into European material culture. At the same time, entrepreneurs from Marseilles to Barcelona, Amsterdam to London, recognized the broad market for these goods and struggled to match the colours, patterns and price. The British cotton/linen industry was part of this naturalization practice, working to imitate Indian calicoes and chintzes, protected by the legislative ban of 1721 which barred Indian cottons from the market, striving for years to produce reasonable facsimiles, ultimately with some success.[122] Mixed cotton/linen fabrics were manufactured throughout Europe, with the most successful technologies introduced first in Britain. The domestication of Indian cottons was complete when Europe claimed the right to make its own cottons, the fibre grown in colonial plantations and the fabric made with the help of new technologies and modes of production. This subject is fully explored in Chapter 4. Many consumers were ultimately willing to accept these instead of the Indian originals.

Western industrialization is justly celebrated as a landmark event in human history; and Asian goods, when mentioned in surveys of these events, typically appear as the source of inspiration for European ingenuity. However, the iconic history of Western industrial triumph should not obscure the productive genesis of Indian manufacturers and the profoundly important role they played in supplying consumers across the world. Communities of Indian artisans developed techniques of spinning, weaving, dyeing, printing, painting and embroidery that were unmatched. Indian merchants cultivated global markets and sustained this commerce for a thousand years. Francois Pyrard wrote in amazement at the scale of Indian production in the early 1600s, stating famously that the products of India's looms clothed 'everyone from the Cape of Good Hope to China, man and woman ... from head to foot'.[123] The capacities of the West eventually to copy Asian wares and approximate their prices and designs, using new techniques, has been privileged, undervaluing the signal role of Indian manufacturers and traders in the creation of worldwide markets. Indian fabrics set the standard against which all successors were measured. Cotton changed the world. This history begins with Indian commercial and technological capacity and the markets they nurtured throughout Eurasia and Africa. These commodities and Indian capacities built what had not been there before. The historical narrative of the cotton trade must more fairly reflect the weight of these processes.

Likewise, the absorption and adaptation of Asian commodities owes something to Europe's wives and daughters. Women were advised in a 1540 Italian needlework book to 'write with their needle'.[124] Inspired by Indian textiles, Western women chronicled a new era of global trade with their stitches. The hybrid embroideries mark the critical first response to expanding commerce with Asia, setting the stage for subsequent developments and a continuing preoccupation with these hybrid forms. Surviving artefacts arising from the trade in Indian cottons paint a telling story; the rug in Figure 2.7 testifies to the wider impact of this commerce, with textile designs originating in India employed in the West in other media. Direct trade with Asia transformed Europe, reshaping the economic and cultural context of the West – its economy and its material culture – a singular phenomenon. By 1800, the balance between East and West had shifted in favour of the latter.[125] Indeed, the tremendous importance of export markets for Britain after 1800 signifies the value of established global demand. In this context, the world markets constructed through the thousand-year trade in Indian cottons are surely as important as the various national histories of industrialization that followed. Indian cottons established a powerful global presence, shaping markets and serving fashion, and in so doing sparked the modern industrial age.

2.7 Bed rug. Artist unidentified. Connecticut River Valley, c.1790–1810. Wool on woven wool, 100 × 96 in. (254 × 243.8 cm). American Folk Art Museum, New York.

3.
FASHION'S FAVOURITE
The Social Politics of Cotton and the Democratization of Style, c. 1600-1820

Cotton is uniquely enmeshed in the development of popular fashions. Indian cottons arrived in Europe after 1500 at a time of commercial expansion and social volatility. Hierarchies of dress were being undermined through the spread of new luxuries; social strata were becoming more complicated and more porous as those with newly won wealth challenged placeholders with inherited positions, a contest which took material as well as political forms. Cotton was a fibre untrammelled by associations with tradition, unfettered with allusions to court dress – with little history of use in most of Europe, cotton represented both opportunity and threat. This is a tremendously mutable fibre that can be spun, woven and finished to produce a myriad of weights, textures and prices, suitable for buyers from any rank and attractive to virtually all communities. It was this very flexibility that antagonized critics of popular fashion, as cotton upended the sumptuary hierarchy. Cotton disrupted the established order of textiles and complicated the visual vocabulary of dress, by introducing new options in the marketplace. It undercut sumptuary regulation, formal and informal, and in so doing it advanced the spread of fashion in the Western world. Later, as the first industrialized commodity, cottons of every sort were among the most ubiquitous ready-made clothes, defining and redefining the meanings of democratic dress. My focus in this chapter is largely on England. To fully assess the impact of cottons, I will look first at the early legal regulations shaping consumption, followed by an assessment of the social politics of wearing wool and the status of the iconic wool trade. Fashion politics evolved within this milieu and cotton had a unique role in its development. This fibre reconfigured fashionable dress in the Western world.[1]

REGULATION AND REACTION

Individual choice in dress is a modern concept. Indeed, for centuries men, women and children, living and dead, were legally constrained in what they could wear and how they wore their clothes. Sir Francis Bacon wrote on many issues pertaining to the proper functioning of early modern England, including means for 'the Repressing of Waste and Excess by Sumptuary Laws'.[2] In that era it was widely accepted that legislation was needed on issues of moral and practical concern such as the purchase of food, apparel and domestic furnishings, commodities representing the greatest outlay for most families. Equally these goods signalled rank and status. Rules for approved expenditures, on foods, fabrics or other goods, were widespread throughout Europe, as well as in urbanized Asian societies. In Europe, governments aimed to contain two evils: first, the excessive purchase of foreign imports; second, the blurring of social boundaries and inversion of hierarchy. The budgeting habits of citizens concerned governments, like that of England, which disliked the prospect of gold flowing out of the kingdom to pay for superfluous luxuries like combs and velvet hats from France or neckerchiefs and silk gloves imported through the Low Countries. Indeed, in 1563 official import statistics were assembled on the order of Lord Burghley, Secretary of State and later Treasurer to Queen Elizabeth I (1533–1603). The aim was to uncover the full range of imports and to categorize the useful and the inessential, and in the long term encourage English substitutions for these 'superfluous' foreign items.[3] In the meantime, legislative restraints would curb spendthrifts. Consumption was policed through sumptuary statutes, proclamations and moral injunctions, a combination of pressures deployed from the fourteenth century onwards. In some cases these rules persisted into the nineteenth century. In most urbanized commercial societies, whether in early modern China, Japan, the Ottoman Empire or Europe, governments tried to contain the use of key commodities. Invariably, more people wanted to own these goods than were approved.[4]

Men were the focus of a 1510 Tudor enactment that forbade the wearing of blue or crimson velvet by men below the rank of knights of the garter. English legislation intensified in the reign of Elizabeth I (1558–1608). In the year following her succession, Elizabeth added another proclamation charging magistrates with enforcing sumptuary restrictions. This was followed by instructions from the Privy Council to London authorities, commanding them to establish parish surveillance teams to watch for dress infractions among passers-by. Teams were to patrol the streets of the capital keeping a sharp lookout for audacious outfits on plebeian bodies. In 1560, the mayor of London also prodded his aldermen to 'give a diligent eye' to the dress of residents in their wards. Eventually, several prominent defaulters were brought before the Star Chamber for punishment. At the same time, provincial authorities were urged to implement regulations.[5]

For the government, deviant patterns of dress were a social danger. The introduction of 'watchers' to spot infractions on the streets of London illustrates the determination of authorities to bring offenders to book. Given the freewheeling consumer cultures in many regions of the world today, it may seem extraordinary that so much effort was expended to enforce public conduct. It is useful to recall the many instances in the twentieth century when central governments dictated personal expenditures and prescribed forms of dress.[6] However, the early modern period had one overriding characteristic that distinguishes it from our time – scarcity. This was an era of relative scarcity for all common folk. Thus both political and social hierarchies were manifested through material difference and unsanctioned indulgence signalled a potentially subversive disorder. As Susan Vincent observes: 'Apparel was important business'.[7] Joan Thirsk further illustrates this point, outlining the extraordinary measures taken to check a passion for Italian-style hose showcasing the nether regions of men's bodies. Hose could be constructed either in two separate pieces attached together, or seamed at the crotch combining leg-covering and upper hose in one garment – trunk hose and melon hose were among the fashionable Renaissance designs. The upper segment, precursor to breeches, was voluminously padded and covered the lower torso, ending mid-thigh.[8] How better to show off one's legs than in striped, clocked or patterned silk hose in the Italian style, emerging from a voluminous pair of trunk hose? Thirsk recounts that: 'A remarkable system of surveillance was called into being in 1566, involving the stationing of four "sad and discreet" persons at the gates of the City of London from 7a.m. to 11a.m. and from 1p.m. to 6p.m. daily, watching for people who might be wearing prohibited styles of hose.'[9] The dimensions of these leg coverings, as well as the fabric and its colour, were the points at issue. Tailors and hosiers were enjoined to make hose 'to lye juste unto their legges, as in ancient tyme was accustomes' – with no additional stuffing of any sort about the hips. Authorities claimed this fashion was driving some 'to destruction'.[10] A servant, Richard Walweyn, was arrested about this time for disporting himself through London's streets in 'a very monsterous and outraygous great payre of hose' and was detained until he could dress himself in 'a decent and lawful facyon'. A merchant tailor wearing the proscribed garment suffered a more painful humiliation, being led through the streets to his home, where the stuffing in the hose was publicly removed and the outer fabric left to flap against his thighs.[11] Elsewhere, Oxford and Cambridge students remained defiant in their choice of attire and disregarded all attempts at their reform.

Negley Harte asserts that sumptuary law was the 'identifying characteristic' of the age.[12] Those born to the purple, members of the nobility, should dress the part and no others should presume: plebeians should not wear silk or cloth of gold, they should not wear hose that showed off their legs or framed genitalia in immoral ways. They should dress in a modest manner or face the consequences.[13] Silks of virtually all types were the focus of intense bouts of legislation. Silk was the first luxurious Asian import and as a result sparked the greatest official reaction.[14] However, in time, bans on the general wearing of silk were rescinded in one jurisdiction after another as regional silk industries developed in Europe. This change was slow to arrive in England. The 1530s English enactment, for example, permitted those of middle rank to wear silk ribbons, although other restrictions remained in place.[15] Dress remained a flashpoint.[16] In 1585, a Lancashire magistrate issued a presentment against the jurymen who arrived for court duties, charging all of them with infractions of sumptuary laws. Their crime was to wear silk facings in their hats, an indulgence forbidden their social class.[17] Nonetheless, all formal sumptuary legislation was repealed in England in 1604.[18] That startling turn was unique in Europe, but reflected tensions between Parliament and the monarch on matters of privilege, rather than a renunciation of the sumptuary ethos. Repeated efforts were made to revive such legislation, with no results. However, neither English moral nor political theorists subscribed to unfettered consumer choice and sumptuary laws remained close to the hearts of many legislators, if not on the books.[19]

Support for dress hierarchies remained a foundational belief in many quarters. Edward Chamberlayne, writer, member of the gentry and occasional diplomat, reflected this perspective in his 1667 publication, insisting that 'According to the wisdom of our Ancestors, and the custom of the most civilized Nations, some sumptuary Laws may be made, whereby the great Excess, especially in the inferior sort of *English*, may be restrained, and most Degrees and Orders may be discerned by their Habit or Port, as now in the Universities and amongst the Clergy is partly done.'[20] Profound philosophical and political positions were at issue. Should men and women be able to dress as they pleased, as they were able, without interference from the state? Or, should luxuries be available only to those of inherited position? Sumptuary legislation continued to be debated even as the social reformation of fashion took place on city streets. Jeremy Collier made 'A Moral Essay Concerning Cloaths' the subject of a late seventeenth-century dialogue. One of the disputants insisted on the essential merit of rank, noting that: 'A Gentleman's Mien and Behaviour is sufficient to discover him, without any great dependence upon *Shops* and *Taylors*'.[21] The author reassured readers that even without legal injunctions the good taste intrinsic to the elites would maintain a buffer against encroaching social classes: '[Fine] Cloaths don't suppose a Man considerable, so neither can they make him so'.[22] The politics of clothing distilled profound moral and political debates.

Merchants and professionals were the most troublesome, as in many instances their material ambitions exceeded their birth; likewise they might be far wealthier than many nobles.[23] City dwellers were another problematic group, living within a more ambiguous social setting. People from different backgrounds rubbed together and the complex material milieu polished ambitions as people jostled for position. This produced what contemporaries called 'the confusion of degrees of all estates'.[24] Inconstancy, ambition, innovation and aspiration were derided and despised by champions of custom and hierarchy. Defenders of the status quo skirmished to contain those pushing against restraints. However, they failed to quash the effects of disruptive fashion among the commonality.[25]

Indian cottons entered a complex textile ecology in northern Europe. Systems of knowledge, of production, of sale and use were long established and dominated by the two major fibres in Europe: flax and wool. Silk imports had disrupted these twin elements over the previous centuries, as imports of Asian silks were followed by the genesis of silk industries in Italy, France and elsewhere in Europe. This fibre trilogy was then confronted by a fourth, further disturbing patterns of manufacture. The industrial ramifications are discussed in detail in Chapter 4. In the main, cottons were a largely alien import into northern Europe. As quantities of imports grew, cotton unsettled the wool trade, which was at the foundation of England's manufacturing, and international trade. The bolts and bales of heavy, warm English cloth comprised the single most important export in the late 1500s. By 1600 this staple was under pressure as a result of a variety of forces outside its control. From the 1570s, the port of Antwerp – once 'the warehouse of all Christendome' – was enmeshed in war between Spain and the defiant Netherlands Republic.[26] Antwerp had previously sold almost all the cloth England made. Now Dutch privateers at the mouth of the River Scheldt were strangling Antwerp and confounding the English merchants.[27] At the same time, the wider preference in Europe was shifting to lighter fabrics – thinner worsted or mixed-fibre goods known as the New Draperies.[28] England benefited from the chaos wrought by the religious wars in northern

Europe, as this led to the settlement of refugees in England able to produce New Draperies, and this trade flourished. But the changing commercial forces unsettled established certainties for the wool industry. Cotton imports added to this disruptive/creative process. Thus, there is no better way to understand the realpolitik of early modern textile and fashion politics than by juxtaposing cotton with wool. In this long transitional period, wool epitomized hierarchy, tradition and even anti-fashion in unique ways, even as it struggled to find its fashion footing. Cotton is best assessed through the cultural relations and periodic intense political antagonisms with wool.

CULTURAL AUTHORITY, THE WEARING OF WOOL AND THE ADVENT OF THE COTTON ERA

The fleece was a commanding symbol of cultural authority, with unequalled ties to convention, hierarchy and skill. Emblematic of European dynasties and countless artisanal guilds, the fleece also represented wealth, industry and commerce to generations of Europeans from all social ranks. Wool epitomized order and its fabrics were employed in the habit and symbolism of European life.[29] Competition among wool-producing regions boiled up periodically – the turmoil surrounding the seventeenth-century New Draperies is a case in point.[30] But whether woollens or worsted, wool was a foundational industry. Generations of men and women laboured in the production of these cloths and, like the landowner dependent on the wool clip for wealth, or the merchants who amassed wealth through trade, they celebrated and defended their connections to the wool staple. This fibre carried extraordinarily rich associations of custom and social allegiance.

Tradition was a powerful factor in the marketing of wool. During the late Elizabethan debates on sumptuary issues, the English moral critic Phillip Stubbes honoured the honest men of his generation who cleaved to wool in the face of tempting alternatives. In his view, wool had everything to recommend it.[31] However, the established connection between wool and tradition now fell within more anarchic circumstances. Fashion's mounting influence among the elites, the urban middle classes, and even young artisans or servants, resulted in fads for new commodities, for goods capable of a more individual style. This phenomenon embodied what Gilles Lipovetsky calls the 'instability of appearance',[32] reflecting individualism, group or social markers articulated through dress. Despite periodic crises in the late sixteenth and early seventeenth centuries, a growing part of the population could now afford to purchase a wider array of goods. Moreover, articles now came in a growing variety of qualities and prices.[33] Joan Thirsk comments on the 'speed with which the new-style consumer goods penetrated the length and breadth of the kingdom'.[34] England was among the vanguard of social change sweeping north-west Europe. However, these innovations antagonized those favouring sumptuary restraint. The power of tradition and fashion collided.

Despite the repeal of sumptuary law in 1604, wools of various sorts continued to be prescribed for much of the population. Wool dominated sartorial discourse.[35] Englishness was still epitomized by woollen fabrics, the product of English sheep and domestic industry, solemnized and celebrated by the Woolsack in the House of Lords (Figure 3.1). Wool was autochthonous, a fibre rising from local soil and entwined in its culture and economy. Lipovetsky contrasts the temporality of fashion

3.1 Palace of Westminster, with the king presiding and the Members of Parliament seated on wool sacks, engraved *c.*1610. Guildhall Library Print Room.

with concepts underlying customary dress as a 'repetition of models inherited from the past, a seamless conservatism in modes of being and appearing'.[36] Thus, the common 'honest kersie'[37] was perceived as the antithesis of foreign cloth. Phillip Stubbes reflected on earlier times when men 'went clothed in black or white Frieze coats' and he concluded that men were now being 'transnatured' through the wearing of new garb. Stubbes insisted that: 'Men were stronger, healthfuller, fairer complexioned, longer lived and finally, ten times harder than we be now' when wearing English wool. The fibre itself infused their bodies with strength and their outer habit was the source of this potency. In contrast, those men swathed in laced shirts and velvet cloaks were a 'nice and womanish kind of people'.[38] The valorous claims of wool resounded.

The culture of dress was imbued with powerful social and cultural significance. Ann Rosalind Jones and Peter Stallybrass argue for 'the animatedness of clothes, their ability to "pick up" subjects, to mould and shape them both physically and socially, to constitute subjects through their power as material memories'.[39] Specific vestments instilled wearers with a distinctive authority in the Renaissance era. In this respect, it is important to recognize the intersecting clothing practices of this period. One garb might reify position, place and custom reinforcing traditions of hierarchy and the other celebrate innovation and self-fashioning in ways antithetical to tradition. Ceremonies of investiture, with distinct casts of players, filled the seasonal calendar, whether civic, trade, military or religious events. Robes embodied position. It was widely accepted that office holders should be identifiable, as should those in the professions or in service to monarch, prince or nobleman. For those in office, when attending meetings, the day and event dictated the colour and form of the wool robes worn: for instance, codified regulations dictated that on the first day of the quarter sessions court in midsummer, the Lord Mayor and sheriffs of the City of London wore violet-coloured wool cloth robes and scarlet cloaks; while at the election of the governors of Christ's Hospital in London, both the Lord Mayor and aldermen wore black robes only. These regulations persisted through the 1700s.

Tiers of coloured wool coats, hoods and sashes, worn by men and women, marked routine public spectacles. In 1661, the Dutch visitor William Schellinks described the Lord Mayor of London's Easter procession and illustrated how easily he could measure social standing through wool garments. 'First', records Schellinks, 'came all the apprentices ... shoemakers, weavers, tailors and all kinds of crafts dressed in blue with grey hoods, each with their master, walking in pairs'. Children from Christ's Hospital were 'all dressed in blue coats and yellow undergowns', to be followed by surgeons wearing green with white sashes. The Lord Mayor came last, decked out in a red wool tabard, surrounded by aldermen and sheriffs similarly dressed in red wool.[40] Processions such as these punctuated public life, where the practice of sumptuary distinction was manifested in wool. Daily observances as well as grander rituals required this cloth.[41] Edward Chamberlayne was one of many members of the elite who affirmed this belief. Chamberlayne was a confirmed Royalist who had lived outside the country during the mid-century Interregnum. Popular enthusiasms were things to be avoided, in the view of men like Chamberlayne, who feared that the arrangements of everyday life were becoming too variable and too subject to whims. Wool was the prescription to calm this fever. Livery was a case in point. Blue cloth was long associated with servants' dress, and was chosen by the squire Nicholas Blundell in 1706 as part of his male servants' livery: grey cloth coats 'faced with blue serge [and] blue serge waistcoats'.[42]

Wool was allied with orthodox values, with an investment in proper training and habits, its national utility uniting the moral allegiance of maker and wearer. 'Wool', declared another writer, 'is the Flower and Strength, the Revenue and Blood of England'.[43] What other commodity could claim so clear an affiliation not just with commerce, but also with the bodily essence of the English nation? Periodic alarms arose when the wool trade was endangered. In some instances these were external threats, such as the wars in northern Europe that rolled into the 1600s. On other occasions the disruptions had internal causes, such as the Cockayne Plan. An immensely wealthy London alderman, Sir William Cockayne, proposed the scheme in 1615 to increase employment in England, dyeing and finishing English wool cloth locally rather than in the Low Countries. The plan was a failure and the resulting crisis shook the foundations of the English economy.[44] England's vulnerability through its dependence on the wool trade was wholly apparent. Competitive industries in Italy, France and Spain, whose textiles flowed into England, further dismayed legislators.[45] This was the context in which the East India Company launched its first voyage to the East Indies in 1601, at a time of ardent debates about nationalism and dress, social status and fashion.

THE EARLY CALICO TRADE IN ENGLAND AND NORTH-WEST EUROPE: INTRODUCTION AND INNOVATION

Cotton has a unique role in the development of popular fashions. Cotton textiles were not embayed by pre-existing expectations about use and wear – for this cloth was not a component of traditional dress practice. Neither was it constrained by long-standing sumptuary associations with luxury, as with silk. It was an afterthought in the impetus to Eurasian trade. Yet, almost immediately, cottons began to change local dress habits in parts of Europe, an impact that rippled from region to region. Cotton was used in ways comparable to some linens and similar to varieties of silks, fustians and light wools. It was chameleon-like in its capacity to take on roles previously served by other textiles. Moreover, the varieties and prices of Indian fabrics enabled innovations in style and innovations among consumers.

The early calico trade was characterized by a measured process of interaction and accommodation. Tastes in Europe changed further as familiarity with this product grew. I have called this the domestication of an exotic, whereby a once rare commodity gradually became an accepted part of the material world.[46] Naturally, this history varied by region. Lisbon led the field, as discussed in Chapter 2, with numerous shops specializing in Indian textiles by the mid-1500s.[47] In northern Europe, the diffusion of Indian textiles took a slower pace. Indian quilts were among the early fashionable goods, the history of which is explored in Chapter 5. The focus in this chapter is on clothing. Examples of calico appear among the extensive wardrobe of Henry VIII, in particular a calico shirt embroidered with silk. A generation later, his daughter Queen Elizabeth acquire 'a kirtle of whit Callacowe bounde with riben' in 1594.[48] In the interim, calicoes arrived in small quantities in Southampton and other communities in proximity to ports. Though still relatively scarce in the mid-1500s, these foreign imports arrived more routinely as the century ended. Both like and unlike familiar linen fabrics, cottons hovered between existing categories of cloth. Through its intrinsic qualities and the associations it garnered, these Indian fabrics inevitably became embroiled in the social politics of fashion. This would be its liability and its strength.

The sale of cheap Indian cottons to ordinary folk is more difficult to discern than the fads for calicoes among courtiers and their ladies. However, we know that 'callacow' was being peddled on London streets in the 1590s.[49] Windfall cargoes of Indian goods also made a splash in English markets as when a great Portuguese ship, crammed with Indian merchandise, was seized in 1592 – the unification of the Portuguese and Spanish crowns in 1580 made Portuguese vessels fair game for Protestant privateers. Pepper flooded the market as the cargo was sold off,[50] but there were also plenty of textiles in the hold of this craft, as by this period the value of Portuguese textile imports from India far exceeded that of any other commodity. For example, in 1593, textiles comprised over 80 per cent of the value of cargoes in the two carracks that arrived safely in Lisbon. Portugal continued to be one of the major importers of Indian fabrics well into the 1600s, despite the arrival in Asia of competing English and Dutch traders.[51] Early in the 1600s, even as the first voyage of the East India Company was under way, English privateers seized another Portuguese craft. This ship contained a dizzying wealth of products from green ginger, cloves and cinnamon to cotton quilts, cushions, leather 'carpets', calicoes and painted 'pintadoes'.[52] Auctions were arranged in London and we can imagine the buzz of activity surrounding the sale of this booty. Sir Fulke Greville, a prominent royal administrator, 'was Thr'er for the sales'. These extended from the autumn of 1602 to the following January and Greville wrote to the Countess of Shrewsbury to see if she wanted anything at all, listing calicoes among several tempting items. The countess's mother, Bess of Hardwick, had already evinced a liking for such items, so perhaps her eldest daughter shared this taste.[53]

Many of the Indian cottons arriving in England were plain white or dyed in the piece, similar in look to linens (with the exception that the Indian dyes were colour fast and improved with washing). Other items included checked and striped cottons in a range of colours and qualities, tie-dyed handkerchiefs (produced in lengths ready to cut and hem), large painted hangings or palampores, and silks of various sorts. Another distinctive part of the cargoes was embroidered, painted or printed cottons. These in particular carried exotic connotations in the motifs, in keeping with elite fascination with foreign rarities of all sorts. Thus it is not surprising that one of the masques arranged for the entertainment of Queen Anne in 1613 featured a figure bedecked 'in a skin-coate [under which was a] ... Green Calico set thicke with leaves and boughs'.[54] The 'leaves and boughs' of his painted calico suit exemplified the verdant exoticism of this commodity. Calicoes were imported routinely by this date, enabling merchants to supply customers and allowing more shoppers to learn about these goods. Thomas Dekker included an observation on current fashions in his 1615 play *The Honest Whore*, when a linen draper served new male clients: 'I can fit you Gentlemen with fine calicoes too for dublets, the only sweet fashion now, most delicate and courtly, a meeke gentle calico'.[55] Fashionable metropolitan men and women embraced this fabric, which became part of their wardrobes. English merchants were also sending supplies to overseas colonial markets, following the lead of Iberian colonizers who had shipped these goods to Caribbean and South American buyers for nearly a century. Thus, during the opening decades of the 1600s there was a steady expansion of cotton consumption. The English East India Company felt confident they could sell 12,500 pieces of Indian cloth in 1614 and ordered the same. By 1620, 100,000 pieces of cotton were shipped from trading factories in Gujarat, western India, to the Company's London warehouses. Five years later, the total shipments of cotton cloth to England reached nearly a quarter of a million pieces – each piece comprising a dozen to several dozen yards in length.[56]

English buyers were very willing to adopt these new products. Nicholas Leate was an experienced overseas merchant and also an investor in the East India Company, and he was sure about potential sales in England, writing in 1619 that: 'they are likely to be of great use here in the land, instead of linen'.[57] Each new report brought further confirmation of the potential of this commodity in the English market. Another merchant testified to Company officials in 1622 about the £10-worth of calico he sent to be sold in smaller towns and rural districts in England. His provincial dealers requested £200-worth of cottons in the next consignment. When King James I enquired about the growing rate of Indian imports in 1623 he was advised that these were 'very useful and vended in England whereby the price of [foreign] Lawns, Cambricks and other linen cloths are brought down'.[58] During these decades, Indian cottons generally cost less than competing European linens, encouraging substitution and a widening consumption. By the 1620s, London's linen drapers and merchants wanted regular consignments and were ready to contract for large quantities.[59] Both rich and poor could afford calicoes, as they came in many qualities and prices.[60] We can get a measure of the material transformation under way in a guide for colonial settlers printed in 1634. The author listed 'Callico stuffes' and 'blew Callicoe' among essential stock for would-be New England 'planters'.[61] Thus, the East India Company felt justifiably confident about the future of cotton imports, with sales encompassing large parts of England, its new colonies, and extending also to Ireland.[62]

The advance of the cotton trade during the early decades of the seventeenth century was disrupted in India and England. Famine in Gujarat during the 1630s scattered artisanal families and the Company was forced to open trading factories on the eastern Coromandel Coast to secure needed textiles, with resulting higher prices and decreased sales. In England, the 1640s and 1650s brought periods of civil war, a republican government and a new governmental interest in colonial trade. The shifting political terrain was a challenge for the East India Company. Amidst all these events, the competing Dutch East India Company remained a power to be reckoned with. But the account book of an anonymous English textile dealer illustrates the persistence of calico as a trade good throughout the years 1639 and 1640. Indian textiles are not the most numerous in this ledger, but 'callicoes' appear intermittently in considerable quantities, such as the 157 pieces bought in November 1640 for over £84, complementing the fifteen pieces previously noted for July of that year.[63] Between 1649 and 1651 the new Commonwealth government was lobbied vigorously by a collection of merchants determined to get a share of the trade with Asia. The English Company lost its monopoly for a time in the 1650s and independent adventurers rushed to fill the void, with good results. The quantities of Indian textiles landed in England and re-exported to foreign markets was so vast that later commentators marvelled. William Petyt, writing in the 1680s, believed that 'Our Merchants sold the Indian Commodities so low, that they furnished more parts of Europe than since we have done ... and ... this very much sunk the Actions of the Dutch East-India Company.'[64] Indian cottons streamed into English and northern European markets in mid-century, even with interruptions, whether supplied legally by English merchants, or as a result of smuggling by English interlopers in India or illicit shipments from the Netherlands. An example survives of the sort of common printed cotton circulating at this time, used on this occasion by an English artisan to cover the bottom of an embroidered box. This cloth was coarsely woven and crudely printed, likely selling for pennies. The box, dated 1656, is housed in the Nordiska Museet, Stockholm and exemplifies the quality of goods available to ordinary shoppers (Plate 7). The same sorts of basic fabric could be used for many other clothing purposes. Indian cottons were noted in Chester in 1654 as part of a legal contest between two local guilds competing for the right to sell textiles in the Chester market, including calico.[65] The English market was broad, not dependent on the tastes of earls and countesses, but enlivened by the purchases of industrious rural folk, urban labourers and middle-ranked families, who wanted to spend their extra money on new clothing and accessories. Cotton flourished in this setting.

This summary of the early English trade in Indian cottons brings us to a turning point: 1660. This date marks the re-establishment of monarchical rule in England and the return of the Stuart monarch Charles II to the throne. It also marks an intensification of efforts by the English East India Company to capitalize on their most profitable merchandise, Indian textiles. The Stuart king reinstated the Company monopoly (following an exchange of gifts). Indian cottons were now set to become a more prominent part of the material landscape. No longer a relative rarity, they were now the stuff of routine commerce and everyday wear.

CALICO AND THE TRANSFORMATION OF THE FASHION MARKET IN ENGLAND

The spring of 1660 witnessed the debarkation of Charles II to English soil. Samuel Pepys described an 'infinite crowd of people and horsemen, citizens, and noblemen of all sorts' at the landing in Dover and in Canterbury he recorded that: 'The shouting and joy expressed by all is past imagination.'[66] Pepys was one of the newly risen men of this age, an able and acquisitive naval administrator, with a deep interest in all sorts of fashions, particularly those that could improve his standing. In 1663 Pepys made a frank comment on the state of his wardrobe. Now a senior member of the naval administration, he resolved 'to go a little handsomer than I have hitherto', expending considerable sums on a velvet cloak, suits, periwigs (a newly introduced male fashion) and clothes for his wife. Although Pepys worried at the expense, he was convinced of his decision and compared his present modish self to the time 'when, for want of [fashionable] clothes, I was forced to sneak like a beggar'.[67] Pepys rubbed shoulders with nobles and wealthy merchants as a matter of course – and on occasion with courtiers and members of the royal household. Thus his priorities were shaped by a powerful compulsion to present a good figure. Pepys's preoccupations were common among generations of middle-ranked men whose numbers swelled the cities of Europe. Their tastes, material objectives and creative fashions signalled the wider societal transformations under way.

Some, like Neil McKendrick, have claimed that emulation was the driving force of fashion and McKendrick assigned this generative period to the eighteenth century.[68] Proximity certainly played a part in shifting material patterns of life. But hierarchical emulation is too blunt a force to explain this complex phenomenon. What Jan de Vries describes as 'New Luxuries' carried with them aspirational qualities that were far removed from those associated with the 'Old Luxuries' of aristocratic life. These new luxuries (or niceties) arose in greater abundance, in growing quantities, to be embraced and interpreted in a variety of settings; they were not singular rarities acquired to reinforce assigned hierarchical positions.[69] These new luxuries complicated and confounded social structures, as we have seen with the spread of Italian-style hose in late sixteenth-century London. Likewise the sentiments, ambitions and social norms of these new consuming groups differed (sometimes dramatically) from those of traditional elite consumers. Emulation alone does not account for the collective and individual patterns of material behaviour that arose in this era.[70] Indeed, Lorna Weatherill notes that the 'consumption hierarchy was not the same as the social hierarchy' in this period; although they were not entirely dissimilar, the distinctions were significant.[71] The material priorities emerging within the swelling middle classes, and even amidst the labouring classes, presaged social and political disruptions as old norms crumbled. Thus, while monarchs set styles for their acolytes, the participants in fashion included more non-elites than elites. Courtiers naturally devised their sartorial priorities, as they had an interest to *be* in fashion, but they were not the spring from which this new flood poured. Herbert Blumer described fashion as 'a continuing process of collective selection from among competing models … a reaching out for newer models which will answer to as yet indistinct and inarticulate newer tastes'. Blumer further remarked that 'the fashion mechanism is woven deeply into the texture of modern life'.[72] Blumer's observations were based on mid-twentieth-century analysis. But, his remarks apply equally to the early modern period when the emergence of popular fashion reshaped the economy and society.

Samuel Pepys exemplifies these features. He was born in a Fleet Street home in London in 1633, the fifth child of a modestly prosperous tailor and a butcher's daughter. Through family connections Pepys secured a good education, completing his schooling at St Paul's, London, going next to Cambridge where he earned his degree. This gave him exceptional training and connections for future endeavours. But it did not provide him with an income. Pepys began his working life as secretary to Edward Montagu, Councillor of State to the regicide and Lord Protector of England, Oliver Cromwell. Shortly afterwards, Pepys married the young impoverished daughter of a French émigré, a skilled carver. As the Interregnum ended, Pepys had a foothold in government administration and made a safe transition with the restoration of the monarchy, accompanying Montagu to the Netherlands to escort the king back to England. By dint of these connections and his growing administrative skills, Pepys rose. He achieved relative security in naval administration by the 1660s, studying the intricacy of weights and measures, learning the skills of accounting and contract negotiation.[73] These were quintessential accomplishments of the 'new man', the philosophy of which shaped some male fashions, as I show below. Pepys was determined to rise higher still – his ambitions were replicated in countless commercial and professional settings. Clothing was part of Pepys's strategy. In this he was not alone. The urge to present an appropriately modish figure inspired spending at many social levels, which collectively animated the marketplace. Sober additions or more frivolous acquisitions were bought to construct a decent or stylish look. Second-hand markets or more intensive labour represented two routes to increased consumption among plebeian folk. Pepys himself borrowed a silk banyan or dressing gown for his portrait, wanting to be commemorated in what he could not yet afford. He wrote of the future that: 'I shall with more comfort labour to get more [clothes]'.[74] Investors in the East India Company hoped that more painted, printed, striped and plain Indian cottons would figure among this mix.

MEN REFASHIONED

Men wore particular types of cotton clothing, the most notable of which were informal robes. Elite Western European men abandoned floor-length robes for everyday wear over the fifteenth and sixteenth centuries, adopting various forms of hose, short jackets and breeches that showcased their legs. Robes remained in use for ceremonial occasions such as with the sitting of Parliament (Figure 3.1), or in judicial, clerical or academic forums. Judges' robes and scholastic gowns are reminders of formerly typical elite clothing that retained symbolic importance only in selected settings.[75] But the geopolitics of early modern Eurasian trade reformulated the wearing of gowns by men, as nobles and merchants, gentlemen and genteel aspirants embraced a garment infused with Asian symbolism. This item had no connections to the venerable, formal garments of old, now worn only on official occasions. Rather, this new-style robe was emblematic of a new era, redolent of sea voyages, scientific enquiry and the commercial desires so often tied to these endeavours. The prototype for this robe came from Japan, where the Dutch had exclusive trading rights from the 1630s. Once a year the Japanese shogun presented a single kimono to the Dutch East India Company representative, the garment folded beautifully and presented on a lacquered tray. The recipient, honoured among European merchants, attracted immediate notice when he donned this garment.[76] The cachet attached to this robe spread to Europe in the wake of East India galleons. The patterned silk gown had honorific connotations. But this article was not born of entitlement; rather, its receipt marked initiative, endurance and commercial perspicacity, ethics of the mercantile middle classes. Investiture in this garb alluded to individual achievements that complicated the existing social system. So many European men yearned for these marks of distinction that new sources for robes were found in India, where they were made in a variety of fabrics, including painted and printed cotton. Blumer's observations on fashion are particularly apposite here. He wrote that: 'It is not the prestige of the elite which makes the design fashionable but, instead, it is the suitability or potential fashionableness of the design which allows the prestige of the elite to be attached to it.'[77] This innovation in male vestment spread from the commercial classes to encompass middle-ranked and aristocratic men in its folds.

This garment was designated a 'banyan' in the English-speaking world, an intriguing cross-cultural eliding of terms. Duarte Barbosa employed the word in his 1518 account of his voyage to the Indian subcontinent, describing a 'caste of Heathen merchants whom they call ... Baneanes ... and trade in goods of every kind from many lands ...'[78] Thus, the term employed for the merchants of western India became the English name for a garment in vogue among those who likewise toiled for riches. In France, this article was given an Armenian provenance, Armenian traders being long established Eurasian intermediaries.[79] The Dutch whose commercial zealousness gave birth to this fashion employed two names: 'Japonsche rocken' (Japanese robe) and 'Cambay', the second term reflecting the commercial power of the Indian port of that name.[80] Each term harkened to the wealth of Asia, a lure to mercantile and philosophical adventures. Regardless of the label, this garment became ubiquitous throughout the Atlantic world. The robes themselves signalled the rational mercantile skills so celebrated in this era, as well as wider cosmopolitan pursuits (Plate 8).

R. W. Connell defines what he calls conventional 'gentry masculinity' as an elite male ethos that 'did not emphasize rational calculation ... being tied to lineage and kin networks'. Gentry masculinity was, in turn, connected to forms of 'Old Luxuries', their acquisition and display. The great social and economic movements of the early modern period, of which the new global trade networks were key, inaugurated a process of change in dominant male cultural forms. This era, as Connell notes, 'saw the displacement of gentry masculinity by more calculative, rational and regulated masculinities'.[81] This new-style masculinity was typified in the expressed aims of the Dutch East India Company (VOC) when the governing council wrote that 'no great attention should be paid to the question of reputation and honour, which is often taken too seriously; in our opinion (for we are merchants) he has the honour who without doing injustice or violence has the profit'.[82] The banyan became the material idiom of this rational ideal, defining urbane, successful and erudite masculinity. Aspiring men embraced this new mode, signalling their affiliations through the use and wear of banyans at home, in their libraries, at their desk, with their cabinets of curiosities or at their ease with friends.[83] Margo Finn finds that middle-ranked English male diarists from the long eighteenth century were keenly active in consumer activities, including in the purchase of clothing that would construct a socially appropriate appearance, while also offering utility. Without a banyan these men's wardrobes were incomplete.[84]

The term 'virtuoso culture' has been coined to define the ethos of the men enamoured with the natural or manufactured curiosities brought to Europe as part of colonial and imperial projects. Science and commerce conjoined in these interests.[85] An affinity for such intellectual preoccupations marked the incumbent as *virtuosi*, an association confirmed for some by membership in a scientific or philosophical society, by the adoption of the new coffee drink, or through the deployment of a banyan for private interactions.[86] There was a powerful imperative to signal standing through the wearing of this Indian robe, like the printed calico banyan worn by the *bourgeois gentilhomme*, Jourdain, in Molière's 1670 play of the same name. Jourdain affected this dress and was derided for his pains by courtiers who resented the threat to their status represented by commercial wealth and knowledge.[87] But whether or not this vogue was approved for bourgeois men at Louis XIV's court, it was a potent cultural form that persisted through several centuries.

Brandon Brame Fortune explores the symbolic importance of the garments worn by eighteenth-century American scholars and scientists in their portraits. Fortune observes that among members of the American Philosophical Society, 'a banyan in eighteenth-century portraiture seems to indicate a body at ease, giving free rein to the mind's work'.[88] However as we have seen this fashion pre-dated the 1700s and can be found in many hundreds of portraits from about 1650 onwards, throughout the Atlantic world. A scan of online portrait collections turns up examples like Louis XIV's chief architect, along with a prominent Dutch sculptor at the Sun King's court and a citizen of Utrecht dressed in the latest style – all of which survive in the Louvre.[89] The Italian, Antonio Verrio, was a contemporary of Samuel Pepys, working as a fresco and portrait painter for the restored Stuart royal household after 1660. For his 1700 self-portrait, Verrio chose a sumptuous flowered banyan, a mode of dress that transcended borders.[90] The political aesthetics established for the Indian banyan after 1650 continued for generations and with this the market for Indian fabrics grew. This robe was a sign of fashionably reformed elite masculinity. Sir Josiah Child, English East India Company director; John Locke, philosopher, member of the Royal Society and appointee to the Board of Trade; Isaac Newton, scientist, inventor and governor of the Royal Mint; British and colonial American painters, William Hogarth and John Singleton Copley; Benjamin Franklin, writer, inventor and revolutionary; Voltaire, Enlightenment essayist, novelist and philosopher – each of these men was memorialized wearing a banyan. They articulated their self-image through the patterns and practice of their dress, as surely as through other endeavours. And although painters typically dressed their sitters in visually more reflective silk robes, the daily use of cotton banyans is beyond question. For example, Brook Taylor, mathematician, was painted wearing a blue and white striped (cotton?) banyan in the 1720 portrait, Plate 9. So entrenched was this style that the notorious London thief-taker, Jonathan Wild, was described as wearing his 'Callicoe Gown' when receiving a genteel client seeking his services in the early decades of the 1700s.[91] Publishers, architects, botanists, chemists, clerics, diplomats, engravers, geographers, merchants, philosophers, politicians, artists, poets, actors, composers, mathematicians and writers – all were painted wearing banyans of one sort or other. These men, and many less august males of the age, wore this garment as a habitual practice and were painted swathed in this garb. The encyclopaedist Denis Diderot wrote a paean to his 'old dressing gown', which 'made me look picturesque as well as handsome', a robe whose hem served as a pen wipe during his hours of writing.[92] The men so attired recognized the links between this hybrid garb and the wider intellectual, physical and commercial worlds with which they were engaged.[93]

East India merchants and local retailers provided ready-made banyans to Europe's retailers, or made-up morning gowns for their clients from the millions of bolts of calico cloth landed at European ports.[94] In central London, Edward Gunn's shop specialized in men's Indian gowns, offering dozens of styles in 1672, which included items such as 'coloured Indian sattin', 'flowered' and more generic and affordable 'ordinary gowns for men'.[95] The breadth of sales exemplifies Blumer's concept of 'collective selection' in the creation of fashions. In the Netherlands, the *Amsterdam Courant* announced the arrival of hundreds of ready-made robes on ships of the Dutch East India Company, as well as ready-to-sew; 317 such items were advertised in 1686, for example.[96] Specialist shops selling these garments persisted well into the eighteenth century, such as the Magazin des Robes De Chambre that opened in 1732 in London's Temple Exchange, the French name of the shop suggesting the transnational reach of this garment.[97] At the end of the century, in 1792, the style persisted with sales of 'Gentleman's Banyans … all Sizes' from a ready-made linen warehouse on London's New Bond Street and advertisements for similar garments appeared at the end of the century.[98] A caricature from about 1800, of a painter immortalizing a sailor in miniature, shows the artist in his printed banyan, a hallmark of his trade (Figure 3.2). The banyan developed as an ever-present feature of dress for men from elite to middle ranks, worn within the confines of their homes, offices or social circles. It ascribed a specific set of social and intellectual mores to the male wearers, very different to those attributed to women in calico.

All imported goods carried political baggage. Imports could elicit a backlash because of the country of origin, the impact on local manufactures or its effect on traditional norms. Indian cottons were vulnerable on all counts. The late 1600s witnessed explosive anti-calico politics and vituperative screeds against female consumers, even as gentlemen lounged in their favourite calico banyans. The gender fault lines permeating society came dramatically to life in the anti-calico campaign. Women held a unique place in the political economy as the domestic managers of textiles and clothing, as well as being the most sexually charged public face of fashion. The nation was called upon to negotiate the tensions wrought by the advent of global trade and the new expressions of consumerism. Caught within contending social forces, plebeian women became the focus of riots, beatings and acid attacks, in a campaign to restore a national sartorial hierarchy. Cotton was the catalyst in this contest; women bore the brunt of the resistance to change.

Come my Hearty mind what you are at make good use of your Eyes - you know the terms on which I set sail - ten golden quids if you come to Anchor in ten minutes, but a minute beyond time, and you have but five you know, so heave a head do you hear - and lay in plenty of the true-blue about the jacket, and Harkee young one - don't forget the beauty spot on the lar-board side of my Cheek - Poll calls it her hearts delight - well this same painting is a fine knack to be sure - but I am rather puzzled about one thing - If you can get my hulk, head, and stern into that there little bit of ivory - d_n me, but I think you would be able to tow a seventy four through one of the cock boat Arches of London Bridge.

A SAILOR sitting for his MINIATURE.

3.2 *A Sailor Sitting for his Miniature*, c. 1800. The Lewis Walpole Library, Yale University.

WOMEN, FASHION AND CALICO POLITICS

A flood of Indian textiles poured into England after 1660, including all manner of cottons from high to low prices. K. N. Chaudhuri has calculated that over one quarter of a million pieces arrived at the Company's London warehouses in 1664, more yardage than in the very best years of early trade. These textiles represented 73 per cent of the Company's commerce. Yet this rate of importation paled in comparison with the years to follow. Import levels peaked in 1684, when more than a million and a half pieces arrived at London docks.[99] The East India Company represented a new source of wealth for its investors and it offered a new source of profits for retailers and wholesalers distributing the imports. In less than thirty years, the flow of Indian textiles altered the commercial atmosphere in England and shook to its foundations the wool and worsted trades. Calicoes were among the provisions supplied in 1662 by a poor law authority in Kent and they appear in a Birmingham shopkeeper's bill in 1668.[100] Notice of a missing wagon in 1683, heaped with cargo and destined for the north-western city of Chester, further illustrates the circulation of these wares. The missing wagon carried:

five Chequer'd East-India Taffatees, 120 yards plain East India Taffatee, two striped Muslins or Callico Lawnes, 17 Pieces of large brancht painted Callicoes … three black and white mixt India Silk, half a yard broad, and twenty two yards long, 10 Striped Bengalls, one yard broad and ten yards long, 60 Pieces of white Callicoes, about a yard broad, some 16, some 18 yards long, 20 Pieces of Dyed Callicoes, and 12 Pieces of Romals or Sea Handkerchiefs.[101]

The 'Sea Handkerchiefs' or 'Romals' listed were among the most popular, affordable accessories, brightly printed in many patterns; 'Bengals' referred to cottons from that region of India; muslins were among the finest of cottons; 'Taffatees' were a plain-weave glossy silk; and the 'large brancht painted Callicoes' were likely palampores, a painted hanging popular in the decoration of bedrooms. This cartload of goods exemplifies the diversity of products landing in Britain, while the planned destination of this shipment confirms the geographic breadth of demand. Indian calicoes amounted to one quarter of all imported textiles by 1700.[102] This position in the national market drew as much political fire as it did consumer acclaim. A series of duties followed, steadily raising the price of cottons in the hopes of damping enthusiasm for what seemed, to some, an unaccountable phenomenon.

A flourishing East India trade was one of several shocks for the British wool industry in the 1600s, including as well the success of fustians (linen/cotton fabrics) and lighter New Draperies.[103] The response by wool's defenders was to re-emphasize customary values and legislate what could not be gained by persuasion. In both 1660 and 1678 enactments required all English subjects be 'buried in wool'; 'sheep's wool only' would shroud English corpses in their earthly repose.[104] One fictional goodwife insisted: 'The thoughts of a [wool] Flannel-shift are so odious to me, that I'le never Dye at all rather, if I can help it.'[105] Symbolism and practicality combined in this legislation, with all things English returned to the same soil.[106] The mercantilist sentiment that inspired these policies aimed to limit imports and encourage local manufacture.[107] The murmuring against the East India trade grew louder year by year. Sir Josiah Child, a major stockholder and later director of the East India Company, was moved to publish a treatise in 1681 insisting that 'the East-India Trade is the most National of all Foreign Trades'. Child offered a comparable mercantilist argument in its defence: '*England* may be said to be Rich or Strong, as our Strength or Riches bears a proportion with our Neighbour Nations, French, Dutch, &c. and consequently whatever weakens or depopulates them, enricheth and strengtheneth *England*.'[108] However, the rage for Indian cottons precipitated political crises throughout Europe, as governments struggled to defend local manufactures and local interests.

Debates swirled around coffee houses and merchant haunts and increasingly became the subject of political controversy among Members of Parliament. France banned the domestic printing of cotton and followed the next year, in 1687, with the first of many enactments barring all Indian and Chinese textiles, in defence of the French silk industry. Olivier Raveux uncovered the dynamic spread of calicoes in late seventeenth-century Marseilles, illustrating the wider vogue in France. Probate inventories indicate a substantial growth in the use of calico garments, rising from 10 per cent in 1667–8, to 27 per cent in 1680–81 and 43 per cent in 1692.[109] In the 1680s, however, France sought to impose a sweeping proscription, although in a few enclaves like Marseilles these injunctions did not apply. Nonetheless, the French ban resonated with European legislatures. But French consumers were disinclined to accede to this law. In 1695, a Parisian merchant ruminated on more direct ways of enforcing the ban on calicoes, offering 500 *livres* to men willing 'to strip ... in the street, any woman wearing Indian fabrics'. As a further suggestion he recommended prostitutes be paid to be stripped of their calico gowns in a public spectacle blending punishment and ridicule, as an object lesson for female consumers.[110] This French proposition was not the only expression of mercantile misogyny. In England, by the close of the 1600s, women were likewise singled out as the source of unnatural, unpatriotic, corrupting fashions inimical to the health of the nation.

Women were the principal buyers, managers and manipulators of textiles and clothing as housewives, domestic servants, needlewomen or retailers. They bought, made, repaired, pawned and reclaimed garments, negotiating family budgets to optimize wants and needs through the purchase of new and second-hand goods. By 1700, more women also worked for wages in the increasingly industrious society and they made their choices apparent in the marketplace.[111] Daniel Roche observes for Paris that by the end of the eighteenth century, 'it was women who were chiefly responsible for circulating the new objects and the new values of commercial fashion'.[112] The chronology for these changes was possibly earlier in southern England, certainly in London. And from the later 1600s through the next century, urban women from many social milieus engaged in creative self-fashioning, investing their time and money in ways that upset moralists, mercantilists and special interests. Women's choices were displayed in gowns, petticoats, jackets, handkerchiefs, headwear and stockings as they walked to markets and shops, to visit family or friends, or travelled to and from work. Plate 10 shows a printed calico petticoat from the early 1700s with a painted design that is its most prominent feature. Calico bedding, cushions and curtains, like men's banyans, were privately enjoyed. Women's dress choices were publicly displayed and more routinely discussed and dissected, a fact true for genteel as well as plebeian women. Their material behaviour now elicited a vituperative rhetoric, emphasizing ancient tropes of female corruptibility. Female dishonour was a recurring theme in this society and it was argued that women could most easily assure honour and respectability through a cloistered obedience. In contrast, the marketplace bespoke potential indulgence, material seduction and possible social transgression. Laura Gowing observes that for early modern Englishwomen, 'the possibilities of dishonour seem almost to erase those of honour'.[113] The play of fashionable Indian cottons offended critics at every social level. The 1699 verse, *Prince Butler's Tale*, exemplifies these complaints, crafted in a form that may have been put to music for strolling ballad singers.

> Our *Ladies* all were set a gadding,
> After these Toys they ran a madding;
> And nothing then wou'd please their fancies,
> Nor *Dolls*, nor *Joans*, nor wanton *Nancies*,
> Unless it was of *Indians* making;
> And if 'twas so, 'twas *wondrous* taking.
> This Antick humour so prevail'd,
> Tho' many 'gainst it *greatly* rail'd,

> 'Mongst all degrees of *Female* kind,
> That nothing else could please their mind.
> Tell 'em the following of such fashion,
> Wou'd *beggar* and *undo* the Nation,
> And *ruin* all our Labouring Poor,
> That must, or starve, or beg at door,
> They'd not at all regard your story,
> But in their *painted* Garments glory;
> And such as were not *Indian* proof,
> They *scorn'd*, despis'd, as paltry stuff:
> … What *mischiefs* to our Trade befel;
> How both our *Men* and *Bullion* went
> To work in *India*, and be spent
> In needless *Toys*, and gawdy *Dresses*,
> For *Ladies, Madams, Trulls,* and *Misses*.[114]

In the late 1690s, weavers rioted outside the House of Lords as a bill was considered to ban Indian textiles. The 'great Tumults of the multitude' involved London weavers and their wives and supporters, who feared that the influence of the East India Company would derail this legislation. These interests achieved a partial victory in 1700 when Parliament banned printed and painted Indian textiles; henceforth only plain Indian fabrics would be allowed into the country. But this legislation had little effect, as by this time England, French and Dutch artisans were fully able to print counterfeits of Indian wares almost as pleasing as the originals. The Lords Commissioners for Trade and Plantations expressed frustration that: 'The calicoes now painted in England are so very cheap and so much in fashion that persons of all qualities and degrees clothe themselves and furnish their houses in great measure with them.'[115] With the failure of the 1700 Act, the abuse against English women shoppers intensified, a process encouraged by scurrilous texts of every sort. A 1703 verse characterized the women who bought and used calicoes as 'Jilts', 'Satyrs' and 'Patched, painted powder'd Drury Whores'. The author proposed to 'tear your Gawdy Cloaths, and pay your Backs'.[116] The invective was poisonous, an incendiary diatribe against the most visible actors in the marketplace. It employed the hackneyed terms of sexual misconduct, immorality and vice and claimed any women who bought or wore foreign-produced textiles deserved the lash, the penalty of a convicted wanton.

> More Patched Misses, with their Muff and Fans
> Came posting there, like Ladies in Sedans,
> To buy a hoard up for their wanton Pride,
> Leave all their Money and a Pawn beside,
> A Card-Match Woman, with a Brimston's funk
> Did much disturb a Common Garden punck,
> Faugh, nasty Beast, away, I'll kick your Britch
> *You kiss my Ars,* you Common-Garden *Bitch,*
> *You Town-bred Miss, that paint your outward skin*
> *And seems so fair, yet pockey soul within;*
> *Pray hold your-Brazen Tongue, what's here to do*

I'm come to buy up Goods as well as you:
I have a Taylor that will work all Sunday;
And you may see me wear my Gown on Monday.
Next fat Arse Sarah, lives in Turnbull-street
Who pawn'd four Smocks, wrap'd in a Flaxen-Sheet,
To buy a Suite of Calicoe most rare,
And on her Back had ne'er a Smock to wear.
Four Oyster Wenches went from Billingsgate,
To buy up Calicoe e're went out of date
That each may have a right *East-India* Gown,
And look as great as Misses of the Town.
Some Country Wenches ... to *London* comes,
With scarcely Cloaths enough to hide their Bums,
Cooks, Scullens, Servant maids, when they have Places,
Will Flower their Buttocks, to set out their faces ...[117]

This verse was street fare, bawdy, the language of libertines, designed to get a laugh when rhymed on street corners, taverns or anterooms, but also to spark anger against women whose appetites were deemed so unruly. That same year, a comedy at the Theatre Royal included a similarly scathing portrayal of the 'strange Trollops in Callicoe Gowns ... Women of no Fortune, that have made a good figure in an old Sheet printed black and white'.[118]

Misogyny flowed through early modern society and was largely unremarked on, notable to our eyes in the anti-female aphorisms that circulated casually throughout the culture.[119] The sentiments evident in these and later tracts are directed specifically at women, at their independence in the market and at the fashionable judgements they employed. At the century's turn, about 1700, there was a high rate of unmarried women, higher than in previous generations. Single women needed to work and their involvement in many areas, including domestic service, was very apparent and especially in the great city of London, a magnet for labour. Women predominated in new consumer trades, from the stitching of cheap, ready-made clothes, to the making of buttons, pins and ribbons. Women worked in the growing numbers of shops, coffee houses and market stalls or hawked ballads, broadsheets, fruit or second-hand goods in the streets.[120] The earnings of single and married women brought about what Jan de Vries calls 'the industrious revolution', where the possibility of new material benefits encouraged more women to take up paid work and prompted others into longer hours of work as opportunities arose. The money these women earned opened a new world of options for their families, or for households of single or widowed women who pooled their resources.

Indeed, de Vries remarks that 'The industrious revolution has as its social pendant female earning power'.[121] However, wage-earning women, along with their wealthier sisters, materialized fashion choices in a manner that left them open to accusations of indulgence and even treason. The anxiety surrounding the influence of fashion was widespread. For example, Antwerp experienced a series of anti-fashion riots in 1701 and 1702 during which 'Indian cloth and cottons' was seized from shops and warehouses and burned in crowd actions.[122] An anti-fashion backlash was evident in many parts of Europe. In England, the author of *Pride's Exchange* accused women of robbing weavers of their 'Birth-right'; Daniel Defoe termed the female calico buyer 'An Enemy to her Country'; another writer deplored 'the Folly of our Women'.[123] Attacks on foreign imports did not begin with Indian cottons. Roze Hentschell notes that 'Clothing and cloth from which it was made was not only associated with specific nations, but also helped to create sentiments of nationhood through the linkages of clothing with a particular country.'[124] The great difference in this case was that Indian textiles were not part of the mercantile contest among European neighbours but arose from global trade. The wares channelled into Europe brought unique material characteristics in their wake and precipitated broad geopolitical repercussions. The ban on printed Indian goods resulted in the growth of local textile printing and the flow of calicoes continued unabated. Opponents were determined to stop the trade and stop female consumers. Ballads and verses excoriated 'Callico Madams', drawing an equation between sexual depravity, heartless treason and the wearing of this fabric.[125] In legislative circles another bill was debated, aiming to ban virtually all Indian fabrics and the East India Company mounted a weak defence against these attacks. By 1719 the scene was set for a second crusade against Indian cottons. The onslaught of weavers against female consumers moved from metaphor to menace.

On a bright summer evening in June 1719, thousands of disgruntled weavers and their supporters assembled to protest against their slack trade, laying the blame on Indian imports. In London alone, an estimated 40,000 weavers were working on worsted wool and mixed silk and wool fabrics.[126] The crowd on that June evening numbered about 4,000 strong and it ranged from the weaving district of Spitalfields through the old City of London. Pouring through the streets and alleyways, the men 'tore the English and Foreign Callicoes from off the Backs of all the Women they met, and proceeded to such Irregularities that the Lord Mayor caus'd the City Gates to be shut'. The tumults continued the next day and women attired in calico (or what appeared to be calico) were mobbed and beaten. The trouble spread as protesters crossed the Thames to the south side, where calico printers were based, aiming to smash the printing workshops. The Lord Mayor called for help and a troop of cavalry was sent to disperse the throng, after which the Riot Act was read, requiring the crowd to disperse within the hour. Several leaders were arrested and one man was killed on attempting to unseat a cavalryman.[127] This was the beginning, not the end, of the disorders. Printing presses churned out pamphlets and broadsides by the dozen; petition campaigns organized by the Company of Weavers in London generated reams of pro-wool, anti-calico entreaties from across England. Trades dependent on printing the calico, weaving cotton/linen cloth, making calico quilts or selling cotton commodities likewise produced pamphlets, but with few results. Meanwhile, ballad singers fired up the crowds. One such song jibbed that: 'None shall be thought / A more scandalous Slut / Than a taudry Callico Madam'.[128] This and other such verses were loudly recited, as one newspaper reported, 'to encourage the Mob and the Weavers to tear and burn the Callicoes'.[129]

Women's dress was an incendiary topic, a gendered contest between old consumer wares and new commodities. Few personal attacks resulted in charges or left legal evidence of the events, though some records remain of generalized assaults. In July, a young woman looking for lodgings in east London was targeted when 'some People sitting at their Doors' noticed a printed gown under her red wool riding hood. The simple sighting of a printed pattern was enough to spark an eruption. Despite the prominence of the red cloak, a traditional emblem of English womanhood, the local people took up the cry: 'Callicoe, Callicoe, Weavers, Weavers!' And within moments she was surrounded, pummelled, her clothes torn: 'Her Gown off all but the Sleeves, her Pocket, the head of her Riding Hood, and [she was] abus'd ... very much'.[130] Newspapers recount the most notorious episodes. This was not a passing storm. Rather it inaugurated a long-running, recurring campaign that spanned urban Britain, aimed at disciplining female consumers regardless of social rank. The tenor of the anti-calico pamphlets matched the anti-fashion misogyny. All women in public were vulnerable, like the alewife who ran the White Lion Alehouse in Whitechapel, in the East End of London. An anti-calico supporter came into the tavern and, seeing the landlady dressed in patterned cotton, 'he pulled out his Knife to cut it to pieces, but being prevented and turned out of Doors [by the company], he whetted his Knife upon his Shoe, and swore he would either cut the Callicoes, or stab her to the Heart'. Several weeks later in another incident, a man stumbled across a woman in a calico gown on her doorstep and attempted to slice it with his knife. When she ran indoors he swore 'he would cut her Soul from her Body'.[131]

E. P. Thompson observed that 'It is possible to detect in almost every eighteenth-century crowd action some legitimizing notion ... grounded upon a consistent traditional view of social norms and obligations, of the proper economic functions of several parties.'[132] Thompson focused on food riots and the tensions surrounding the transformation of eighteenth-century English markets in provincial towns. The politics of wool and cotton, tradition and fashion, are equally symptomatic of a charged economic and cultural conflict that wracked English society. The genesis of fashionable consumption was predicated in key ways on a global commerce that undercut the privileged national position of an English staple. The evident hatred of Indian cottons and systematic attacks on fashion actors reflect the unprecedented and painful transitions under way. As the violence spread in the summer of 1719, the Company of Weavers scrambled to damp the fires they had stoked, cautioning journeymen weavers to 'live quietly and peaceably'.[133] But the ensuing months were neither quiet nor peaceable. In Norwich, in the heart of the worsted industry, parades of weavers and their supporters strode through the streets, searching out offending women and ripping their calico gowns to shreds wherever they found them. One man, brought before a local magistrate, was allowed to escape to prevent an angry crowd from overrunning the court. A greater throng mustered the next day in Norwich, marching along the streets 'in great Numbers, and cut and tore all the Callicoes they met with'. The alliance of wool, worsted and silk weavers deployed a host of well-known rituals of protest, sometimes hiring a bell-ringer to bring out supporters; raiders wrapped looted fabrics around their waists and waved the cloth in triumph, like banners seized in combat, as they raced down the streets; others nailed shreds of torn calico on a gibbet by a London thoroughfare as a simulacrum of the traitors' heads that bedecked the city's bridges for generations. Locals thought to be opponents were threatened, one with having his house pulled down around his ears – and another suffered that fate.[134] One assembly of Norwich weavers was described as 'carrying in a triumphing Manner the Callicoes they get upon the Top of Poles and Sticks; and they are so very bold, that they go into People's Houses, and tear them off of their Backs, and even walk in that manner by the very Doors of the Magistrates'.[135] Money was spent to enlist men willing to act. John Humphreys was later charged and convicted for this disorder. No mention was ever made of the source of the substantial £20 he disbursed over the first days of the London riots.[136] The wool cause had support far beyond those directly involved. Patriotism, in their view, demanded the severest sanctions against 'all those Women that were seen in Callicoe Gowns, or with Painted Callicoes for their outer Habit'. Another fictional householder described the fate he wished for all calicoes:

> My Friends in Spittlefields I heartily apply to, and must let 'em know, I don't suffer any of my Family to wear Callicoe. I had made up four [calico] Dresses for a Dance, but in Justice to their Complaints, I have made a Burnt-Offering of 'em to the Silk and Woollen Manufactures . . .[137]

Despite the intermittent presence of troops in Norwich and London, attacks continued through the summer and autumn of 1719. In London, shops and warehouses selling Indian textiles were repeatedly looted and some destroyed, the weavers acting in small bands, to strike quickly and escape. In September 1719 the first reports of acid-throwing appeared in a London paper. Aqua fortis, or nitric acid, was hurled at women seen wearing calicoes 'in Houses or Coaches'. Acids were used in industrial processes and could evidently be obtained for other purposes. This liquid could be tossed from a distance and still be effective. The number and ferocity of assaults on women shocked some contemporaries and a few charges were laid where perpetrators were caught, though not all juries were prepared to convict. In some circles, there was such an abhorrence of women who wore calico that many were prepared to countenance the use of acid, or look the other way when women were accosted and their clothes ripped from their backs. Records reveal only a fraction of such encounters, summarized in general comments like: '[The weavers] dispersed themselves in small Parties thro' most of the Out-parts of the Town: They destroyed a considerable Quantity of Callicoes in the Shops, and tore all the Callicoes Clothes they met with abroad'.[138]

Women in printed garments were at risk whenever they walked and wherever they wore these items. Why did they continue to wear such dangerous articles? Some doubtless wore what they owned and they could not afford to replace a favourite gown. Others defied the weavers' attempted censorship. Pamphlets contain fleeting references to the ideal of 'Liberty' in dress, including 'Wearing what we please, and Thinking or Believing what we please'.[139] It was a contentious claim. Over the course of weeks and months of attacks, husbands, friends or neighbours attempted to defend spouses, friends or relatives, resisting vigilantes wherever possible. But through the winter and into the spring of 1720, even as a new calico bill was debated in Parliament, the violence spread.[140] The West Country port of Bristol experienced disturbances in the summer of 1720. One heated encounter led to a weaver's death and the trial of the assailant, Thomas Singer. Singer was an excise officer, living in Bristol, who in the company of his wife was strolling through town when she was assailed by a group of men who saw her printed gown. One glimpse incited attack. The incident ended with Singer being tried for the murder of this weaver, but the final verdict was less severe and he 'was found Guilty of Manslaughter only; because he did it in Defence of his Wife, [who] was Assaulted by a Gang of Weavers who tore her Callacoe Cloths off, and used her very Unmercifully'.[141] In another instance, an observant husband spotted a man who had been in a crowd that 'strip[ped] his Wife of a Suit of Callicoe in the Month of March [1720], and set Fire to it before his Face, so that she was oblig'd to go home two Miles without it' – the assailant was charged by a constable and taken into custody. In June 1720, Dorothy Orwell was caught 'by a Multitude of Weavers in Red-Lion-Fields in Hoxton [London], who tore, cut, and pull'd off her Gown and Petticoat by Violence, threatened her with vile Language, and left her naked in the Fields; that she was in such a Fright that she did not know them again'. But her friend identified the ringleader. John Web recounted that to protect his companion he 'took her in his Arms to save her from their Rage', being knifed in the ensuing melee. When it was over he covered Orwell with his coat before guiding her to shelter in a local tavern. A few attackers were convicted. But most apprehended in the summer of 1720 were released with a reprimand – evidence of sympathy from court and civic authorities.[142]

The legal cases are singular in that they offer slightly more detailed narratives of outbreaks replicated many hundreds (possibly thousands) of times when women were mobbed, beaten, their clothes torn or skin burned with acid – incidents erupting on the streets of the capital and major provincial cities like Norwich and Bristol. It is likely that skirmishes played out in other locales, but were unrecorded in newspapers, or are still buried in local archives. The vilification of women for their looks, for their simple choice of clothes, represents a broad-based attempt to enforce a collective material discipline and impose a traditional moral economy over a large female population. These women were visible members of urban societies, prominent in numbers if not always in social position and uniquely reflective of new cultural sensibilities. Their collective fashion practice became exceptionally politicized – 'The Fashion is the Grievance', confirmed one anti-calico pamphleteer.[143] The denigration of this group encouraged extreme measures. In contrast, the voices protesting this gendered violence were rare and more muted than the champions of wool. However, the British linen industry denounced the systematic attacks on women, possibly because at least some of those attacked wore printed linens or linen/cottons, locally made. 'These Violences will lay a … Restraint upon the Wearing of Printed Calicoes and Linens. This [violence] is a Distemper in the Blood, and if not timely checked will end in a raging Calenture.'[144]

Almost inevitably, all light, printed textiles became embroiled in this anti-calico campaign, even the hybrid linen/cotton or linen goods, British made and British printed. Printing on textiles was a uniquely Indian aesthetic form, applying decoration through inexpensive processes that could be easily varied in line with changing tastes. European techniques of textile decoration involved patterning in the loom or embroidery, which were more costly, labour-intensive and time-consuming than printing. Printing added colour and design to even inexpensive stuff and was an exceptional system of embellishment ideal for a burgeoning consumer society. Not surprisingly, European artisans worked to replicate the Indian style, with some success. Thus, printed textiles, regardless of their origins, symbolized the new fashion-driven economy abhorrent to those dependent on the making and sale of more traditional commodities. A printed petticoat, gown or jacket signalled the implacable rivalry between old and new political economies. Indian cotton imports disrupted existing hierarchies of trades, encouraging more varied and demotic fashions among a highly visible population. As Jan de Vries observes: 'The diffusion of fashionable dress followed a different dynamic from that of durable goods'– or old commodities.[145] Urban women adventured in this new sociopolitics. Women worked not only for basic subsistence but to be able to buy more of the new niceties and small luxuries. They added crucially to family budgets and they also spent more on items of their choosing. The marketplace in which they bargained was made flexible through mediums like the second-hand trade, which enabled greater market participation by all social sectors and gave a broader choice to non-elites.[146] Thus, middle-ranked and labouring women became important consumers, frequenting retail shops in many urban areas.[147] Would the fashion impulse be extinguished in the campaign against cotton? There were certainly many who wished for that outcome, along with a return to ordered material behaviour: 'As the general Wearing of Callicoes is the Complaint, the general Leaving them off will be the Cure', opined one writer.[148] Could sumptuary standards be legislated and enforced? France found it difficult to enforce the repeated anti-calico decrees, adding increasingly draconian punishments, including servitude in the galleys for those caught dealing in Indian textiles. These policies were widely reported. Meanwhile, British legislators agreed to limit consumer choice in defence of a staple industry, as the country painfully adjusted to an increasingly consumer-driven economy.

The wool trade achieved its goal in the short term. An Act was passed in March 1721 banning most Indian textiles after the coming Christmas, in keeping with similar laws passed elsewhere in Europe. The Act championed old values and weavers celebrated in a traditional manner, with the 'Woollen Manufactures of Southwark' organizing a great bonfire. A broadsheet of the day depicts these events (Figure 3.3). The image commemorates the protection of wool and includes in its

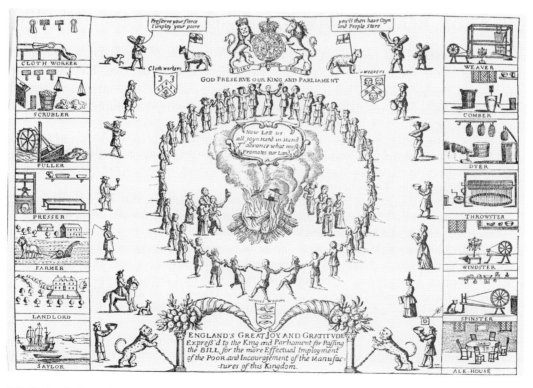

3.3 'England's Great Joy and Gratitude', broadsheet printed c.1720.

borders every social emblem of the trade from the landlord through to the weaver, suggesting the organic relations underpinning this alliance. Thanks were extended to the king and Parliament while the weavers danced about the fire, alight with burning calico. On the actual occasion, an effigy of 'an old Woman drest in Calicoe' was carried round the neighbourhood, exciting jeers and catcalls. At the climax of this procession the figure was thrown on the flames, to great cheers and celebrations.[149] At the moment the effigy was set aflame, the customary moral balance seemed restored. The real and symbolic assaults on women consumers culminated in a great pyrrhic cleansing, with crowds rollicking around the burning form. A real-life immolation took place later in the summer, before the ban was in effect. One July evening, a woman dressed in calico walked through London's Haymarket, passing a group of linkboys waiting about in the square to light pedestrians home. Her defining feature was that she was wore a calico gown. The linkboys set her ablaze.[150] This was neither the first nor the only death attributable to the anti-calico campaign and the linkboys' brutal certainty in their actions speaks to the social politics at work. But customary practices could not be so readily restored in the wider society, even with such tactics. Indian cottons and women consumers in combination were part of a powerful dynamic that challenged traditional material behaviour, inaugurating fashion-driven, popular consumerism that destabilized older industries and older hierarchies. The antagonisms that resulted and the persistence of these antipathies suggest the depth of the struggle under way.

LEGISLATION, REACTION, INVENTION – FASHION RENEWED

Daniel Defoe, novelist and polemicist, was a resolute supporter of the English wool and silk industries and wrote innumerable articles and pamphlets in their defence. He also registered distaste for new female shopping habits.[151] Yet despite this position, Defoe introduced the fullest account of the plebeian woman shopper. Like her actual counterpart, this fictional female character would not be checked.

> We are oppressed and insulted here in the open Streets, – we are abused, frighted, stript, our Clothes torn off our Backs every day by Rabbles, – under the pretence of not wearing such Clothes as the Weavers please to have us wear.
>
> We always thought, and have been told by our Grand-fathers, that English people enjoyed their lawful Liberties above all the Nations in the World; that it was their Honour to do so, and that our Ancestors fought for those Liberties.
>
> What, did they fight for Liberty to abuse us, and that we should not have Liberty to go about Streets ... Never tell us of National Liberties! If our Sex has not a Share in the Liberties, how can they be National? We think we have Liberty little enough, *as we are Wives*, consequently Drudges. Shall we have less Liberty, *as we are Women*, than our Mothers had before us? This is Tyranny and Partiality, and we neither can, nor will bear it.[152]

We cannot assume that this defiant posture reflected Defoe's attitudes; indeed, the female claim for gender equity in the market may have generated further rebuttals. That may have been its rhetorical intent. But it is equally possible that, as a father of six daughters, Defoe heard these sentiments expressed at his own table or among his many female acquaintances. Defoe's fictional creations included characters such as the Londoner Moll Flanders (1722) and he was fully cognizant of the gendered machinations that animated her world.[153] Thus it may not be surprising to see so pointed a claim for consumer independence in a female speaker of his creation. There is no record of an actual martial cry such as this from any woman of that era, or not in so many words. Women's actions, however, suggest a staunch resistance to sumptuary censorship and many continued to wear printed cottons (or lookalike printed linens and fustians) at the height of the campaign and after the prohibition, whether for budgetary reasons or as statements of defiance. In response, groups and individuals continued to monitor women and those found in printed garments risked penalties. This style of patterned textile was not normalized for a generation.

In fact, during the lengthy calico debate, local British manufacturers of linen/cotton fabrics and local textile printers, who made imitations of Indian cottons, faced repeated demands that their trades be banned in the national interest. Linen weavers made facsimiles of Indian goods composed in whole or in part of linen; fustians made of linen and cotton yarns were also crafted to look like Indian fabrics. This business had grown in the past generation and the linen industry wished this to continue. One representative rebutted critics, stating that: 'Our Linen Manufacture is as much a Staple Manufacture of the Kingdom, as the Woollen, and hath as much right to be encourag'd'.[154] Mixed linen/cotton fustians were not banned by the 1721 Act and English weavers and printers continued with their trades, the one weaving new types of linen/cotton cloth and the other devising new patterns and printing methods. They aspired to serve the widest markets and they prospered with the forced departure of competitive Indian products. The fustian trade, centred about the north-west county of Lancashire, and the linen trade in south-west Scotland, took full advantage of the ban to advance their growing industry.[155] But despite native credentials, they were enmeshed in continuing political hostilities.

The marketplace was difficult to police. There were too few officials to monitor regulations and authorities relied on informers to enforce rulings. Such was the case with the 1721 enactment, which promised £5 to any informer who brought a calico-wearing miscreant before a magistrate, the sum to be paid by the person convicted. In the days following the Act, a flurry of cases were reported of women brought to justice for their fashion crimes. Some thought they were exempt if they only wore calico 'round the bottoms of their Petticoats' – a supposition held by 'ignorant People' according to the press. Not all could pay the fine and they were imprisoned for their pains. The elite, too, suffered betrayals; in one case a disgruntled ex-footman rushed to a magistrate, following his dismissal, to lay information against his former employer. This lady did not appear in court, but paid her fine and surrendered her calico gown in the privacy of her home.[156] An enthusiastic early report stated that 'The Effects of the Act of Parliament for suppressing Callicoes are visible; none of the Female Sex having ventured to wear them since Christmas-Day.'[157] But the issue was far from resolved, for although there was an initial decline, locally made printed linen and fustian grew in popularity. At the same time, a campaign of harassment and intimidation persisted against women in printed garments. Riots were at an end. But actions by small groups and individuals continued and men threw sulphuric or nitric acid 'and other corrosive Liquids' wherever they saw 'Flower'd Linnen'.[158]

Informers were key to the suppression of calico. So keen were these men in their hunt that they accosted women wearing printed apparel whatever the fabric. We can only guess at the numbers week in and week out: records survive only occasionally and usually deal with elite women. In the spring of 1723, several skirmishes were recorded in London neighbourhoods, in one instance the man 'laying hold of, and insulting' the lady involved.[159] Discretion drove many women to substitute printed linen for Indian wares; yet despite or possibly because of this, London journeymen complained in 1728 of their 'Miseries and Hardships', blaming 'the wear of printed Linnens; as was formerly their Case when Calicoes were worn'.[160] Several dynamics were in place. In the first instance, fashion worked to the advantage of lighter, cheaper fabrics; these were now produced in Britain from linen and cotton blends in growing quantities, varieties and prices (see Chapter 4). Lighter worsted wool and silk textiles also profited from this trend and the former produced printed worsted fabrics in recognition of the prevailing style. Cotton equivalents of all sorts remained a major factor in the market. Second, textile prices in general continued to fall. Beginning in the seventeenth century, the price of fabrics declined substantially and the trend continued through the eighteenth century, a phenomenon attributed to competition from cheaper European and Asian fabrics. This decline did not depend on new technologies, but on the lighter qualities of the new textiles themselves, bringing added pressure on wages among English cloth workers.[161] Workers in the wool trade undoubtedly suffered, especially in the sectors making traditional cloth. National regulation offered a temporary panacea. But it could not stifle the broader market reorientation.

Nonetheless, protests persisted along with efforts to enforce the calico ban. Edinburgh was the next city to see an attempt and in 1730 'several Women were apprehended in the streets with Gowns of the same [calico]'.[162] During the mid-1730s, prosecutions reached a fever pitch across Britain and were reported in even greater numbers than in the year immediately after the 1721 Act. In Norwich, the calico miscreants included a female tavern-keeper, the wife of an innkeeper and the owner of 'Manchester Warehouse' in the city. In London a vintner's wife and a butcher's wife were charged, along with several anonymous 'Mrs' and a few highly placed ladies, all 'for wearing a Chints Callico'. Most paid their fines; all forfeited their clothing. Many of those charged were middle-ranked folk, the sort whose participation in the consumer market is well documented, and whose prosperity was often connected to the new commodities through trade or manufacture. Local magistrates heard complaints and at the same time acid-throwing revived as a tactic, a practice that spread to Dublin by at least the 1730s. In the fall of 1735 there were reports of renewed 'Gang' activity, 'squirting Aqua-Fortis' on unlucky women's clothes. As in other British cities, weavers and their supporters launched public protests along with targeted punishments. One report suggests that acid was reserved for actions against 'Ladies', with more direct strokes taken against 'the meaner Sort'. The 1735 report from Dublin continued: 'We are inform'd, they not only cut ... [labouring women's] Cloaths, but have used them very scurvily, by abusing them otherwise'.[163] In the mid-1730s the tempo of protests quickened, matched by a resurgence of petitions to Parliament from wool and worsted representatives. The aim was to ban all printed cloth entirely. As before, the uncertain state of the wool trade was blamed on competitive fustians and the skill of local printers. One pamphlet objected that 'by the artful Contrivance of Printers and others, a sort of Stuff mixt with Cotton, has been since found to supply the Place of India Callicoes'.[164] The allegations against

British manufacturers were accurate in one sense, as a 1736 testimony before a House of Commons committee confirmed, for the British cotton/linen trade had grown in the last decade, their goods replacing previously imported German linens, as well as Indian cottons. As one witnessed testified:

> Great Quantities of the said Manufactures have, for several Years last past, been printed, and, when so printed, have been used in Apparel and Furniture; and that Eight Parts out of Nine of the Goods he manufactures are printed, and, according to the best of his Judgment, One-half or Two-thirds of the Cotton Wool brought into this Kingdom from the *British* Plantations is used in the Fustians that are printed; and that the greatest Part of them are sent up brown, from the several Countries in which they are made, and printed in or about *London*.[165]

In the face of this success, provincial retailers received leaflets and read advertisements claiming that British-made printed fustians were banned along with Indian cottons. Retailers were threatened with prosecution if they sold the controversial fabrics.

The wool interests did not prevail in this instance. In April 1736, Parliament decided in favour of the British cotton/linen trade, specifying that British-made fustians of cotton/linen blend were exempt from the 1721 legislation. The cotton/linen industry had grown to such an extent and employed so many that, like the wool trade, it could demand the favour of legal protection. The nascent cotton trade and its printing industry received the security it sought. London's textile printers celebrated. A group of a hundred travelled in a barge from the House of Commons at Westminster up the Thames to the suburb of Wandsworth, accompanied by a small band of musicians playing trumpets and drums. Wandsworth was one of the centres of the printing trade and the locals were jubilant. On shore the printers were greeted with a salute from several gunners and a larger company of men and women joined them to parade through the streets to Bowling Green House in neighbouring Putney. The celebrants waved flags made of printed fabric; women of the trade dressed in brightly printed gowns, jackets and petticoats and church bells rang as they marched along. The day ended with feasting, dancing and 'other Demonstrations of Joy'.[166]

Legal ambiguity was at an end; but this did not end policing by the wool trade and their sympathisers. Throughout the spring and summer of 1736, newspapers describe the relentless crusade against women in printed garments. In some instances the women were attired in the forbidden calico – smuggling provided continuing supplies for discerning customers. Mr Morris, a very active informer, accumulated a number of £5 fines extracted from women infringing the Act. His success encouraged others to patrol the streets with a sharp eye on women's clothing. However, the court looked unfavourably on the harassment of gentlewomen, falsely charged. One such informer was convicted of perjury for 'swearing falsely against a Gentlewomen' when her gown was found to be printed linen and the would-be informer was jailed. In the winter of 1737, Mr Morris found himself in similar straits. The previously successful informant was committed to Newgate prison for swearing information against Miss Gough, sister of Sir Henry Gough, 'whom he had dogged home to her Dwelling House' after spotting her in St James's Park, a popular resort for fashionable Londoners. This locale was evidently one of several where he hunted. The case itself became a brief cause célèbre, widely reported, with legal council employed on both sides. Morris evidently had the backing of people with money to pay for his attorney. He was lucky.

3.4 Wrapping gown for a young child, made of cream-coloured English cotton printed in red, c.1750. Victoria and Albert Museum, London.

Ultimately his fulsome apology was accepted and he buttressed this by acknowledging that 'the most experienced Man might be deceiv'd at a Distance, by Reason of the great Improvements made in our Linnen Manufactures'.[167] The London jury acquitted him, accepting the excellence of British printed textiles as the basis of his error. Figure 3.4 shows an example of printed British cotton from mid-century in a simple wrapping gown for a child. It could have been cut down from a larger adult garment – this fabric would have suited a woman equally well.

CONCLUSION

Fashion's force produced social and economic reverberations that at times generated heated polemics and violent confrontations. An ever wider range of men and women embraced fashion priorities, working and budgeting to engage in new forms of consumption and display. The landscape of fashion now involved a diverse collection of individuals and groups carving out new styles and representative looks, asserting their position through symbolic and material variations in dress.

3.5 *Quite Ripe Sir*, Bodleian Library, Oxford.

The collective choices made by these new consuming classes inaugurated economic opportunities for some, leaving others fired with resentment and the desire to punish. Calico-wearing women epitomized new, more demotic styles, embraced by a visible heterogeneous assortment of women. The figure of a strawberry seller from about 1780 shows a young woman wearing a printed gown, likely of British-made cotton (Figure 3.5). However idealized this image may be, there is no doubt of the numbers of women from this rank who made similar choices in dress over the century. She epitomizes the generations before her who worked, budgeted and bought clothes to their taste.

For Gilles Lipovetsky, fashion 'helped unsettle the immobility of tradition'. Writing about the nineteenth century, Lipovetsky notes that: 'Fashion was able to become the permanent theatre of ephemeral metamorphoses because the individualization of appearance had won a new status of social legitimacy.'[168] Change of this sort did not come easily or without controversy. Indeed, the systematic violence against calico-wearing women reflects how ruthlessly traditional materials and material precepts were defended, particularly when innovations were associated with female practices.

Indian cottons were the catalyst that sparked a broad social process. Their entry into the European marketplace encouraged the expansion of a heterogeneous fashion-driven consumerism, a process already under way. This phenomenon engaged a growing cohort of shoppers, users and wearers. In turn, societies and economies adapted to the broader dictates of this system. Choice was a crucial factor enabled by the new commodities; choice allowed the crafting of new public personae, materially complicating the social strata inherited from previous centuries. Women from various social ranks asserted their right to create fashionable styles of many sorts and they employed cottons in this exercise. They persisted despite the extraordinary public penalties enforced by vigilantes. The calico crisis reflects profound societal adjustments as politically charged popular fashions were negotiated in British society.

The impulse to renew sumptuary laws persisted throughout this era, advocated as the solution to disorienting practices that undermined the old certainties. Virtually every European territory, except the Netherlands, legislated against Indian calicoes in a paroxysm of anti-fashion, anti-consumerist activism. The Netherlands profited by printing plain Indian cottons and linens – it also served as a staging post for smugglers moving cargoes of Indian textiles to various European landing sites. In Britain, paradoxically, the nascent British linen/cotton industry benefited from the fashion catalyst. The unintended consequence of the 1721 Act was a market virtually free from competitors, where local innovation and invention was encouraged in an effort to match the quality, look and cost of the Indian exemplar. By 1736, when Parliament legislated in their favour, the term 'calico' came increasingly to refer to British-made fabrics, created by British men and women in communities from London to Lancashire to Scotland. The anti-calico frenzy abated by mid-century. At the same time, the fashion phenomenon was increasingly accepted as a facet of British society that could profit local manufacturers. Several witnesses before a Parliamentary Committee in 1751 remarked on the success of some Lancashire textiles on account of 'Fashion'. Witnesses seemed rather surprised by this development.[169] However, cotton manufacturing was inextricably linked to fashion markets in ways that would evolve in the generations to follow. A printed English cotton gown, made up in the 1780s, reveals the later achievements of the British cotton industry (Plate 11). Manufacturers learned the value of pervasive, demotic fashion cravings, serving a range of needs, a process already well under way during the middle decades of the eighteenth century. A reference to local calicoes in 1736 charts these shifting attitudes. The young woman celebrated in this song was not vilified, but described in admiring terms as 'Never loud nor craving', for Pretty Poll chose 'callicoe, or lowly chints, to be more saving'.[170] The female character's modest expenditures are applauded and her ambitions approved. This idealized pattern of consumer behaviour, multiplied many times over, formed the foundation of a new fashion era and a new industrial era that came to full flower in the 1800s. The women who navigated these rough waters defined the new parameters of a fashion-driven consumer economy.

4.
COTTAGE, MILL, FACTORY, PLANTATION
The Industrialization of Cotton and the New World Order, c. 1400-1860

Cotton production in the West evolved from a minor subsection of the linen industry to become the world's first mechanized and industrialized trade. The process took centuries and the impact reshaped the world. Over this long time period, men, women and children in Western regions learned how to work with this fibre, discovered how to print on the fabrics and developed new craft and trade practices. Cotton manufacturing grew in prominence despite the opposition of its European opponents. The continuing international competition with India pushed the newcomers to this trade to devise new technologies during the eighteenth century to improve spinning and to accelerate weaving, giving birth to what is known as the Industrial Revolution. The Industrial Revolution began with the British cotton trade. Karl Polanyi described this event in very stark terms as producing 'an almost miraculous improvement in the tools of production, which was accompanied by a catastrophic dislocation of the lives of the common people'.[1] Research surrounding the Industrial Revolution has generated a more complex list of gains and losses since Polanyi made this statement more than sixty years ago. But debate on this subject continues. Library shelves are filled with analyses of the inventors, businesses and communities shaped by these new forces. The application of original technologies began in Britain but spilled out to many other parts of the world, sparking interest, acclaim and opposition with the passing years. Innovation was not restricted to the United Kingdom. American inventor Eli Whitney and his cotton gin improved the cleaning of raw cotton, facilitating the continuing growth of the industry in many locales. The insatiable demands of the industry encouraged the cultivation of this crop across the tropical and temperate zones of the Americas, tended by a growing cohort of African slaves.[2] Cotton was celebrated and decried. During the nineteenth century it became a ubiquitous medium of self-expression, a symbol of liberal entrepreneurship, or evidence of moral turpitude. Amidst these political conundrums, every independent nation sought to establish a cotton industry during the nineteenth and twentieth centuries as a sign of economic development, industrial prowess and national dynamism. By this time, the manufacture of cotton was synonymous with prosperous modernity. The long-running evolution of cotton manufacturing in the West brought with it new social and political relations. That history is the focus of this chapter.

EUROPE'S EARLY TEXTILE LANDSCAPE

The manufacture of cotton cloth in Europe was not a natural outgrowth of regional resources and, thus, the integration of this fibre into the panoply of European textiles took generations. Cotton was a little-known substance in north-west medieval Europe. Linen and wool provided the foundation of European textile culture and the cotton industry eventually grafted on to this stock. In the medieval period, in the territory running from the Black Sea to the Atlantic, the Mediterranean to the Baltic, millions of men, women and children toiled in the production of linens, woollens and worsted fabrics for all manner of functions, military to matrimonial. The medieval organization of production varied widely and it is essential to appreciate the foundation of Europe's fabric culture to grasp the impact of cotton's progress in this region. Wool cloths had become an increasingly capitalized product during the twelfth and thirteenth centuries, linking together Italian, Hanseatic, French, Low Country and other merchants with guild-based producers and finishers. Guilds were secular city-based institutions providing training for young apprentices and overseeing the guild workshops of journeymen who laboured in the trade. Guild apprenticeships were typically the prerogative of boys. Guilds likewise enforced restrictions on who could practise within city precincts, policing workshops and ensuring that only those who had served apprenticeships secured employment. These bodies were ubiquitous institutions in Europe's cities, providing an organizational basis for production at the same time as they allowed for competition among masters. Fortuitous connections through family or marriage, plus diligent effort, might elevate a journeyman to master status, as head of a workshop. But most journeymen remained waged workers, practising their craft as weaver, finisher or dyer.[3] The wool cloths they made became a major commercial commodity during the medieval era and the cloth trade itself was among the largest industries of the age.

Great fairs were held about six times a year in north-eastern France during the thirteenth century, most prominently in the towns of the Champagne region. These provided a safe venue for the cloth trade, drawing together merchants from far afield eager to supply or buy the wool fabrics so much in demand. Some of the most luxurious textiles were made from English wool imported in great volumes into the Low Countries. The fairs allowed the circulation of commodities moving along commercial networks extending across Eurasia: spices from the islands of the Java Sea, silks from China and manufactures from Italy were exchanged for wool cloths and other assorted goods at these venues. Italians had the closest connections to the great Asian trading networks that culminated in the eastern Mediterranean and North Africa. This intermediary position enabled merchants from Venice, Genoa and Florence to grow to a degree unmatched by other regional merchants. Throughout the thirteenth century, Italian merchants assumed increasingly prominent roles as suppliers of capital and virtual bankers at the Champagne fairs, with profits rising steadily.[4] The exemplar of this phenomenon was the wealthy fifteenth-century merchant Francesco Datini, of Prato, whose surviving cache of 125,000 letters reveals his extensive dealings in Italy, France, Spain and northern Europe.[5] Datini inscribed a motto on the front of his account books: 'In the name of God and of profit'.[6] Fernand Braudel observed that 'All the international and above all most of the modern aspects of the Champagne fairs were controlled, on the spot or at a distance, by Italian merchants'.[7] Commercial dynamism rippled out from this hub across the developing regions of thirteenth-century Europe. This era saw adaptations in technology and production in many facets of agriculture and manufacturing, and the textile trades in particular thrived as a consequence. Workshops multiplied in the urban centres of Italy, north-east France and the Low Countries and artisans found ready employment. With time, the social structure of this regional wool trade became increasingly hierarchical, with merchant manufacturers operating virtual 'factories', precursors of later production sites. The organizational services provided by Europe's guilds were critical to this growing prosperity. Steven Epstein notes a sermon preached in the thirteenth-century Italian city of Siena in which the speaker singled out particular trades for their contributions to the public good; the wool guild received the orator's highest accolade as being 'of greatest usefulness to the city'.[8]

Manufacturing regions rose and fell over this time as a result of competition and geopolitics. By the fourteenth century, Flanders superseded Champagne as the site of the most important commercial fairs, as well as being the principal location of high-quality wool cloth production.[9] At this time, the Low Countries were among the most heavily urbanized regions in Europe, with equivalent activity in manufacturing and commerce. Ghent and the coastal city of Bruges thrived through industrial and mercantile activities, the latter benefiting from extensive seaborne traffic. These regions were now more closely intertwined with the markets of the eastern Mediterranean and Asia Minor, through the intercession of Italian merchants. Ghent was the more populous of the two textile cities with approximately 80,000 residents, with Bruges numbering half that number, drawing in men and women from the surrounding regions. Estimates suggest that between 26,000 and 32,000, or as much as 40 per cent of the population of Ghent, worked in the textile trade in the mid-1300s, both men and women.[10] Women were not routinely admitted to guilds, but their work preparing fibres and spinning thread and yarn was indispensable and the number of women and children involved in fibre preparation and spinning exceeded by many times those dedicated to weaving and finishing. The finest cloths required the best thread, in consistent quantities, necessitating a proximate workforce with the time and skills to generate the necessary materials for warp and weft. Spinning thread demanded a dexterity that differed to some degree with the fibre being spun and the methods applied also varied somewhat. The tremendous concentration of female labour in spinning was a function of the dynamism of the medieval European textile industry, but was equally a consequence of earlier technological developments with profound implications for women's daily work. Constance Hoffman Berman argues that one of the great transformations of the early medieval era was the introduction of water mills and windmills for the grinding of grains, an arduous job that otherwise devolved to women. Freed from this chore, women could then engage in more profitable tasks, among which was the spinning of yarn. The fabrication of textiles involved more and more communities across Europe, presenting opportunities for potentially profitable employment for women.[11] Drop spindles were the commonest spinning tools, a basic technology with many variations. Prepared fibres were often mounted on a distaff or held under the arm; drawing out a segment of fibre attached to the spindle, the spinner would drop and twirl the spindle, extending the filament, the rotation of the spindle introducing twist to the extended fibres. At the right moment the thread was wound up, the spinning complete. A spindle was cheap to make, highly portable and could be employed in conjunction with other tasks, sitting or walking, or picked up and put down as required. In other words, the practice of spinning was suited to women whose family, seasonal and perennial homely tasks involved variable duties. Housewives were instructed: 'Let thy distaff be always ready for a pastime, that thou be not idle'; but the author acknowledged 'It needeth not for me to show, for they be wise enough.'[12] The drop spindle proliferated in countryside and town, as the demand for textiles expanded along with Europe's population and economy. Spinning wheels arrived in Europe in the later thirteenth century, spreading from east to west, another Asian innovation. Many varieties of these wheels developed over time, suited to different types of thread production, for standing or sitting spinsters, modified by local technicians. These wheels were more commonly employed in urban settings, or in households with the resources to invest in this equipment (Figure 4.1). They were more costly than the simple drop spindle and although they increased the rate of production it would be many centuries before the generality of spinsters could afford this technology. Hence the spindle prevailed. Spinning assumed powerful cultural connotations with the feminine, as a staple of women's lives, and their thread was an equally essential component of the cloth trade, as well as an invaluable support for individuals, families and communities. A sixteenth-century author illustrates the cultural value assigned women's production of thread with a description of the 'good housewives spinning a thread of small thrift'.[13] Women's endless industry was signified by the practice.

Spinning was organized in various forms. Most spinners were rural outworkers, supplying merchants who issued them the raw fibre. However, another kind of female secular institution arose in the Low Countries from about 1200, described by some as equivalent to male guilds, and its female members became prominent in the textile trades. The intent of the widows, single women and wives who assembled together was to create religiously inspired communities; these came to be called *beguinages*. These women in general could not afford the considerable sums given as gifts on entering formal monastic institutions, so from the outset it was clear that the members of beguines would work for their bread. Textile trades became a major focus. Walter Simons observes that: 'The beguines' engagement in the textile industry was far more extensive than that of religious women in traditional nunneries.'[14] The women in the beguines undertook tasks as spinners, weavers and cloth finishers, some establishing themselves as retailers. The 1304 will of a wealthy member illustrates some of the entrepreneurial functions found within these communities.

4.1 *Woman Spinning*, about 1648–50. Engraving. Museum of Fine Arts, Boston.

Margritain, a beguine *des Prés* of Tournai, made a bequest to forty beguine spinsters in her employ; she probably was a draper … rather than a weaver, that is, an entrepreneur who hired other (beguine) workers, supplied her employees with raw materials and traded the finished product on the local market.[15]

Within the walls of these medieval institutions, women worked in trades customarily the purview of men in the secular world. The range of female enterprises that flourished in these communities contrasted with the normative female practices in the wider world. Moreover the capacity of beguines to flourish for nearly a century and a half is testimony to the wider importance of the textile trades in generating income and employing labour in different contexts.

Wool was a staple, but it was not alone in providing a substantial trade. Linen was the other major fibre whose variations in quality and use perhaps surpassed even those of wool. Flax and hemp were grown extensively, adaptable to a variety of cool, humid conditions and moist soils. However, transforming the flax plant into cloth involved considerable labour, with the greatest effort expended in fibre preparation. The mature flax crop was typically pulled up by the roots and bundled into small stacks, after which the plants would be submerged in water or wetted repeatedly if left on land to initiate the process of 'retting', which dissolved the structural component that bound together the vital fibres in the stems. Only when this element was sufficiently rotted could the valuable internal fibres or 'lines' begin to be processed. At that point the flax was set out to dry and, once dry, a three-stage procedure began with the 'braking' of the outer layer through a distinctive beating process in an effort to loosen the fibre bundles; only when the outer covering was removed could the valuable 'lines' be processed. Straightening the filaments was the final step in preparation for spinning. These stages were dirty and laborious, while at the same time requiring a fair degree of strength and proficiency to access the fibres.[16] Spinning was next performed by a predominantly rural female workforce; thereafter the thread was woven and the cloth bleached or finished for uses from veils to sailcloth. Europe's growing economy, before the mid-fourteenth-century Black Death, absorbed thread and fabric of many weights and textures and linen production became increasingly important.

Innovation in the linen trade began in Italy, evolving most dramatically from the 1100s onwards, as products were adapted in response to new materials and markets. Most significantly, Italian manufacturers incorporated cotton in the production of linen goods to produce what came to be called fustians – fabrics made of mixed fibres, usually linen and cotton. It was no coincidence that the Italian linen trade incorporated cotton in their manufactures at a comparatively early stage in European history. First, cotton was easily available from eastern Mediterranean sources and the examples of Ottoman, Persian and Indian cotton manufactures were much in evidence to Italian merchants. Second, cotton was much more easily processed prior to spinning than linen – easier too than wool – and took dyes more readily. Few manufacturers would prefer linen to cotton if both were available at similar costs, given the time spent in linen fibre preparation.[17] Italian artisans did not model their products on printed Indian fabrics, although they did copy a number of Islamic prototypes. As Maureen Mazzaoui observes, 'there was a high level of product differentiation', with striped, checked and geometric designs along with plain-weave and napped fabrics, among 'a broad category of affordable, serviceable cloth for apparel, household décor, and industrial use'.[18] Cotton was the quintessential consumer product and the northern Italian region of Lombardy produced outstanding varieties of linens, cottons and fustians. Full cotton fabrics were also produced, from the finest lawns to the most robust velveteens and corduroys, shipped to centres from Spain and France to North Africa. Cities like Venice, Genoa, Milan and Bologna also promoted the manufacture of fustians and cottons, the local guilds acting to enforce quality. Peasant women supplied the quantities of yarn demanded by this trade, spun to the length and fineness specified by guild intermediaries who organized the putting-out and collection of materials across rural communities. The result was a robust medieval trade that competed successfully for markets in the Middle East, North Africa and southern Europe.

Italian fustian and cotton cloth production reached its height about 1300. By this date, Lombardy's success had spawned imitators throughout the Italian peninsula and into southern

Germany.[19] This pattern of diffusion would be repeated throughout the coming centuries, as the benefits of manufacturing lighter fustian fabrics became evident to guilds, merchants and consumers in one new region after another. Large swathes of central Europe from the Rhine through to Hungary developed expertise in these fabrics, with the southern Rhineland in particular specializing in fustians. Following the deaths and devastation of the great plague in the mid-1300s, there was a gradual recovery and demand for lighter fabrics eventually rebounded. However, the balance of manufacturing shifted in favour of central and northern Europe. These competitors undercut the price of goods made by urban guild workers in Italy and successful manufacturing endeavours arose where rural labour or other labour-saving costs could be employed, portrayed in the depiction of cottage production in Figure 4.2. Linen and fustian trades were well established in northern France and the Low Countries before 1500 and a generation later, the religious turmoil

4.2 Ostade, Adriaen van (1610–84). *Reading the News at the Weavers' Cottage*, 1673. Pen and brown ink, watercolour, white heightening, traces of graphite; framing lines by the artist (?) in brown ink and gold, 9⅝ × 7¹⁵⁄₁₆ in. (24.4 × 20.2 cm). Metropolitan Museum of Art, New York.

drove Protestants from these regions to England, carrying their craft to the next fertile ground.[20] By the 1620s, English exports to France, Spain, Holland and Germany included goods described as 'Venetian fustians English making' and 'Milan fustians English making', as well as 'ordinary English fustians'.[21] The production of fustian fabrics, combining cotton with linen, wool or silk, proved profitable at a time when more people wanted textiles of varying weights, designs and textures. During the 1600s fustians became a greater part of the material repertoire, at the same time as unparalleled volumes of Indian cottons also entered the market, carried by European trading companies. The gradual northward spread of fustian manufacturing by 1600, centred within the expanding linen industry, combined with the significant flows of Indian cottons into these same markets, bringing about an extraordinary conjunction of events. In combination, a second-tier sector of the textile industry grew to become an unparalleled agent of change.

TEXTILE POLITICS IN BRITAIN: COMMERCE AND INNOVATION

The English fustian trade carried none of the political prestige of the wool industry. Fustians were a foreign innovation, without the storied cultural and economic associations of the wool staple (see Chapter 3). Fustians varied in fibre composition, width, weight, look, length and quality, presenting a variable, adaptable appearance that unsettled some contemporaries. A 1613 commentary reflects this unease.

> There is also a late commodity in great use of making within this kingdom, which setteth many people on work, called Fustians, which for want of government are so decayed by falsehood, keeping neither order in goodness nor assize, … what a shame is this to our Nation, to be so void of reason and government …[22]

The material philosophy of fustians was anathema to those who believed in guild-based production, with highly regulated standards. In these lights it was reprehensible that a trade encourage the sale of non-standardized wares in such a variety of qualities and prices. However, fustian weaving had grown substantially over the 1600s, migrating north and setting roots in the Lancashire hill country between the towns of Bolton and Blackburn where it proceeded to prosper, spreading to neighbouring parishes and towns including Manchester and the lands to the east and south. The linen industry also flourished in this region, especially in the lowland and central regions of Lancashire. An English correspondent bemoaned the fact in 1662 that England was becoming 'the poor man's clothier'.[23] But the success of these fabrics was part of broad underlying changes. All textiles sold in the British market became less costly over the seventeenth and eighteenth centuries, with increased demand for lighter-weight cloths. This allowed for a greater consumption among a wider cohort of buyers, further stimulating overall production, a pattern that persisted despite the inflationary pressures of the seventeenth century.[24] Lower prices were possible in part because of a predominantly rural workforce, including a vast pool of female labour spinning warp and weft. Lancashire's advantage was proximity to key supplementary supplies of linen thread from Ireland and proximity to west coast ports with easy access to the Atlantic and its wealth of growing markets. Merchants and small middlemen carried raw fibre to cottages and farmsteads for cleaning and spinning, and finished materials were collected or returned to a central store for later distribution to rural weavers. Sometimes two crafts met in one household, with husband as weaver and wife as spinner. Textile production became a mainstay of a growing portion of the Lancashire population.[25] At the same time, weavers in certain districts developed specializations for which they became known. Locally, the town of Manchester came to prominence as a finishing and distribution centre, described in the seventeenth century as 'the very London of those parts, the liver that sends blood into all the countries thereabouts'.[26] Thus the linen and fustian trades grew in tandem largely overlooked by national legislators, who were far more interested in the pre-eminent national industry: wool.

The 1600s closed with a great political contest between the supporters of the English wool trade and the English East India Company, the debate centring on Indian cottons. Aside from cottons, linen imports from Europe accounted for about 15 per cent of all imports in 1700, a factor of periodic concern to officials. Yet there was no lobby for the British linen trade equivalent to the alliance of landlords, merchants and manufacturers who agitated for the protection of wool. Negley Harte notes that linen imports declined over the eighteenth century in part as a consequence of rising duties, at the same time as linen production increased dramatically across the British Isles and Ireland. However this was not a national strategy, but a serendipitous consequence of rising tariffs to pay for a string of wars from 1689.[27] The linen and fustian trades were almost entirely sidelined in the contest between English wool and Indian cotton, only occasionally gaining notice for the similarity of some printed linens with printed cottons. Nonetheless, the outcome of the dispute between these textile titans was critical to the future of the fustian trade.

A great debate took place intermittently between the late 1690s and 1720 about the contours of the national textile market, and questions were raised about the status of the British linen and fustian sectors. As mentioned in the previous chapter, a series of exchanges took place in 1720 proposing that British printed linens be banned along with Indian cottons, regardless of their national origins. One pamphleteer deemed the whole sector too petty to deserve serious attention, insisting that 'the Linnens made in *Britain*, and which are used for Printing, are so small a Quantity, that they really cannot be worth naming in Competition with the *British* Woollen Manufacture'.[28] Manufacturers and 'dealers in Cotton Wooll', or raw cotton, from Manchester navigated these troubled waters, supporting the proposed interdiction of Indian cottons, provided 'a clause may be incerted in the said Bill that all cloths and stuffs manufactured in this Kingdom of Cotton Wooll of the produce of his majesties plantations in America may be confident allowed to be printed, painted, stained or dyed and wore in Great Britaine'. The Lancashire petitioners were convinced that a ban on Indian cloth would be to their benefit, 'employing great numbers of his majesties subjects', but in the local linen/cotton trade.[29]

The fustian industry prospered, despite recurring campaigns by wool interests (see Chapter 3). It expanded in scale and scope 'without any trace of regulation' and with none of the restrictions typical of guilds in corporate towns. Lancashire had few incorporated towns, and thus few guilds, and the principal expansion of manufacturing occurred outside such regulated environments. This was in sharp contrast to equivalent fustian-producing areas in Continental Europe, which retained guild oversight throughout the eighteenth century.[30] The fluidity of labour migration into the British linen/cotton regions, and the innovations that resulted, contributed to the success of this initially modest sector. The trade had another long-term advantage within the domestic market, as steadily rising tariffs gradually squeezed out some of the most competitive products from Germany and the Low Countries. Imported linens declined from 15 per cent of imports in 1700 to 5 per cent in 1800.[31] It is also noteworthy that Britain was the largest free trade zone in Europe, with a functioning national market where the appetite for consumer goods grew steadily across the social spectrum. Finally, the legal ban on most Indian textiles provided perhaps the greatest advantage to local manufacturers.

Fustians were divided into two general categories: plain weave and napped, the latter having raised surfaces that were cut. These varieties were similar to others made elsewhere in Europe. Utilitarian fabrics included checked and striped cloth, a routine portion of British production, modelled on equivalent fabrics from Europe and India. Small patterns of checks or stripes, in a light cloth, were used in aprons, petticoats and shirts; larger patterns woven in heavier cloths found uses in furnishings such as bed curtains, cushions and upholstery, depicted in a later eighteenth-century caricature of a London labouring woman in her lodgings (Plate 12). St Giles was a close-packed neighbourhood in the heart of eighteenth-century London, which was as well known for its proliferation of shops as its local residents. This *St Giles's Beauty* epitomized the demotic fashions that most perturbed authorities and the print suggests the corruptibility of those working women who succumbed to the lure of new commodities, the tears in the curtains perhaps equivalent to metaphoric rents in her moral character. Checks hang across her foldaway mattress and drape her shoulders. Both categories of cloth were bought in growing quantities as bedding and soft furnishings became more popular and affordable across the social classes, along with greater quantities of clothing. These were unproblematic fabrics, useful and profitable, made both in linen and linen/cotton varieties as the century unfolded. Quantities of cheap checked and striped cloth were shipped to colonial markets for the working clothes of slaves and freemen, and traded as well in West Africa. Samuel Touchet, a merchant and financier active in the trade, testified before a Parliamentary committee in 1751 and explained that even prior to 1740, 'the Demand for these Goods was very great'. Touchet's concern was competition from European rivals like the French, Dutch and Germans, all of whom served Iberian markets along with Atlantic plantations more fully than did the English. Access to cheap yarn was the key to their success, opined Touchet. He hoped for policies that would encourage the shipment of greater quantities of Irish yarns to England, or failing that, the importation of yarn from the central European region of Silesia if the price was right. Foreign-made checked and striped cloth had been virtually eliminated from the British markets in the past generation, reported Touchet, 'now supplied by our own Manufactures'.[32] In sum, Touchet hoped for greater future profits and the Lancashire industry seemed an excellent vehicle for his ambitions.

Yarn was a perennial problem. Great merchants and local weavers alike were preoccupied with obtaining sufficient quantities, reliably available at a reasonable cost. There were weavers aplenty and more entered the trade as demand for linen and fustian textiles grew. Weavers could acquire their training informally or through apprenticeship and no authority could gainsay practice of this craft in these regions. The only practical impediment was securing timely sources of yarn. Samuel Touchet himself became involved with the administrators of Lewis Paul's roller spinning machine, securing rights to this technology in the 1740s,[33] one of a series of experiments at that time. By mid-century, solutions remained elusive. Moreover, the imbalance in the production process was intensified as John Kay's shuttle mechanism was more widely adopted during the middle decades, increasing the rate of weaving output. In the interim, spinners developed specialist skills in support of the production of cotton/linens and all cotton fabrics like velvets and corduroy, which became a popular speciality. The Lancashire region became renowned for its textiles, attracting the attention of a French industrial spy in the 1750s.

John Holker was an English political exile living in France, an adherent of the failed Jacobite plots to restore a Catholic Stuart monarchy in Britain. He was a calenderer by trade, part of the finishing of cloths using rollers, key in the creation of the right look and feel for finer fabrics. By the 1750s, Holker had risen to become inspector general of foreign manufactures in France, a prominent bureaucrat and an active agent in the importation of new technologies wherever and however he found them. Britain was the site of a number of innovations in finishing technologies, which predated major developments in spinning and weaving.[34] Holker was energetic on behalf of French industry and risked imprisonment to make several trips to British textile districts, assembling a report for his French patrons in the hopes of advancing the industry in his adopted homeland. France clearly felt the pressure from competing manufacturers and Holker assembled extensive samples of the most successful British fabrics. Both his report and the fabric swatches survive in a French archive and illustrate the diversity of products available, the colours still vibrant after 250 years. Of the 115 cloth samples, ninety-nine came from Lancashire and sixty-seven of these were a mixture of cotton with other fibres, with nine made entirely of cotton.[35] The cotton velvet received particular praise, a fact attributed to 'the greater skill of the manufacturers in mixing the raw materials in order to produce the best stuff at the lowest price'.[36] Competitors spied on each other and lured away skilled workers quite routinely. Two Lancashire spinners were enticed to move to France in 1754 in an attempt to transmit the specialist spinning techniques needed for cotton velvet. Their testimony confirms that there were dedicated spinning workshops in some parts of Lancashire for velvets, where a division of labour was in operation, whereby carded cotton battens or rovings were prepared by one woman allowing three spinners to proceed without interruption.[37] Specialization and subdivision of tasks were among the innovations designed to improve output – strategies that predated advances in the mechanics of spinning.

The towns and countryside of Lancashire hummed to the rhythm of the textile trades. From the 1750s onwards, farmhouses and cottages became virtual workshops as men, women and children adjusted their agricultural work to devote more time to textile labour, attracted by the income this provided. Figure 4.2 exemplifies the spatial combination of workshop and home that characterized this stage in textile production, a pattern that persisted for generations. There was money to be made, not only by merchants putting out the raw materials, but also by families who could devote time and care to their tasks. Samuel Bamford has left a wealth of detailed reminiscences from his Lancashire youth, along with tales he heard from family and neighbours. Born in 1788, Bamford summarized this mid-century era, writing that:

When [farm work] … was finished, they busied themselves in carding, clubbing, and spinning of wool, or cotton, as well as in forming it into warps for the loom. The husband and sons would next, at times when farm labour did not call them abroad, size the warp, dry it, and beam it in the loom; and either they, or the females, whichever happened to be least otherwise employed, would weave the warp down. A farmer would generally have three or four looms in his house, and thus, what with the farming, easily and leisurely though it was performed, what with the house work, and what with the carding, spinning, and weaving, there was ample employment for the family.[38]

Bamford paints a picture of comfortable industry, independent of the discipline and oversight of later factories. However, the seeds of mass production had already been sewn; the number of spinners employed suggests the scale of the manufacturing enterprises. James Livesey employed 2,400 rural spinners in 1743 and another Manchester entrepreneur kept 5,000 in his employ at about the same date. Investors organized where opportunity allowed, such as a group who pooled their resources in the 1750s in south-west Lancashire to arrange for 'spinning cotton and taking in cotton woof [warp] and weft upon commission … for the use of Richard Cough of Manchester, who is a large dealer in the fustian manufacture'.[39] Lancashire hosted a variety of textile trades, including silk and wool, allowing a cross-fertilization of experiences and techniques. Districts became known for specific varieties of cloth, as well as varieties of yarn. Some innovative individuals in the small wares trade reorganized weaving workshops, buying a quantity of new Dutch looms, used to make ribbon or tape, and installed these in workshops under direct supervision of the owner or overseer. For a period in the 1750s, an effort was also made in Manchester to power the Dutch loom by water – an unsuccessful effort, but one that indicates the experiments routinely attempted. Buildings described as a 'Factory or Weavers' Shop' or another holding 'forty Looms' were advertised in 1759, among the many sites with concentrated machinery even if still operated by hand.[40]

The first successful large-scale spinning mill in England arose within the silk, not the linen/cotton, industry. John and Thomas Lombe recognized the potential in producing reliable quantities and qualities of silk thread – English framework knitters for one would be delighted to have stocks on hand rather than pay the price of imported yarn from Italy or use inferior thread. The Nottinghamshire framework-knitting trade represented a growing sector whose stockings were gaining wide acclaim.[41] In the early 1700s John Lombe travelled to Livorno in northern Italy to prise local secrets from that community. He succeeded and carried drawings of Italian machinery back to England. With English patents in place, the Lombe brothers prepared and equipped a large mill in Derby centralizing the winding and twisting stages of silk thread production. The twisting mills differed from hand-worked machines only in the size and the numbers of spindles on the machine; but that innovation ensured a large and regular output of thread. Regularity and consistency in production were the two main challenges dogging the textile trades, especially when it came to thread. Centralized, mechanized production addressed this problem. The mill opened in 1721 employing 300 workers and proved hugely profitable, earning Thomas Lombe the immense fortune of £120,000 on his death in 1739. Within a generation, silk mills of three or four storeys opened in half a dozen locations across England, evidence of the impact of this mill as an inspiration to other entrepreneurs. Large, capital-intensive mills became the model of industrial thread production and the silk mill in Macclesfield employed 3,500 by the 1760s, while one in Stockport had 2,000 hands.[42] Silk would never have the market impact of a more democratic fibre such as cotton or more versatile fabrics like fustian, as silk was fundamentally a luxury or semi-luxury product. But the standard of production represented by these mills laid the ground for the more dramatic innovations to follow.

'THE APPLICATION OF MECHANICAL PRINCIPLES ... TO SHORTEN LABOUR'[43]

The 'machinery question' became one of the most hotly disputed issues of the late 1700s, generating riots as well as volumes of debate. Controversy would continue into the next century. Should new machines be adopted that would disrupt established work patterns and reorder customary employment? The answer may seem obvious to readers in the twenty-first century. But the case then was not clear-cut. Tradition and law still supported the concept of regulated, restricted employment in certain trades, founded on a hierarchy of skills and epitomized by skilled male artisans. Guild standards remained in many trades and male artisans valued their status and income, resisting any infringement on their privileges. The law still required all who practised certain trades within incorporated cities to have served an apprenticeship and city guilds were still empowered to search out those working illegally and bar them. But the guild writ extended to city boundaries and no further; the suburbs and countryside developed different employment models, pulling women and children into paying work along with their menfolk, with informal training as the foundation of their skills. The linen and fustian trades thrived in Lancashire and neighbouring regions of Derbyshire and Cheshire in large part because restrictions on trade could be ignored. Industries flourished and the population profited through a combination of natural and human resources. Nonetheless, even in these less regulated locales, new technology could be seen as a threat to present and future livelihood. Some celebrated the advent of new machinery, while others opposed it.

Merchants were constantly frustrated by delays in production. There was a loose and extended production chain, running from the importers of raw cotton or suppliers of linen yarn through to rural spinners, weavers, finishers and then back to distribution warehouses. Every step involved the physical circulation of goods across country. Enforcing production standards was difficult or impossible, embezzlement or customary claims on waste materials were rife and timely deliveries often frustrated. Peach & Pierce, a Bristol merchant company, exemplify features of this eighteenth-century trade, explaining to a customer in 1753 the difficulties in meeting his order: 'I have been as exact to patterns as the times will allow[.] Our Manufacturers are under no Command and 'tis impossible to get them to make all small and dark Patterns [such as you require] without extraordinary price.'[44] Merchants could not obtain special orders from suppliers, never mind guarantee delivery of routine stock. Weavers often waited for sufficient yarn, sometimes walking miles to assemble the needed supplies, while Kay's 'flying shuttle' accelerated the imbalance between weaving and spinning. Geopolitics also affected industry. During the Seven Years War (1756–63), trade with German linen-producing areas was disrupted and the price of linen yarn rose steadily as overseas supplies dwindled, putting added pressure on Lancashire fustian manufacturers. Ultimately, the cost of linen made cotton a more economic choice, intensifying the push for reliable supplies of quality cotton yarn.[45] General conditions stimulated technical innovations.

The Society for the Encouragement of Arts was established in 1754 with the aim of promoting invention through the offer of premiums or prizes, with the ultimate goal of 'the employing of the Poor'. In 1760 this society turned its attention to spinning, offering prizes for 'a Machine that will spin Six Threads of Wool, Flax, Cotton, or Silk at one time, and that will require but one Person to work it'.[46] Several such machines were demonstrated before this society, though no prize was awarded. But these prototypes demonstrate the serious attention given to improved spinning technology. For example, Lewis Paul's mid-century spinning machine 'would spin, in the most perfect manner' and could be powered by water or animal. Unfortunately, its mechanisms were 'easily disordered', in the words of one contemporary, and the experiment was a failure.[47] But the need was evident and the demand was great. British reliance on Indian cotton yarn was virtually at an end by this date. In 1707, the imports of cotton yarn from India amounted to nearly 220,000 lb; this commodity had declined markedly by the 1760s, as local spinners embraced cotton spinning and in 1760 a mere 2,814 lb of cotton yarn was imported.[48] In contrast, over this same period retained imports of raw cotton increased in volume, feeding local industry (see Figure 4.3). This appetite for raw cotton rebounded across the Atlantic, reshaping American agriculture as planters responded to demand. Meanwhile, in Britain, the introduction of new spinning devices proceeded rapidly from the 1760s forward, with James Hargreaves's spinning jenny developed in the mid-1760s and Richard Arkwright's water frame patented in 1769. Later innovations by Samuel Crompton capped this key trio of technologies.

James Hargreaves (c.1721–78) launched the new spinning devices. Hargreaves lived in the village of Oswaldtwistle outside Blackburn, amidst the textile trades of central Lancashire, and he was well acquainted with leaders in this industry, like Robert Peel who made a fortune in the trade. Hargreaves worked with Peel to devise a more efficient carding machine in 1762 and he was clearly intrigued with mechanical challenges. Several years later, Hargreaves invented what came

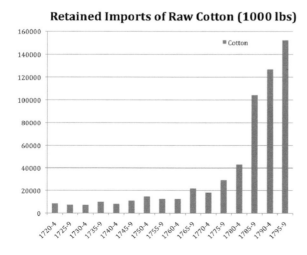

4.3 The British cotton industry showed its growing manufacturing power in its appetite for raw cotton.

to be called the spinning jenny, a machine placed on a horizontal axis that enabled the number of spindles to be increased and thus the output of each spinner to be dramatically augmented. This spinning machine was devised specifically for cotton thread, though it was subsequently modified for other fibres. It was also conceived as a cottage technology. Large jennies could also be assembled in workshops, an innovation that Hargreaves himself attempted on farmland outside his village. Within a short time, Hargreaves's invention attracted the notice of his neighbours and some of these folk, fearing it would reduce the work for local spinners, made their objections known. In 1770 Hargreaves left the area, but not before setting up a partnership with merchant hosiers in Nottinghamshire, where he relocated. The new machine was welcomed enthusiastically in that stocking-knitting region. The same year Hargreaves applied for a patent, describing the wonders of a mechanism that 'will spin, draw and twist sixteen or more threads at one time by a turn or motion of the hand and the draw of other'.[49] Hargreaves may have patented his invention, but copies were soon widely available throughout the cotton and wool sectors, adapted wholesale without his approval. The technology itself stimulated further innovations, although Hargreaves saw no profits.

The spinning jenny transformed the context of spinning at the same time as it changed women's labour. The jenny was the first robust machine that could consistently produce multiple spindles of thread from the effort of a single spinster. The smaller jenny was soon widely employed, with the result that weavers no longer waited for yarn. Maxine Berg argues that those to benefit first from spinning jenny were 'the cottage producers and those who ran small centralized workshops … [They] reaped the first gains in efficiency from the jenny, and they did so until the merchants and factors saw the gains to be had through setting up their own larger jenny factories'.[50] The greater flow of yarn attracted more weavers to the trade in the 1770s and the pace of manufacturing visibly accelerated. About this time, cotton manufacturers finally resolved their legal position in Britain. Most cotton textiles were still subject to the 1721 provisions as only fustians had been recognized as legal in 1736. However, by 1774 Parliament had no objections to the obviously buoyant and growing cotton trade and in that year manufacture of British cottons was legalized. Growth continued at an extraordinary pace. The leap in retained raw cotton imports illustrates, in part, the acceleration of production and hints at the repercussions to follow (see Figure 4.3).

Throughout the 1770s, Richard Arkwright (1732–92) introduced a series of innovations, some of which were later said to be the work of other inventors. Arkwright, like Hargreaves, moved from Lancashire to Nottinghamshire to profit from the demand for thread within the dynamic stocking-knitting community. Arkwright's innovation was to add a system of rollers, which further perfected the spinning process. This power-driven roller or water-frame system incorporated the preparatory stages of carding and roving, as well as spinning, and this machinery was solely designed for factories. Arkwright envisaged this as a large-scale machine (despite his small-sized prototype) and he patented this device under those specifications and refused permission for anyone to build to a smaller scale. This invention marks a crucial stage in the rise of the factory system, as the new processes could only be realized in a large enclosed site. Arkwright collaborated with a number of men to bring his dream to fruition.[51] The first Nottingham mill was operational by 1772 and a second mill was proposed among the business partners about that same time, to be built at Cromford, Derbyshire. Each advance in the capacity of his machinery encouraged Arkwright further. He described his cotton thread as 'soft and as Even as silk' and it soon became clear that this thread could be used to weave calicoes, and in 1773 they began selling their yarn for this purpose. In Britain, linen thread had traditionally been used for warps in British 'calicoes', as it could better stand the high tension when tied on the loom – few hand spinners in Britain could equal the tensile qualities of Indian cotton yarn. Producing cotton thread suitable for warping the loom was a notable achievement and, as Elizabeth Arkwright wrote, they could 'Sell them ... as fast as Cou'd make 'em'.[52]

The hills and valleys of Nottingham, Derbyshire, Cheshire and Lancashire were soon dotted with spinning mills, most of them powered by water and located alongside fast-running streams. One new mill, operating in 1774, employed 600 workers, mostly children.[53] The first generation of textile mills typically needed a water source to power the machinery and this was more imperative than proximity to willing workers, though some sites had both. The Arkwright Cromford mill was described by him as boasting 'a remarkable fine Stream of Water, And in a Country very full of inhabitants vast numbers of whom & small Children are constantly Employed in the Works'.[54] Farm buildings were converted and new mills constructed in the hope of cashing in on the cotton bonanza. Contemporaries realized they were witnessing events with great significance for good or ill. In 1779, local communities rallied against the proliferation of 'patent machines'. There was a deep-seated antagonism in many neighbourhoods against innovations that threatened customary patterns of work and at this juncture, new technologies affected all stages of fibre preparation and spinning. Carding 'engines', twisting mills and spinning 'engines' were targeted by machine-breakers during the autumn of 1779 and among the arrested protesters were weavers, spinsters, colliers, labourers, nail-makers, joiners and one cotton tradesman.[55] These men and women represented a cross-section of occupations in the area and all felt beleaguered by the changes that engulfed them. By 1780, Parliament had begun to receive petitions outlining the grave events troubling the cotton manufacturing regions of Lancashire, the epicentre of the new modes of work. The petitioners acknowledged that war with the American colonies had interrupted overseas trade. But in their view the real 'Evil in Question is the Introduction of Patent Machines and Engines, of various Descriptions, which have superseded Manual Labour to such a fatal and alarming Degree, that ... many Thousands ... with their Families, [are] pining for want of Employment'.[56] In the months previously, crowds had assembled in various districts, sometimes in their thousands, and turned their anger and frustration on the machines they blamed for their troubles, smashing jennies of more than twenty-four spindles and attempting to destroy others. In the town of Wigan, local authorities tried to diffuse public anger, holding a meeting and promising they would suspend 'the use of all Machines and Engines worked by Water or Horse, for carding, roving, or spinning of Cotton'.[57] This reprieve would last until Parliament decided the merits of the case. These outbreaks were among repeated cycles of complaint brought before national and local authorities, protesting the new conditions of work and the erosion of known and accepted patterns of labour.[58] The burden was not borne equally by all those in the textile trades, as some suffered for a considerable period of time as rates for spun yarn declined, while others flourished in the new conditions.

Parliament reacted to the spinners' petitions with a special report in 1780. This acknowledged that the price of yarn had dropped markedly, affecting all who previously earned their bread spinning or carding cotton before spinning. Even the jenny spinners saw their income drop by about a third from earlier rates. It seemed astonishing that in just ten years, returns on jenny-spun yarn had fallen so dramatically; yet they fell further still with each passing year. Those worst affected could least bear the burden, a fact the report stated bluntly: 'Jenneys are in the Hands of the Poor, and the Patent Machines are generally in the Hands of the Rich.' Some claims could be made for the superior quality of the jenny-spun yarn.[59] But the final resolution of the Parliamentary report was clear: 'It is the Opinion of this Committee, That the Increase of the said Manufactures is owning to the Introduction of the Patent Machines, which are used in carding, roving, spinning, and twisting Cotton; and that a very valuable Manufacture of Callicoes has been established in the said Country by the Use of the Patent Machines.' That said, the report concluded: 'The Cotton Manufactures could not possibly have been supplied without the Use of the Patent Machines; and that there is no Want of Employment for the Industrious Poor.'[60] Parliament's response was not unexpected. Moreover, the report pointed out that there was sufficient work in the burgeoning cotton industry to employ all those seeking employment. However, the poor had to accept new conditions of labour over which they had little control and long-standing practices were extinguished – often a painful process. One local magistrate called for calm and published a widely circulated appeal, insisting that both workers and masters profited when trade was 'in so flourishing a state'. This author tackled the question of machines head-on, reminding readers that some had also opposed the jenny when it was first introduced, although it was now hotly defended. This tract epitomized the new liberal philosophy of trade that accepted few interventions in the market and defended new technologies over customary practice:

> Trade, in general, will soon find its own level. Those who were thrown out of their old employments, will find, or learn new ones. Those, who now get less by their labour, will be aiming at the more profitable branches. Those who, by striking early into new inventions, get a disproportionate gain, will soon find so many rivals, that they must sink their terms, and reduce their profits ... In fact, the cotton manufacture is now almost a new trade. The fabrick, the quality of the goods we make, is amazingly changed. How many new kinds of cloth are made, in very great quantities, which could not possibly, have been made, at least in any quantity, or so cheap as to sell, without our machines?[61]

The dispute over machinery took oral, written and physical form even as the tempo of innovation accelerated. There were no further outbreaks of violence in the cotton districts, at least for a time. Female spinners did turn to other work and the expansion of new forms of employment served as a substitute for lost trades, at least for some.

In 1783, Richard Arkwright incorporated the first steam engine in a spinning mill, a new application of power to the production of thread. By 1785, Arkwright succeeded in powering carding and spinning, making it one continuous mechanized process, with every stage under one roof. Whether or not investors chose to use Arkwright's machinery or combined other technologies, there was steady take-up of new equipment and adaptation of existing models. Within the mills, spinning machines became a male technology and new cohorts of male spinners entered mills to oversee this equipment, becoming the first generation of elite industrial workers. They were well paid and worked with technologies that brought them considerable prestige. But these new 'engineers' were a minority of mill workers. Women and children represented the majority, an attractive workforce from many perspectives, not least as they were thought more inherently biddable and easier to manage. They could also be employed more cheaply than men – although women's industrial wages were routinely higher than in agriculture, the main alternative employment for the rural poor. Women and children picked and cleaned cotton, prepared fibres, minded machines, replaced full spindles with empty and tied broken threads. Some support tasks remained as outwork and an alliance of mill and cottage labour persisted for some time. Mills and factories introduced a new style of work: a new pace of labour, direct oversight by supervisors, enforced quality control, restrictions on customary access to waste (now seen as embezzlement), new powered machines and new types of discipline. In cottage production, authority was vested in the family hierarchy and while discipline may have been harsh, it was set within a family context. Some early mills also employed whole families as working units, transferring old social practices into new settings. Advertisements calling for workers sometimes included enticements like 'a number of convenient cottages' suitable for large families. But the new work setting was fundamentally different, with a supervisory hierarchy that had little in common with the older labours based in cottages and farms. Workers entered new surroundings, with some new mills of an exceptional scale having hundreds of windows and rows of machines. For generations, the soundscape of cottage workers had been the rhythmic clatter and beat of the loom, underscored by the hum of the spinning wheel. The roar from water mills or the loud, pulsing cadence of steam engines now joined the powerful mechanical rumble and thrum of machinery cementing a new acoustic environment, supplanting the older sonority of work.

Samuel Crompton (1753–1827) furthered the mechanical transformations under way. Crompton was another local Lancashire inventor, son of a farmer-weaver, who began his years in the trade while still a child. As a young man, Crompton produced his own yarn on a spinning jenny and was continually frustrated by the quality of the yarn. These deficiencies inspired invention; but, like many, Crompton kept his experiments a close secret, especially as machine-breaking riots roiled about his community in the autumn of 1779. In 1780 his invention was able to produce a greater variety of thread than could be spun using other devices. Crompton's thread was consistent and uniform, either warp or weft. This represented an unprecedented advance in technology, equalling the Indian yarns that for so long had been the apex of quality. The invention combined elements of the spinning jenny with the use of rollers in a combination that came to be called the mule. Mule spinning inaugurated a whole new stage in the industrialization of the cotton industry, as for the first time British manufacturers could compete with the finest Indian muslins. Mule spinning technology was rapidly adopted, resulting in a great leap in production, with almost a quadrupling of imported raw cotton over the 1780s (see Figure 4.3). Specialization in production also allowed for small and larger enterprises to flourish, producing thread for a wider range of fabrics than ever before.[62] In 1788, a report from Lancashire announced: 'A total revolution in spinning has happened in these parts, the water engines make such fine level threads; spinning by hand engines is entirely abolished'[63] (Figure 4.4). This author was a little premature in announcing the demise of hand spinning, but there is no doubt that the falling price of cotton thread put extraordinary pressures on those still pursuing this trade. At the same time, weavers and would-be weavers

4.4 *Mule Spinning*, from J. R. Barfoot, *The Progress of Cotton: A Series of Twelve Engravings* (Manchester, 1840). Manchester Archives and Local Studies, Manchester.

flooded into the region to meet the demand for cloth fabrication, including women and children. Those within the handloom weaving trade enjoyed a golden heyday with as much work as they could want and at high rates of pay. The technological imbalance between weaving and spinning worked to the advantage of that generation of skilled and semi-skilled weavers, men and women. At the same time, cotton spinning attracted unprecedented investment. In 1789 the first mule mill was opened in Manchester itself, powered by a steam engine. Water- and steam-powered mills multiplied across Britain and the shift from domestic production to a larger centralized workplace was now unstoppable. As Katrina Honeyman observes, the 'increased scale of production was a feature of the first purpose-built factories, and eventually mass production became the norm'.[64]

SLAVERY, THE BRITISH COTTON INDUSTRY AND THE WIDER WORLD

The impact of the British cotton industry extended across the globe, but it was initially a small part of a wider historical process, integrated into an evolving system of colonial commerce. Europeans hunted for markets and the West African coast offered one of the most dynamic commercial zones from the 1500s onwards, as African and European merchants collaborated in the enslavement and sale of thousands of men and women annually. This trade was based on the perceived need for labour. Plantations constructed by colonial investors produced key consumer commodities – sugar, tobacco, rice, indigo and (later) cotton – and likewise provided important markets for the sale of basic supplies like textiles. The growth of slave labour in South America, the Caribbean and the North American colonies shaped those economies and societies, with profound and ongoing repercussions. Over nine and a half million Africans were transported across the Atlantic between approximately 1500 and 1866, a brutal forced relocation. Over four million were dispatched to the Caribbean, where sugar brought immense fortunes to plantation owners, but where slave mortality rates were punishingly high; nearly five million slaves were carried to Central and South America during these centuries for similar crops. North American slave owners bought approximately 400,000 African slaves according to the best estimates of David Eltis.[65] The growth of the Lancashire trade grew in tandem with this larger colonial project.

The Portuguese began the trade in slaves on the West African coast from the fifteenth century, carrying their human cargo to new sugar plantations established on Atlantic islands like the Azores and the Cape Verde Islands, both previously uninhabited. The pattern of plantation slavery inaugurated in these liminal zones shifted to the Americas after 1500, where land was plentiful but labour scarce. With this model in place, Iberian traders laid the foundations for the Atlantic slave trade, establishing plantations in the New World and peopling these to a great extent with forced African labour.[66] In the 1600s, a host of other European nations joined in the traffic, at the same time as they competed for colonial possessions. Sugar plantations were the first and primary goal of Caribbean colonists. West African merchants supplied the men and women for the new plantations in exchange for the requisite trade goods. Commercial interactions on the West African coast demanded knowledge of local norms and preferences, along with commodities that met regional tastes. Indian cottons quickly became indispensable and remained a staple for the duration of the slave trade. Cotton was not an exotic novelty in West Africa and Colleen Kriger argues that this was part of the reason for its success. Cotton textiles were well known and manufactured locally in West Africa and, thus, the Indian imports fed into an established market. Kriger notes that 'In aggregate, textiles were the largest category of goods that were used to make purchases on the Guinea Coast.'[67]

European traders sold vast quantities of Indian goods termed 'Guinea' cloth; but another aspect of their trade was selling European goods, including fabrics, to local African buyers. As the English fustian trade developed, merchants repeatedly sought to substitute English for Indian wares, especially when they could be sold for greater profit than Indian cloth. But initial attempts were fruitless, as African merchants had exacting standards that English manufacturers could not yet meet. 'East India goods only and not those imitated are saleable', insisted the English representative at Cape Coast Castle in 1706. Other attempts at substitution in the 1720s were equally unsuccessful, with some goods described in 1724 as 'far from being approved on by the natives'.[68] In contrast, checked and striped fustians, made in Lancashire, were more generally successful and both became regular exports not only used in the West African slave trade, but also in provisioning plantations. In West African ports, manufactured goods from all major European nations competed for buyers.

But American colonies were at least nominally closed to direct imports from competing nations and became vitally important outlets for English industry. Samuel Touchet was heavily involved in the Lancashire linen/cotton industry and in the African slave trade. His testimony before Parliament in 1751 on the state of the linen trade involved detailed accounts of the competition among Europeans and the quality and price of the goods brought to West African ports. He feared foreign competition. But Touchet was more sanguine about colonial markets and reported that: 'We send out Chequed Linens to all the Plantations',[69] a growing component of the Atlantic economy. In the five years before his testimony, Touchet exported about £30,000 of linens and linen/cottons; he was one of many merchants dependent on the Atlantic markets for his overseas profits.[70] Descriptions of slave dress, as well as the attire of ordinary working colonists, routinely listed checked shirts as well as linen or fustian breeches.[71] For example, in Virginia in 1768 a runaway slave wore 'a new osnabrugs shirt, Virginia linen short trousers, old cotton jacket, and felt hat'.[72] These garments were part of a long and complex commercial chain. Thus, as the colonial population increased (slave and free) so too did opportunities for European manufacturers. The mercantilist structure of European trade was designed to optimize opportunities for metropolitan industries and provided a critical geopolitical structure for growth.[73] Over the eighteenth century, English exports (including re-exports) shipped to Africa and the Americas rose sixfold; France's trade with the Atlantic world grew tenfold.[74] Atlantic markets contributed to the health of European economies and political structures were set in place to ensure economic pre-eminence in these colonial spheres. European textile industries benefited from these political advantages.

Some historians argue that the economic stimulus provided by the Atlantic slave trade and sugar plantations was critical to capital accumulation in Britain and a causal factor in later British industrialization.[75] The connections were hotly debated among academics, political activists and the media during the 1960s and 1970s in the immediate context of decolonization, the rise of African American history and the flowering of African studies. This subject continues to be debated, although the argument has largely shifted from claiming a direct causal link. At the same time, the quantitative scale of this human traffic has been more fully calculated since the 1970s and the roles played by nations and commercial sectors are more wholly calibrated. The scale of human suffering encompassed by the slave trade has been rightly termed 'a massive and enduring crime against humanity'.[76] This system of coerced labour produced great wealth for some and incalculable miseries for those who survived the trials of enslavement, even as the experience of slavery differed from region to region. Debates continue about the correlation between the profits accruing from the slave trade and (sugar) plantation systems in the Americas and subsequent European development in the 1770s and 1780s.[77] David Eltis and Stanley Engerman ask: 'How important were the slave systems of the Americas to the economic development of Europe, and more specifically Britain?' Their conclusions reveal the complexities of historical forces.

Eltis and Engerman contend that there is no direct correlation between the profits of slave trading, plantation production and British industrialization. Pre-eminence as a slave-trading nation and reaping the highest profits from plantation crops, like sugar, tobacco or indigo, did not produce an equivalent industrial superiority at the imperial centre. In the case of Britain, their slave trade and associated Caribbean sugar plantations ranked among a large number of profitable sectors within the economy, many equally or far more profitable, and comprising a far larger fraction of the total British economy in 1780, as for example the woollen industry. Indeed, only about 1.5 per cent of British ships were involved in the slave trade, representing 3 per cent of shipping tonnage. Eltis and Engerman note that Portugal carried the largest number of slaves to the New World until 1650, after which British traders equalled and surpassed this traffic until 1807. Thereafter the Portuguese once more controlled the bulk of the transatlantic slave trade. They note that: 'Strikingly, the Portuguese were responsible for far more slaves leaving Africa in the first half of the nineteenth century than were the British in any 50-year period.'[78] In turn, this commerce and the associated slave plantations in Brazil accounted for a far larger portion of the Brazilian-Portuguese economy than did the British equivalents. Yet, these Portuguese revenues did not precipitate industrialization in Portugal. Equally, the French profits from their Caribbean territory far exceeded Britain's during the eighteenth century; at this time the French produced 43 per cent more value from their crops than did the British Caribbean by the mid-1770s. It is clear that the first industrialization in Britain was not a direct consequence of the traffic in African slaves or the profits from the sugar plantations, both of which grew dramatically prior to the 1780s.[79] However access to land and resources in the New World, as well as the allocation of coerced African labour, increased the profitability of this region and contributed significantly to British and other European economies.[80] A more direct link would be forged between the British cotton trade and plantation slavery in the nineteenth century, after the American Revolution. The model of African plantation slavery was then redirected to the expansion of cotton plantations in the new republic in service of the British cotton industry, to the profit of the American economy.

The mechanization of spinning technology accelerated the hunger for raw cotton to an exceptional degree. Mediterranean and West Indian sources of cotton were stretched as demand grew. Tragically, the expansion of slave-produced cotton in the United States took place at a time when heated campaigns were already under way, demanding an end to the slave trade and the very existence of slavery itself within British territory. Quakers led the denunciations of slavery throughout the eighteenth century. By the 1780s, a prominent cohort of British reformers, like William Wilberforce and Thomas Clarkson, along with thousands of humble activists, worked to transform public and parliamentary attitudes to the traffic in African slaves and the infamous middle passage across the Atlantic. The British Parliament responded, ending the slave trade in 1807.[81] However, this legal and moral victory coincided with circumstances that linked slavery and the cotton industry more tightly than ever before.

The cultivation of cotton in the tropical and southern temperate regions of the Americas was encouraged almost from first settlement. Early colonists transported Old World species of short-staple cotton to their new homes and, although sugar supplanted cotton as the principal Caribbean commodity in the 1600s, it remained a useful crop for smaller planters without the resources to invest in sugar production. In the last two years of the 1600s, British colonies in the Caribbean shipped 67 per cent of all the raw cotton imported into Britain.[82] Through the eighteenth century, the West Indies and eastern Mediterranean provided the growing quantities of fibre needed by the linen/cotton trade. The flood of cotton at the end of the century would dwarf these early shipments, while the source of this fibre also shifted to mainland America.

Plate 1 Ceremonial cloth, block-printed, made in Gujarat, western India, for the Indonesian market. Design features the goose or *hamsa* motif. Radiocarbon dated 1510±40 years. Victoria and Albert Museum, London.

Plate 2 Chintz palampore, Coromandel Coast, India, cotton painted and dyed, *c.*1700. Victoria and Albert Museum, London.

Plate 3 Cotton palampore, Gujarat, India, embroidered in silk thread in chain stitch, c. 1700–20. Victoria and Albert Museum, London.

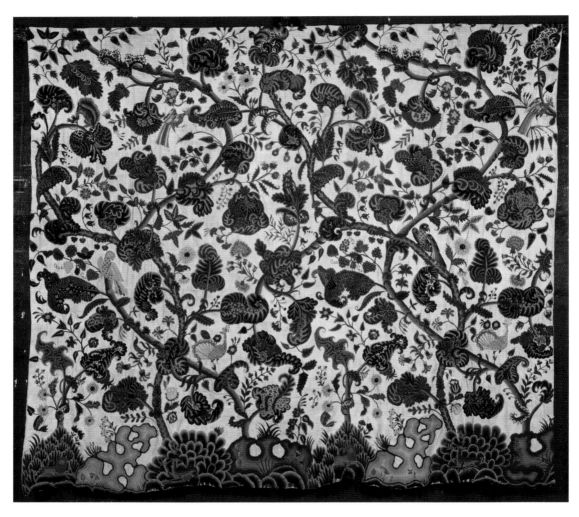

Plate 4 Late seventeenth-century bed-hanging. Linen plain weave with wool embroidery in stem and coral stitches, crewel work. Philadelphia Museum of Art.

Plate 5 Small purse or pocketbook with basket of flowers, Pennsylvania (possibly Chester County) *c.*1720–50. Silk and metallic thread over linen with spangles, 4½ × 5½ in. (11.4 × 13.9 cm) (closed). American Folk Art Museum, New York.

Plate 6 Embroidered pocket, Pennsylvania, c.1740–70. Crewel work on linen with cotton and linen binding, 10¼ × 8¼ in. (26 × 20.9 cm). American Folk Art Museum, New York.

Plate 7 Printed Indian cotton on the bottom of an English-made embroidered box, dated 1656. Nordiska Museet, 183.511, Stockholm.

Plate 8 Banyan or gown, painted cotton, lined with red and white checked cotton, mid-1700s, textiles made in north-west India. Rijksmuseum, Amsterdam.

Plate 9 Brook Taylor, mathematician, *c*.1720, attired in a blue and white striped (cotton?) banyan. National Portrait Gallery, London.

Plate 10 Indian painted petticoat, c.1725, textile made on the Coromandel Coast, India. Victoria and Albert Museum, London.

Plate 11 Printed cotton gown of English-made cloth, lined with linen, hand-sewn, c.1785. Victoria and Albert Museum, London.

Printed for & Sold by Carington Bowles.

Nº 69 in Sᵗ Pauls Church Yard London.

A Sᵗ GILES's BEAUTY.

521

Publish'd as the Act directs 14 Feb 1784

Plate 12 *St Giles's Beauty.* The Lewis Walpole Library, Yale University.

Plate 13 White cotton coverlet, quilted and embroidered with red silk, with the coat of arms of the Portuguese family Lima da Villa Norvada Cerveira. Made in India or Bangladesh, c. 1600–25. Victoria and Albert Museum, London.

Plate 14 Bedcover or hanging, made in India for the Portuguese market, seventeenth century. Overall embroidered design in yellow silk in chain stitch on linen, central coat of arms, surrounded by scenes from marine and land battles. Museum of Fine Arts, Boston.

Plate 15 Bedcover or hanging, made in India for the Portuguese market. Cotton ground, embroidered in silk with chain stitch. Seventeenth century. Museum of Fine Arts, Boston.

Plate 16 Lying-in room in Petronella Dunois's doll's house, decorated in chintz, *c*.1675. Rijksmuseum, Amsterdam.

Plate 17 Whole cloth quilt, eighteenth century, the Netherlands (textile made in India). Hand-painted, pieced, quilted and embroidered cotton, with silk border, 108 × 99 in. (274.3 × 251.4 cm). Los Angeles County Museum.

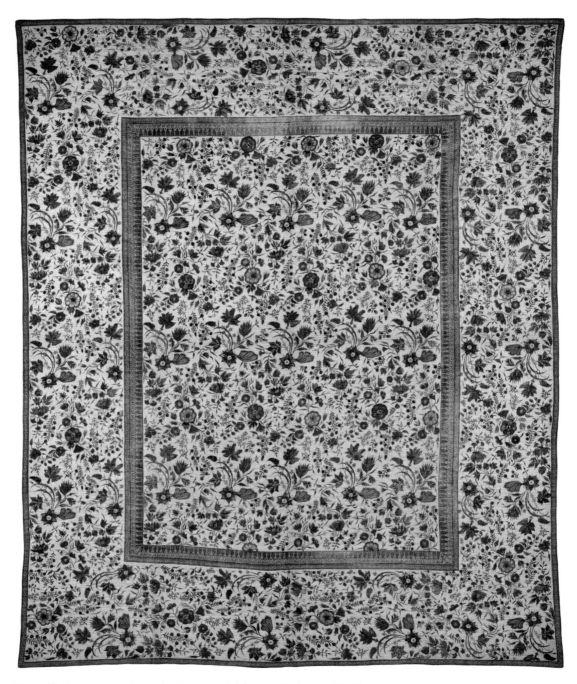

Plate 18 Bedcover made on the Coromandel Coast of India, *c.*1725–50, painted and dyed, cotton wadding, quilted. Victoria and Albert Museum, London.

Plate 19 Bedroom with calico coverlet from the doll's house owned by Sara Ploos van Amstel-Rothé, 1745. Frans Hals Museum, Haarlem.

Plate 20 Bedcover, quilted, patchwork top of printed cotton, hand-woven linen backing and wool wadding. English, dated 1801. Victoria and Albert Museum, London.

Plate 21 Star quilt. Cotton in beige, brown, red and blue printed cotton patches appliquéd on to a cream ground, with green border. Rhode Island, 1843. University of Alberta, Canada.

Plate 22 Pictorial quilt made by Harriet Powers (1837–1910) *c.*1886. Cotton, plain weave, pieced, appliquéd, embroidered and quilted. Museum of Fine Arts, Boston.

Plate 23 Diamond in the Square quilt, c. 1900–1950s. Made from white striped shirting material with multicoloured printed and plain red triangles, all cotton. Letter 'T' embroidered in the corner. University of Alberta, Canada.

Plate 24 Jacob's Ladder variation quilt, c. 1900–1950s. Hand-pieced, multicoloured cotton, on cotton flannel backing. University of Alberta, Canada.

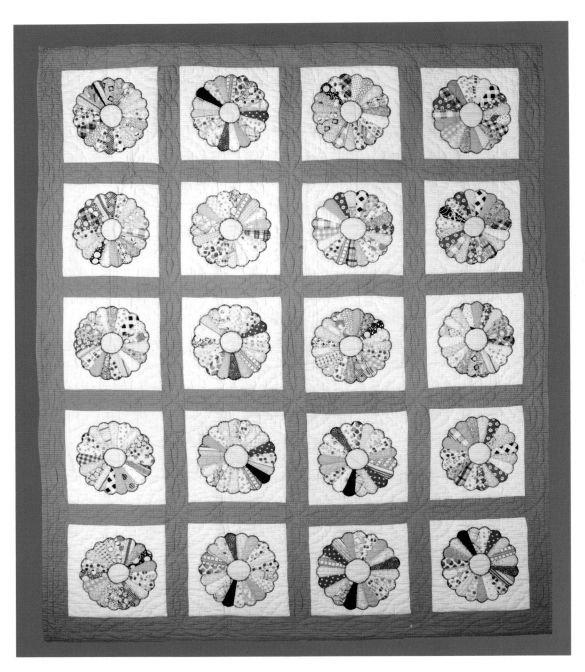

Plate 25 Dresden Plate quilt made by Martha Ruby Sills in 1935, Handel, Saskatchewan, Canada. Cotton, Dresden plate blocks with a variety of 1930s cotton prints. White backing of bleached sugar bags. University of Alberta, Canada.

The state of slavery is a variable condition, the characteristics of which are shaped by time and location, as well as the gender and ethnicity of the enslaved. Slavery in eighteenth-century North American colonies encompassed a range of labour experiences, from task allocation to gang work.[83] This variability allowed slave men and women in some Virginia communities to engage with the market as local suppliers of eggs, chickens, tobacco and other wares, which in turn enabled them to buy goods of their choosing. Equally, in New Orleans, slave men and women might attend occasional dances arranged by their fellow slaves. In pre-revolutionary Boston, some male slaves protested their status to the Governor and in New York other activist slaves were among the revolutionary leaders of the day. These histories reflect the various states of discipline, labour practices and lived experiences, as well as individual and collective cultural articulations of slavery, all of which have been the subject of considerable new research.[84] In antebellum America, enslaved men and women of African origin were also instrumental in producing limited commercial stocks of raw cotton for export, working on large and small properties. The conclusion of the American Revolutionary War brought about the resumption of trade relations between the newly independent republic and Britain, at a time when the mechanization of cotton spinning accelerated year by year. The Caribbean had grown long-staple Sea Island cotton since the early colonial era, transplanted by the Dutch from its place of origin in the Amazon river basin.[85] This long-staple cotton was ideal for the fine velvets and muslins now made in Britain. This species of cotton was also grown in the islands and coastal regions of Georgia and South Carolina and during the 1790s, there was an explosion in exports of the fine long-staple cotton to Britain, rising from 93,540 lb in 1793 to over 8,300,000 lb in 1801. Premium prices were paid for this commodity and many planters converted their holdings to cotton. However, Sea Island cotton could not be cultivated successfully away from the coast, so short-staple varieties were substituted, becoming the basis for new levels of wealth in the southern territories.[86] It was this fibre that would feed industrial mills and factories in the coming decades.

The hunger for cotton recast the nature of slavery in the American South. During the 1790s Eli Whitney's cotton gin became a celebrated American innovation, further contributing to the profitability of cotton crops. Improved ginning technology stepped up the rate of seed removal in heavily seeded, short-staple cotton, a laborious process not fully addressed by the ginning engines and equipment previously employed. Thus, with this new technology in hand, investments in slaves, land and cotton seed could realize substantial profits.[87] Joseph Clay, a plantation owner in Chatham County, Georgia, switched from growing rice to cotton in 1793, borrowing US$32,000 to invest in new ginning machinery and to buy more slaves. His returns were so large that he had repaid the loan and built new slave quarters by 1800, while also lavishly refurnishing his house.[88] Planters bought more slaves in the hopes of realizing profits in the new agricultural lands to the south and west. New settlements arose wherever good farmland was identified. This great migration marked the rise of a 'Cotton Kingdom', accounting for 'the heaviest use of slave labour, a sharp southward and westward movement of the slave population, and a relative movement to larger units [of production] than a century earlier'.[89] The Napoleonic Wars (1790–1802, 1803–15), and particularly the War of 1812, interrupted but did not alter the commercial ties between southern planters and British mill owners. Over the later eighteenth and nineteenth centuries, cotton cultivation spread out along belts of rich agricultural land, like the Mississippi Delta, to every region with the requisite temperatures and rainfall, transforming the landscape and shaping the culture (Figure 4.5). Sea Island cotton was grown wherever feasible for premium prices; however, short-staple cotton was a mainstay. Generations of slaves powered this expansion and, as Gavin Wright observes, 'slaves were concentrated primarily in areas where farmland was most valuable'.[90] Florida was another region that attracted planter-pioneers from the Chesapeake and the Carolinas. This new territory boasted swathes of rich alluvial soil and seemingly boundless possibilities, and the new century began with a steady flow of settlers to the new cotton lands. What Edward Baptist described as a 'spirit of emigration' fired many planters in the old colonies of the South to try their luck south and west of the Appalachian Mountains. The Louisiana Purchase in 1803 brought

4.5 *In the Cotton Fields of Georgia.* Photographic print on stereo card, St Paul, MN: T. W. Ingersoll, 1897, c.1898. Library of Congress, Washington, DC.

additional vast tracts within the scope of US control, including what are now the states of Arkansas, Missouri and Louisiana. The value of the new territories was further enhanced after the 1820s, when a worldwide drop in temperature extinguished the hopes of cotton farmers in Virginia and north-east North Carolina. In 1827, a Florida settler offered a poetic vision of 'Forests falling before the ax [sic] of industry and fields of cotton blossoming where they stood'.[91] Writing from Jefferson County, Florida, Achille Murat presented the perceived equation between land, labour and profits, asking: 'How are great capitals to be employed in agriculture, in a new country, without slaves?'[92]

Slave management was a critical dimension of plantation profits. Harvest time brought the triumphal realization of investments. Picking cotton was a skill best learned in childhood and the learning started young. During harvest, the weight of cotton picked in a day was routinely in the hundreds of pounds per person, 200 lb at a minimum. One mid-century Mississippi planter who paid bonuses to the best pickers recounted the prowess of one slave woman who picked 600 lb in a day, using two hands as she went down the rows.[93] The perspective on cotton picking differs when recounted by a former slave. Solomon Northrup was kidnapped into slavery in the mid-1800s and worked on a Louisiana cotton plantation for a dozen years. The daily weighing of picked cotton was fearful process, as Northrup recounts: 'The day's work over in the field ... the cotton is weighed – a slave never approaches the gin-house with his basket of cotton but with fear. If it falls short in weight ... he knows that he must suffer.'[94] Collectively, the mass of cotton picked, loaded on barges, weighed in port warehouses and shipped to industrial centres on the Atlantic set the pace of life and the characteristics of commerce, persisting into the next century long past the emancipation of America's slaves. Figures 4.6 and 4.7 show examples of the infrastructure built to move the vast quantities of cotton, powered by African American labour.

In the decades between the 1840s and the 1860s, approximately one half of the value of US exports came from the sale of cotton; much of US economic growth and prosperity depended on demand for American cotton from international manufacturers. Most of the cotton plantations were mid-size with between sixteen and fifty slaves; vast plantations were the exception, as were the very small. A few farmers produced cotton without the use of slave labour. But they were a minority, accounting for only 10 per cent of production in 1850. The 'Cotton Kingdom' was based in the South, but its power was felt throughout the new republic. When the price of cotton rose, the entire US economy benefited, with northern regions providing equipment and other supplies to support the growing planter territory. Short-staple cotton was the economic backbone of nineteenth-century America and by the mid-1800s, by virtue of the expansion of cotton production, more slaves resided in the new South than in the original colonies.[95] As Stanley Engerman notes: 'Slave labor dominated cotton production, and US cotton production dominated the world cotton market, accounting for over three-quarters of the input into British textile production.'[96] At the same time, the moral taint of slavery impelled more protests of all sorts within the republic, despite the apparent national benefits of slave-grown cotton. In spite of the vehement protests against slavery, a web of intersecting forces tied together American cotton plantations and spinning mills in Europe and America. The structures set in place during the industrialization of the British cotton trade reshaped the world, from the Mississippi Delta to Lancashire, from lowland Scotland to the hinterlands of Madras.

4.6 *Cotton Warehouse, Carrying Cotton, Charleston, South Carolina.* Stereograph card, Kilburn Brothers, *c.*1879. Library of Congress, Washington, DC.

4.7 Louisiana – the business boom in the South – a scene on the levee at New Orleans. Wood engraving from a sketch by Joseph Horton. Illustration in *Frank Leslie's Illustrated Newspaper*, 9 January 1881, p. 320. Library of Congress, Washington, DC.

MILLS, FACTORIES AND THE FIRST INDUSTRIAL WORKFORCE

By about 1815, according to contemporary estimates, approximately one quarter of a million women, children and men worked in the Lancashire cotton industry, employed in spinning mills, managing machines as 'engineers', and labouring in the weaving trades.[97] In the preceding decades spinning mills had been built from existing warehouses, workshops and any other sort of mill available, in the drive for profits. Partnerships were forged; some fortunes were lost and others never realized. But investors' passions persisted.[98] The newly mechanized mills did not immediately extinguish domestic manufacturing. On the contrary, these systems worked symbiotically for a generation or more, as the mills churned out mountains of yarn and handloom weavers wove as many varieties of cloth as could be conceived. Women who once worked as spinners took up handlooms, as did men of many other trades. William Radcliffe was one of many masters who came to employ an immense number of such weavers, men and women. Radcliffe himself was the son of a weaver, of modest origins, and learned the trade from his parents, carding and spinning with his mother, providing weft for his father. By 1789, in his words, 'I was well established, and employed many hands both in spinning and weaving, as a master manufacturer.'[99] By the end of the 1790s, Radcliffe employed over 1,000 weavers in three counties, at a time when they earned wages that enabled respectable comforts. Radcliffe described the weaving families he came to know: 'Their dwellings and small gardens clean and neat, – all the family well clad, – the men with each a watch in his pocket, and the women dressed to their own fancy'.[100] By 1800, Radcliffe and his fellow masters 'employed every person in cotton weaving who could be induced to learn the trade'. The 'want of hand, and want of looms' was a constant worry.[101] In response, Radcliffe turned to invention. He was among the innovators now determined to increase the pace of weaving. Weaving presented a challenging bottleneck that would not be ignored and attempts had already been made to more fully automate the process.

The demand for labour came at a time when the war with France drained away the male workforce – an estimated 20,000 handloom weavers enlisted from Lancashire in about 1800 and their places were filled by women and children.[102] The extended periods of warfare had a material effect on the evolution of the new industrial sector and on Britain more generally, at one period drawing off labour, at another time fomenting spiralling prices or cutting off markets. Within this turbulent environment, innovation continued unabated. Owners of mills and weaving masters sought out workers, soliciting 'hands', calling for whole families together. Within the mills, the workforce was predominantly female and young. Adult male workers made up a scant 17 per cent of those in spinning mills in the years between 1815 and 1820.[103] These men acted to consolidate their positions with trade associations and later trade unions, based on their select gendered positions within the plants and the expertise they developed in 'tuning' the mule spinning machines. In the nineteenth century, some public houses reserved drinking rooms for 'Mule Spinners Only' – a mark of their status. These men reinforced the gender hierarchy within the new industrial precincts, expecting their assistants to be of the opposite sex or a younger age, similar to their subordinates at home. Mule spinners, mechanics and 'overlookers' in weaving factories formulated the characteristics of male industrial labour.[104] However, industry relied on children and women.

Society approved of an industrious childhood, which was seen as essential training for the life to come.[105] Moreover, children were a particularly large proportion of the population in this period. England and Wales numbered about 8,600,000 by 1801, up from 4,960,000 a century before; more than 600,000 children would be added in the next five years and the population continued to grow. In 1826, children under the age of fifteen accounted for nearly 40 per cent of the population, with young adults a further 18.5 per cent.[106] Providing work for pauper children was a great concern for parish administrators tasked to provide for orphaned or abandoned children. Urban parish officials faced a particularly difficult problem. Cities were unhealthy places and death rates were high, taking adults of all ages; illegitimacy rates were also on the rise, while infant and child abandonment was a long-standing solution to the travails of unwed motherhood. A steady stream of infants and children were left to the care of local authorities, which in turn looked for trades where they could place their young wards. Orphan apprentices would become one of the most contentious segments of the growing industrial workforce, a solution to labour scarcity, trained up in new industrial terrains.

London parishes provided a regular stream of young apprentices to distant manufacturing enterprises, the ancient title of 'apprentice' now applied in an entirely different context. London districts like Tottenham and Bermondsey formally assigned their charges to factory masters many hundreds of miles away, seeing this as a good alternative to other options. From the mid-1780s and for the next thirty years, London discharged a steady stream of pauper orphans to northern industry, establishing routine connections with industrialists. Katrina Honeyman notes that, 'A number of large firms … were regular and substantial customers, who, judging from parish discussions were accorded priority treatment.'[107] One South London parish arranged 90 per cent of its apprenticeships with textile mills in the north of England over a thirty-year period. But cities and rural districts closer to these industrial regions also planned for some of their orphaned poor to enter factories. Even Birmingham, centre of the metal trades, found it had 'surplus' female orphans for a time. These girls were dispatched to large spinning facilities in Lancashire: for example, 115 were sent between 1796–8 and about 200 between 1808–13.[108] The story of orphan apprentices has been associated with the 'start-up' period of industrialization. However, Honeyman's wide-ranging study indicates the continued dependence on this type of labour well past the first decade of the nineteenth century, continuing to a surprising extent through the 1840s and 1850s. Figure 4.4 depicts mule spinning, the child worker on the left side of the image poised beneath the spindles to tie broken threads. In 1833, Parliament officially barred children from working in spinning mills before the age of nine and stipulated that those between nine and thirteen years of age could work only nine hours per day. That legislation in itself confirms the centrality of child labour within the industrial workforce. Various Acts were passed throughout the nineteenth century, further refining the official hours and conditions under which children could work; but only in 1901 was the minimum age of work raised to twelve years, deemed to be above the age of childhood.

Present-day sensibilities are offended at the thought of children shipped by the cartload to distant manufacturing sites. Contemporaries were similarly uncomfortable, but not in general because of the long hours enjoined on these boys and girls. Poor children were expected to take work – and often unpleasant work at that. Nevertheless, some critics found the harsh reality of their labours too stark a contrast to the highly romanticized articulations of childhood common in the literature of the age, now shaping middle-class sensibilities. Frances Trollope wrote of a fictional factory boy, Michael Armstrong, and the 'fearful evils inherent in the Factory System'.[109] More pragmatic reformers were concerned about the moral and physical care of the orphans, vulnerable without the immediate care of a benevolent authority. Indeed, in 1802, the first legislation addressing the condition of factory apprentices attempted to address those issues. This initiative was a joint project of mill owner and social activist Robert Owen, along with Robert Peel, one of the wealthiest members of the cottonopoly. Despite the widespread acceptance of liberal laissez-faire philosophy opposed to state regulations, paternalism and social idealism could ally for the benefit of child workers.[110] However, parishes providing apprentice labour did not slough off their responsibilities and many routinely checked on their charges. Honeyman argues that in general 'the process of factory parish apprenticeship was much more controlled than conventionally believed'.[111] It is equally important to recognize the significant role played by children in the course of industrialization. In Honeyman's words, the 'system of parish factory apprenticeship was important in the construction of an industrial labour force with the general and specialized skills required for textile factory employment'.[112] Children from distant regions, speaking with different accents and with various ancestries, helped build new industrial communities across the Midlands and north of England. They were not voluntary migrants. They had limited options. Some suffered serious privations. Nonetheless, factory work was often no worse and might sometimes be better than life in a workhouse, an option that few would choose but which many could not avoid. Between 1835 and 1850, about 50 per cent of all textile workers were under the age of eighteen, stark evidence of the structural dependence of this factory system on young labourers.[113] At the end of their apprenticeships, many remained within the trade and settled in current communities. Itinerant English and Irish workers, drawn by wages higher than those in agriculture, likewise moved into industrial districts in England, while Scottish cotton mills drew workers from the Highlands and Northern Ireland. The lives of these adults have been more routinely studied. But the contribution of children to the new industrial society was considerable and critical. Sentiment has often obscured the extraordinary contributions of many small hands.

Cotton became a byword for the extraordinary changes taking place in British society, impelling recitations of praise by local worthies like Edward Baines who asserted that 'The Cotton Manufacture of England presents a spectacle unparalleled in the annals of industry.'[114] Figure 4.8, a view of Summerseat cotton mills, reflects this celebratory tone, the middle-class viewers seated on a hillside amazed by the evidence of industry spread below them. By 1838, steam engines powered four-fifths of all cotton mills, a rate that rose to nine-tenths by 1850. Power-loom weaving followed as an inevitable offshoot of spinning mechanization, the technology improving with each generation. In 1803, 2,400 power looms were operating in Britain, a figure rising to nearly 15,000 in 1829 and to a quarter of a million by 1845.[115] The technologies launched within the cotton industry spread out to other sectors, like the worsted industry, generating an ever larger industrial workforce. At the same time, social and physical landscapes were remade under the pressure of industry. Many foreign contemporaries decried the British model of manufacturing, so much at odds with smaller workshops and guild structures, still common in many parts of Europe. The last vestiges of the old

4.8 *Summerseat Cotton Mills, Near Bury, Lancashire.* Russell and Cowan, 1850. Manchester Archives and Local Studies, Manchester, UK.

apprentice regulations were repealed in England in 1814, ending all restrictions on trade practices, allowing market forces to swell the ranks of weavers when work was plentiful, but leaving them to be starved out of the trade when the power loom ultimately became pre-eminent. In fact, in many ways there was no uniform industrial practice at this time; conditions varied with the size, specifications, locale and inclinations of the mill owner and staff, and the reaction of labour. Moreover, many of the worst conditions associated with factories were a consequence of unregulated urbanization. Residents of industrial cities, along with social commentators, looked with bewilderment at the speed and scale of urban growth, as haphazard housing for tens of thousands of people sprang up with no adequate water supplies and non-existent sanitation. Manchester grew from about 84,000 in 1801 to nearly 370,000 in mid-century, with working-class housing commonly 'offensive, dark, damp and incommodious'.[116] The noxious stink emanating from these neighbourhoods became notorious, described by one resident as 'bad enough to raise the roof off his skull'.[117] These were reckoned unfortunate side effects of industrial success. The nineteenth century would be spent addressing the consequences of urban expansion, as by mid-century half the nation's population lived in towns and cities. However, some industrial workers found communities especially built for the purpose, benefiting from the moral or philosophical tenets of the mill owner.

Robert Owen was pre-eminent among early industrial visionaries. Owen's drive brought him from relatively humble beginnings to become a major figure in industrial Britain. He bought out his future father-in-law, David Dale, who operated a series of four mills along the River Clyde, thirty miles south of Glasgow. Dale emphasized humane working conditions and this continued with

Owen. The latter enthusiastically subscribed to this perspective and advanced both the thinking and practice around industrial labour in exceptional ways. This was no small-scale enterprise but one of the largest mill complexes in Britain, employing more than 2,000 workers in 1800. By 1820, there were about 2,600 employed. Owen believed that environment shaped the individual and was determined to provide as equitable a setting as possible, while also reaping profits. New Lanark provided quality housing to its workforce, offered an infant school to working mothers and introduced a general store run at cost price. Owen also employed sophisticated management techniques to encourage quality control in his mills, emphasizing training over punishment. New Lanark attracted visitors from near and far and became a byword for benevolent industrial development. Paternalism among employers, along with cycles of legislation and labour pressure, contributed to improved living conditions over the century.[118] But more generally, improvements in living standards depended on the wealth unleashed by the immense power of industrialization and how this wealth was deployed.

Industrial communities developed a variety of characteristics as they sprang up in new locales.[119] Britain did not retain its technological monopoly for very long. Spinning jennies spread across international borders, despite efforts to curb their migration, and within years spinning mills were established in various regions of Europe (although the long period of war with France delayed industrialization in many areas).[120] Technology transfer crossed the Atlantic in 1789 when the young Samuel Slater took himself to America. Slater had been apprenticed with a leading cotton spinner, learning the latest secrets of production. With this valuable knowledge, Slater easily found a US partner and soon opened the first American spinning mill in Rhode Island in 1790, utilizing the new water-frame technology, employing local children as mill hands. Spinning mills gradually spread throughout New England, wherever water power could be employed, a number of which were the work of Samuel Slater.[121] Early in the 1800s, Slater collaborated with family members to build another cotton-spinning mill on the Branch River in Rhode Island, building as well a village for the families working in the mill. This came to be called Slatersville, the entrepreneur's response to the persistent problem of organizing and maintaining a stable workforce.[122] Here, too, a new style of industrial community took shape, with varying characteristics specific to local circumstance, one that would be replicated in other regions of the new republic.

Handloom weavers prospered in parts of Rhode Island and Pennsylvania as mills poured out ever larger quantities of yarn. In and around Philadelphia, in particular, the industrial production of cotton yarn sustained thriving handloom manufacturing communities where industrial and craft production worked in harmony for generations. The skilled male immigrant weavers drawn to this region could produce goods far beyond the technical capacity of early power looms, and these artisans remained a productive force even as handloom weaving was being extinguished in Britain. Pennsylvania moved towards full industrialization in very different ways from New England, highlighting the fact that, as Adrienne Hood observes, 'industrial growth in America followed distinctive regional paths'.[123]

In New England, as in Britain, industry relied extensively on young female labour. The hundreds of water-powered and then steam-powered mills that dotted the north-eastern states also pulled in workers from surrounding farms. In 1810, cotton mills numbered 102 in the US and in 1831,

795. In addition to the Rhode Island locales, cotton mills were dispersed across the states of Maine, Massachusetts, New Hampshire and Vermont, with the greatest concentrations along the Merrimack River in New Hampshire and in the north-east region of Massachusetts. Lowell was one of the major Massachusetts mill towns. Many of the young women who signed on at these mills were already experienced in domestic outwork. Mill towns promised attractive wages and independence. One New England daughter listed the benefits to her father quite bluntly: 'I want you to consent to let me go to Lowell ... I could earn more to begin with than I can anywhere about here. I am in need of clothes which I cannot get if I stay about and for that reason I want to go to Lowell or some other place.'[124] The experience of the Fowler sisters typified the women attracted to these industrial jobs. The Fowlers' New Hampshire farm could not support all the children in the family and the house was crowded. One by one, beginning in the 1830s, the daughters moved to Lowell for work, fifty miles from their home. For most this was a temporary option, allowing young rural women some adventure and good wages prior to marriage. Four of the five Fowler sisters worked in the Lowell mills from 1831 into the 1840s, after which they married, several returning to live near their home, others staying close to Lowell. On a broader scale, half the Lowell millhands were young women aged between fifteen and nineteen when they started work. Outside work hours, over two-thirds lived in company boarding houses, the rest boarding privately. The prominence of boarding houses is another distinctive feature of mill towns like Lowell, where the company provided safe, respectable accommodation for their female employees.[125] The young women could live safely and frugally, many saving and sending money home. There was evident pride among these women in the wages they earned. Thomas Dublin uncovered the story of one millhand, trained as a teacher, who entered the mill in 1850 following family financial troubles. Anna Mason celebrated her contributions, writing: 'I am not living upon my friends or doing housework for my board but am a factory girl.'[126] She sent home significant amounts earned from her labours. Some years later, Harriet Robinson recounted the importance of millwork for girls and women. The most basic task was as a 'doffer' – removing the full spindles from the spinning frame and replacing them with empty – but even doing that, 'doffers' were paid 'two dollars a week'. Weavers made more, tending multiple looms. Hours were very long; strikes and protests arose sporadically as mill girls pressed for better conditions. But the income from this job could be life-changing, as Robinson noted.

> We can hardly realize what a change the cotton factory made in the status of the working women. Hitherto woman had always been a money *saving* rather than a money earning, member of the community. Her labor could command but small return. If she worked out as servant, or 'help', her wages were from 50 cents to $1.00 a week; or, if she went from house to house by the day to spin and weave, or do tailoress work, she could get but 75 cents a week and her meals. As teacher, her services were not in demand, and the arts, the professions, and even the trades and industries, were nearly all closed to her.[127]

Cotton mills expanded the options available to girls and women. By 1860, 62,000 women worked in mills across New England. The sum of their experiences marked the first generations of industrial workers in America. Later in the century, the migration of Irish, French Canadian and Portuguese families altered the demographic and ethnic make-up of New England mill towns. From their inception these plants attracted families and individuals who balanced opportunity against risk. The wages earned and the communities forged created a complex transnational industrial phenomenon that inaugurated the modern era.

CONCLUSION

Eric Hobsbawm stated: 'Whoever says Industrial Revolution says cotton.'[128] The repercussions from the industrialization of cotton resonated across nations and continents, with implications that continue today.[129] In this global equation, India's loss was great. In 1813, in the midst of war, the British Parliament responded to pressures to open a direct export trade in cotton yarn to the subcontinent, heretofore the largest cotton textile-producing region in the world. Yarn from Britain's mills flooded into India. The effect on the mass of Indian women spinners was profound. Indian weavers might use machine-made British yarn and many did, finding it cheaper and of excellent quality. Printers might continue to decorate cloth for local, regional and even distant Asian markets, which in fact they did. J. Forbes Watson was a mid-nineteenth-century civil servant for the India Office employed as 'Reporter for the Products of India'. He undertook an extensive study of the Indian textile industry and his findings reflect some of the complexities within the trade that survived. One of the more intriguing features of his report was the value of cottons India exported, which in 1850–51 amounted to £637,651 and in 1864–5 rose to £1,045,520.[130] The Indian cotton trade was not dead, but it had been badly injured. Narratives of the decline of this signal trade have taken many forms, from contemporary laments to later anti-colonial and nationalist narratives.[131] Yet, the voice of the Bengali widow, echoing to us from the 1820s, reflects the profound effects of industrialization in the Atlantic world and its impact on Indian Ocean societies.

> I was widowed when I was twenty-two years old. I had given birth to only three daughters … I began to spin yarn … The weavers would come to my doorstep to buy the yarn thus spun … and they would immediately advance as much cash money as I wanted. As a result we did not have any anxiety about food and clothing … In this fashion I got three daughters married … Now for over three years, the mother and daughter-in-law are facing ricelessness again. Not only have the weavers stopped coming to my doorstep to buy my yarn, even when I send it … they will not buy at one-fourth of the former price. I am completely at a loss to understand how this has come to pass. I have made inquiries and have learned that the weavers are using English yarn now being extensively imported … When I examined the yarn I indeed found it better than mine.[132]

Prasannan Parthasarathi and Ian Wendt conclude that a full and detailed assessment of the nineteenth-century Indian cotton trade has yet to be written, wherein the balance of continuity, innovation and decline can be more carefully measured. Indeed, the full commercial dynamic within nineteenth-century Asia remains to be fully explored as this region reacted to external forces and local opportunity.[133] But we cannot dismiss the spinner's complaint. As Parthasarathi and Wendt observe, 'The new competition was sudden, forceful, and unrelenting.'[134]

The spinning of thread defined women's working lives for untold generations, blending with the labours of daily life and epitomizing their sex. Industrialization revised the global context of female labour. As mill-wrought thread permeated global markets, spinning was displaced as a profitable employment for women. In some communities this represented a disaster from which they did not quickly or easily recover. In others, spinning had been only one of many daily chores and time once spent making thread was applied to other alternatives. The displacement of hand spinning was not immediate and in regions distant from the power of the market, women continued with this task of necessity. However, wherever yarn was supplied ready-made, cheap and in quantities, weavers and knitters quickly embraced these materials in preference to making their own.[135] The nostalgia that surrounds the spindle and spinning wheel should not blind us to the pressures that previously compelled spinners' industry. Factory production introduced a new form of labour that was infinitely more productive and thereby changed spinning from a necessity for most women, to an option for a few. Hand spinning slowly declined thereafter to become a cultural artefact rather than a means of survival.

The plantation/factory nexus of the Atlantic world developed a powerful synergy over the 1800s, imposing new patterns of work and life on disparate populations, people constrained or enabled by technologies of production and distribution. The plantations of the Americas, and most particularly those in the Southern US, supplied the industrialized world, which in turn depended on these reliably regular shipments. Whether the mills of Alsace or Manchester, Massachusetts or Barcelona, there was a terrible dependency on the bales of cotton arriving from Dixie. By the 1850s, this measured 'a full 77 percent of the 800 million pounds of cotton consumed in Britain, 90 percent of the 192 million pounds used in France, 60 percent of the 115 million pounds spun in the German Zollverein, and as much as 92 percent of the 102 million pounds manufactured in Russia'.[136] But the politics of this dependency were unstable. The origins of the American Civil War are outside the purview of this study. Yet, in very real ways, that event marked the next stage of the global cotton saga. The forced labour of slaves would no longer underpin the production of raw cotton in the US, although the post-war alternatives retained familiar features of the old system. The American Civil War convulsed established industrial and commercial networks and inaugurated even wider investments worldwide, as industries and governments on virtually every continent sought to negotiate the new context of the global cotton network, planting cotton for the insatiable mills and factories of the industrial era.[137] The long transition from spindle to mill and from plantation to factory has rightly garnered the attention of generations of historians and legions of amateur genealogists. Each stage mirrored the character and constraints within which generations survived or prospered. Weighing and balancing the repercussions from these events will engage generations to come.

5.
CRAFTING COMFORT, CRAFTING CULTURE
Cotton and the Rise of Quilt Culture in the Western World, c.1500–1940

In previous chapters I explored the material revolution in the West, after 1500, initiated by the trade in cotton. Effects were manifest in commerce, industry and fashions. But the impact of the early global cotton trade did not stop there. The rise of quilt culture was equally dramatic. Quilts are commonly celebrated for their connections to past times in the colonial or Victorian eras, as well as being a marker of feminine industry and family heritage. Contemporary quilts are recognized as important textile arts and quilt historians seek to unravel the traditions and practice of regional quilting in many parts of America and Europe. Quilts themselves mirror geopolitical events, social hierarchies and the changing priorities of men, women and children. The rise of quilt culture in the West is entwined with the spread of cotton and with the global networks that bound together continents and peoples. From rare elite luxuries, quilts became fundamentally demotic articles, unleashing a largely female creativity, mediated by social and economic forces. These bedcoverings were adapted over time. Close study of these objects allows a better understanding of their roles in the market, in the home and in generations past, even as trade and industry transformed the materials employed.

This chapter explores quilts in the West in three stages, beginning in India. India had a vibrant quilt culture long before Portuguese ships arrived at the subcontinent in 1498.[1] Quilting in various parts of the subcontinent had an ancient history and a wide regional variety, whether appliquéd with dyed cotton, embroidered on a plain ground or made from painted or printed cottons. Not surprisingly, quilts were quickly acquired by early Portuguese traders and carried back to Europe as trophies of their adventures. Among the most unusual of the early surviving quilts to travel along the new shipping routes are those termed 'Indo-Portuguese' – treasured in major museums around the world. Over centuries, the making of quilts, as well as the quilts themselves, assumed a growing importance in the Atlantic world. That diffusion represents the second stage to be studied. The final themes to be addressed deal with the intersection of industrialized textile production and the variable practices of quilt-making that ensued, taken up by women of various ranks, ethnicities and circumstances. Cotton production accelerated in Britain from the later 1700s, dramatically transforming quilt production in ways that continued to evolve over the nineteenth and twentieth centuries. This chapter explores the metamorphosis of quilts from rare foreign exotics to the stuff of everyday family life, enriching material culture in the process.

'THE PRINCIPLE RICHES': INDO-PORTUGUESE QUILTS AND EURASIAN TRADE

A world without quilts seems improbable today, as they are such a vibrant and ubiquitous part of life. Quilts of infinite colour and design have been ever-present in Western society for centuries and remain a powerful material idiom, whether made by family members, stitched collectively for social purposes or bought ready-made as a type of ersatz inheritance. But there was indeed a time where quilts were rare in the West, a time when material scarcity was the norm and the stark dwellings where commoners resided offered few physical comforts. Bedding in the late Middle Ages was confined to coverings regionally available made of wool, down, linen, animal skins and (occasionally) silk. The wealthy and powerful slept warmly, while poor and middling folk made what they could of their goods, using woollen cloaks indoors for warmth. The scant information about quilts from that era suggests their rarity.[2]

The Asian textile trade had drawn merchant adventurers for centuries, most famously along the Silk Road. Silk quilts of several kinds were mentioned in medieval European documents, most frequently in regions adjacent to Eurasian trade routes such as the eastern Mediterranean.[3] Cotton or silk quilts became more common in Europe only after 1500 and they were mentioned repeatedly in the writings of early travellers to India. The Italian adventurer, Ludovico di Varthema, journeying in Asia from 1502 to 1508, described Bengal as having a 'greater abundance of cotton, than any country of the world' and while in a coastal city of Burma he observed the 'good beds of cotton … covered with silk or cotton' on which people slept.[4] The Portuguese trader Duarte Barbosa likewise took note of the rich assortment of goods shipped from Calicut on India's west coast to Cairo.[5] François Pyrard journeyed to Asia about 1600, a century after initial contact, and yet his account reflects the same intense fascination with manufactures as the first generation of voyagers. Pyrard described the 'quilts stuffed with cotton, painted and patterned exceeding prettily … Others are bespangled and painted with various figures. The silk-work is the same of all these kinds, the articles imported being pillows, counterpanes, and coverlets, pinked with much neatness, and cleverly worked'.[6] Pyrard was probably already acquainted with these manufactures, as by this time Indian-made quilts were widely celebrated in Europe – perhaps this accounts for his lengthy descriptions. His observations reflect the intense preoccupation of Europeans with a region rich in wares suited to European tastes. 'In short', wrote Pyrard, 'I could never make an end of telling such a variety of manufactures … For they are all cunning folk, and owe nothing to the people of the West.'[7] The products of Bengal also amazed him, particularly the articles fashioned from the yellow wild silk of the region.

> The inhabitants, both men and women, are wonderously adroit in all work, such as embroideries, which are worked so skilfully, down to the smallest stitches, that nothing prettier is to be seen anywhere … Many other kinds of work … are constructed with extraordinary delicacy, which, if brought [to Europe] … would be said to come from China.[8]

Reference to China was fulsome praise indeed, as Chinese manufactures were accorded the highest accolades in Europe. The descriptions and detailed inventories produced by these men suggest the profits they hoped would follow their new commercial ventures.

The existing networks of Italian and central European merchants, based in Lisbon, assisted the Portuguese in promoting the Indian commodities.[9] This mercantile fraternity channelled cotton products along well-developed internal trade routes through Iberia, Italy, France, central Europe, England, the Netherlands and northern Europe, where they attracted the notice of kings and queens, as well as merchants, clerics and lawyers enamoured by the new exotics. Over the sixteenth and seventeenth centuries, Indian embroiderers crafted distinctive quilts for new European patrons. These elaborate coverlets offer extraordinary visual depictions of cultural, economic and military interactions. Mnemonics of military and commercial relations, the varied subjects were integrated into existing collections of domestic furnishings, bringing a new iconic form to the beds of Europe's elite. Indian artisans adapted patterns to suit the tastes of the European newcomers, with those from Bengal or Gujarat stitching composite images of Europeans hunting, waging war, sailing ships or otherwise disporting themselves. In some cases these images were composed from models provided by European traders or intermediaries, put before Indian artisans.[10] The charm of these bedcovers encouraged an exchange of embroidery motifs between Portugal and the Indian subcontinent and even the migration of skilled embroiderers to Portugal to instruct local needleworkers.[11]

The embroidered figurative patterns blended European elements with established regional Indian designs, including the floral, fauna and religious symbols of their communities (Plate 13). For the most part, however, Indo-Portuguese quilts highlighted themes that Europeans wished to commemorate, including heraldic emblems, Christian iconography and other Western thematic imagery. The ideals and priorities of the male travellers to Asia were materialized in these early quilts, and the ethos of European adventurers illustrated in the stitchery. Collectively, the surviving quilts reveal the leitmotiv of this cross-cultural encounter, recording themes and objects customized to the tastes of European buyers. Ludovico di Varthema travelled through India and Burma between 1502 and 1508, keeping an account of his time and the peoples he saw: merchandise and martial exploits were routinely noted.[12] Similarly, an early voyager, Tomé Pires, listed the qualities he most admired in the societies he encountered on his eastward journey in 1512. A Portuguese court apothecary and later head of an embassy to China, Pires carried with him the attitudes and aspirations of his era. Hormuz he described respectfully as full of 'warlike ... civilized and domestic men', while the men of the Deccan region of India he noted as 'warriors, [and] gallant by nature'.[13] Pires identified these as among the most estimable of all male attributes, recognizable traits that were also celebrated in his home environment. In turn, these facets of masculinity were memorialized in the quilt designs. R. W. Connell describes the predominant features of early modern masculinity as privileging military performance, family connections and honour. These subjects are vividly depicted in the surviving quilts. Hunting, battles, the playing of board games or musical performances, exemplified the interests of Europe's 'warlike ... civilized and domestic men', typical of the skills honed by young gentlemen in the courts, castles and manor houses of Europe.[14] Scenes from classical and biblical tales were also stitched out, 'Indianized', as John Irwin noted, even in the depiction of Spanish and Portuguese dynastic symbols such as the two-headed eagle – the translation of symbols between cultures was often imperfectly understood by both sides.[15] In some quilts, great ships filled with Portuguese sailors are surrounded by fish and monsters from Hindu legends; the borders are luxuriant with the flora and fauna of the subcontinent and punctuated by figures engaged in land-based exploits (Plate 14). Some bedcoverings were notable for hunting scenes that decorated the border, an elite masculine enterprise with deep social significance in both cultures. There was a flourishing trade in these extraordinary objects, memorializing the intersection of cultures and highlighting the priorities of the commissioning agents. Once landed in Europe, these coverlets graced the beds and couches of Europe's political and commercial elites.[16] Traditional patriarchal aesthetics were blended together with a new cross-cultural form.

A variety of bedcovers decorated with needlework travelled the route from the subcontinent to Europe: some we would describe as 'quilts' and others as embroidered coverlets. Contemporaries to this trade were less precise in their terminology, employing a variety of terms, as they saw fit. Quilts known as Bengalla or Satgaon quilts, for the region and town of their manufacture, typically used white cotton grounds as the canvas for embroiderers, who picked out designs with yellow wild silk or red silk thread, quilting through the several layers. These objects are often difficult to photograph because of their relatively monochrome form, but the patterns are stunningly complex and show immense charm in their characterization of European activities in Asian precincts. The Victoria and Albert Museum holds a number in its collection and those embroidered in red silk are most readily reproduced, such as Plate 13.[17] This example typifies the themes portrayed in many similar quilts. European men are shown playing the drum or the guitar, surrounded by flowering shrubs and birds, with a dog and rabbit nearby. Western ships sail along one of the wide borders, with flags flapping, accompanied by smaller Indian Ocean dhows and mythic sea creatures, charting the newcomers' arrival in the southern seas. Another quilt stitched in yellow silk thread depicts more martial encounters, where men in European dress fire muskets at a gryphon and hunt wild game, spearing tigers from horseback, the ultimate aristocratic hunting adventure.[18] Other related coverlets (on cotton or silk) used chain stitch embroidery to create the effect of quilting, with the heavier stitch generating a more vivid pictorial style. The Museum of Fine Arts, Boston, holds an exceptional example with a breathtaking depiction in the centre panel of an artillery assault between two contending forces, with muskets and canon deployed, military banners aloft and the dead or wounded flung bleeding on the flower-strewn ground (see Plate 15). The borders are filled with action in a further mixture of cultural forms. Europeans are on the hunt, spears ready, dogs growling, deer and boar fleeing, birds preening, the whole linear progress entwined with flowering vines and enveloped by leafed branches. Does the military encounter involve Europeans or Indians? We many never know; however the subject matter would likely appeal to both constituencies. Thierry-Nicolas Tschaloff has studied numbers of Indo-Portuguese quilts in collections held in Paris, Bordeaux and the Indian Ocean island of La Réunion, finding striking examples of the genre. One coverlet appears to memorialize a victory or perhaps a treaty between former combatants, in this case depicting Western and Asiatic fighting forces. A later painted and printed coverlet in a similar style from about 1650 commemorates a diplomatic embassy, with the meeting of Dutch East India Company and Golconda officials in central India.[19]

The richly hybrid patterns of these coverlets introduced a form of domestic furnishings to Europe that was stylistically unique. Little wonder that these goods found their way to courtly bedrooms or merchants' couches. These quilts carried powerful iconic imagery, akin to military banners carried into war, or great naval pennants hung from ships' mastheads. The martial culture of this era, whether on land or sea, involved a complex system of symbolic transmissions through the use of flags, pennants, banners and other fabric devices. Religious banners were similarly replete with imagery and were often key adjuncts to ceremonies, or preserved as markers of notable events. Cloth standards with a multiplicity of designs were highly charged symbols with dynastic, religious, institutional and national associations, steeped in the male-led campaigns of the age. The functional uses of quilts did not arise directly from this institutional culture, such as with highly ritualized flag etiquette, for example. But they were created and used within a materially complex cultural context. The embroidered Indian bedcovers mirrored the aspirations and ambitions of the men driving their nations' martial and mercantile agendas. The quilt motifs signalled these priorities and celebrated their achievements in uniquely liminal spaces, neither fully public nor wholly private, transmitting the geopolitical goals of a generation.

Portuguese and Spanish merchants and nobles were innovators, among the first to incorporate these finely stitched objects in their homes. They esteemed these coverlets despite the absence of costly gold thread or jewels because of their imperial associations with Asia and its riches, along with Iberia's new place within this commercial network.[20] The Spanish connection to England, through Henry VIII's first wife Catherine of Aragon, may well have introduced Indian cottons to the English court. Henry VIII included 'quyltes' and 'coverpointes' in his inventory, quite possibly some of Indian origin. Quilts also figured as favoured gifts within the English court at this time.[21] Later in the 1500s, the noted collector Antonio Pérez, Secretary of State for King Philip II of Spain, included eight quilts among his immense ornamental and artistic assemblage, including at least one of Indo-Portuguese design. Until his political fall in 1579, Pérez was a taste-setter in elite Iberian society, with a reputation for artistic acuity that continued into the next century and across the continent. Pérez's lengthy exile in England at the end of the century exemplifies the ways in which tastes and trends travelled with private journeys, as well as through commercial initiatives.[22] The fashion for these distinctive objects spread from Iberia through the northern reaches of Europe. In the 1560s, an inventory from the family of Orange, the stadtholder in the Netherlands, included 'Couvertures d'Espaigne' as well as other bedding, further evidence of the Iberian fashion.[23] The Spanish Marquis of Velada was another who collected textile artefacts with this Asian provenance, as recorded in 1596. The craze for these objects is reflected in a host of inventories from elite Iberian families of this era, as well as in the collections of the Holy Roman Emperor, Ferdinand II (1578–1637).[24] Whether Bengali monochrome quilts or the more colourful appliquéd and embroidered sorts, these coverlets became a sixteenth-century vogue that flourished and evolved among subsequent generations of consumers. This style also crossed the Atlantic. Indian embroidered quilts, called *colcha*, were indispensable in the homes of wealthy Iberian colonists in the New World long before quilts assumed importance in North American colonies.[25]

England was comparatively late getting a trading foothold in Asia, but did not lag in accepting new goods from this region of the world. In 1567, the notable estate of Rothley Manor, Leicestershire, included in its appurtenances a 'best quilt' from the 'best bed', a notation that suggests the value associated with these objects.[26] An inventory of the Earl of Leicester in 1588 included twelve quilted 'counterpointes', all of which were made of silk, one of which was embroidered with his coat of arms – reminiscent of the specially ordered quilts produced for Portuguese grandees.[27] Indian wares are listed in subsequent inventories from that family decades later; however, the quilts owned by Robert, Earl of Leicester, could have originated from many parts of Eurasia.[28] Another noble in Elizabeth's court, Bess of Hardwick, Lady of the Privy Chamber, included an Indian embroidered coverlet among her possessions, which was listed in her 1603 inventory, while a Bengal-made embroidered quilt had been acquired years earlier.[29] It is hardly surprising then that when Sir William More was considering an important New Year's gift in 1595 for the Lord Treasurer, More selected a quilt for this occasion.[30] The 1618 probate inventory of the Dutch Prince of Orange reflects a continuing enthusiasm for Indian soft furnishings; bed curtains and full sets of bed clothes appear in great numbers, as well as embroidered Indian table coverings and decorative Indian furniture.[31]

Quilted coverlets reflected an exotic provenance even while evolving in use and meaning.[32] Attention to domestic comfort was on the rise. Over the seventeenth and eighteenth centuries, sleeping quarters were awarded greater space in the homes built by elite and middle-ranked families. The settings for sleep were in transition. For newly wealthy merchants and traders, as well as for gentry and nobles, new house designs enabled greater privacy. Corridors allowed passage through a house without intruding in private chambers, while great halls – where previously many would have slept – were adapted for other uses. Rooms dedicated to specific uses were becoming the norm, including rooms for sleeping, where beds, bedding and domestic décor were more elaborately conceived. These new areas of the home were shaped at least in part by trade with Asia, through the incorporation of quilts, painted cotton bed-hangings and curtaining, cushions and the like. This long-running transformation represented a commercial opportunity, and this fact was quickly recognized by European companies trading with Asia. Thus, factors working on site for the English East India Company worked assiduously to secure stocks of quilts from various regions of India, often in competition with other European agents. A letter dispatched from Ahmedabad in 1618 noted the writer's valiant efforts to acquire 'quilts party-cullered … according to your order';

but he complained that 'We cannot get taylors enough to work'. In higher spirits later in the year, the factor announced he had found a supply of quilts in another region 'all of one kind [of] chinte [chintz] … such as either side may be used'. He also noted another variety he had acquired, which was 'most used in India, and wee thinke will be most pleasing to England'.[33] His success was evident in London's auction rooms. At one such event in London, in 1618, a Bengal quilt about three yards square, 'embroidered all over with pictures of men and crafts in yellow silk', was bought for over £20 – a considerable sum that would keep a middle-ranked family for almost half a year. One Portuguese writer noted that by 1620, 'There is no ship from India that does not bring at least four hundred [quilts]' in its cargo.[34] Ships' crews employed by the English East India Company, both sailors and officers, routinely bought and traded on their own behalf and were given cargo space for these goods. Legally they were instructed to restrict themselves to a limited number of items, with the most valuable articles reserved for official trade. But moral considerations rarely guided private ventures. In 1631 Charles I finally allowed East India Company servants to lawfully import embroidered quilts from western India.[35] In the years to follow, sums from £5 to £40 were spent by London buyers eager to own quilts described as 'imbroidered with sundry colours' or 'imbroidered upon Callicoe with sundrie silks'.

The passion for Indian quilts in Europe was evident from north to south, east to west. Evidence of this enthusiasm also survives in the collections of the living history museum, Colonial Williamsburg, Virginia. It holds an Indian white cotton quilt embroidered in yellow silk, owned by Catherine Culpeper (d. 1719), daughter of the immensely wealthy second Baron Culpeper. Her son, Thomas Fairfax, included this item among the goods he carried to Virginia when he travelled there in the 1730s, eventually settling on his vast colonial estates.[36] Swedish royalty and nobles also included exceptional Indian quilts among their household wares from the early 1600s. One 1627 Swedish royal inventory describes a fine white cotton quilt embroidered with yellow silk thread in the Bengali style, termed in this document a 'coverlet of linen with Indian work'. When I saw this quilt in Stockholm, the stitches were exceptionally fine, as was the cotton.[37] More colourful Gujarati embroidered quilts are also recorded in Scandinavian documents – perhaps these were cargo from the Danish East India Company, established in 1616 following the success of other northern European ventures.[38] We cannot be sure of the origins of these particular coverlets, whether gift or purchase. One thing is certain – quilt fever engulfed Europe. Indian quilts were initially favoured as a medium to celebrate the triumphs of European adventurers and dynastic agents, and the scenes and images annotated by the needleworkers recorded their triumphs. But the variety of Indian quilts expanded over the seventeenth century, along with the range of buyers, inaugurating the next stage in quilt history.

DOMESTICATING QUILTS, CREATING NEW TRADITIONS

The enthusiasm for quilts was part of a wide transformation in material culture built on the dramatic flow of cotton textiles into the hands of European consumers, discussed in previous chapters. Indian cottons were widely adopted in European homes and these settings reflected the passion for cottons. For example, Olivier Raveux notes the significant presence of calico furnishings in late seventeenth-century Marseilles, the destination for many Indian cargoes channelled through the Mediterranean. The trend towards calico furnishings was well under way by 1667–8, when such goods are found in 62 per cent of local Marseilles probate inventories; this figure jumps to 85 per cent by 1692.[39] The aesthetic and practical features of these cottons won legions of admirers. Quilts from India offered uniquely crafted comfort with distinct visual forms. Although many early quilts celebrated mercantile and military adventures, this type of coverlet was infinitely malleable and came to be valued by less august owners, of more modest means. Beds represented one of the most expensive items of furniture, one of the great costs being the collation of bedding. One of the great innovations of the seventeenth and eighteenth centuries was the increased accumulation of bedding among the general population.[40] Given the response of Europeans to Indian quilts, trading companies expanded and diversified the products they procured. For example, during the 1600s printed and painted calico quilt tops were shipped to Europe, becoming another successful product, with the quilting completed in cities like Amsterdam or London. These items were made for a broader market segment. In 1683 instructions from the London office of the English East India Company encouraged their factors in India to focus specifically on lower-quality bedding, made 'strong, but none too deare'. The letter continued: 'Possibly some of these things may gain that repute here as may give us cause of greater enlargement in them hereafter.'[41] The lists of quilts shipped into London give some sense of the commercial dynamic. For example, a ship arriving in London in December 1670 carried ten bales of large quilts and five of small. Another 1676 London auction offered 920 large quilts and 400 small ones for sale. Similarly, the announcement of cargo arriving on four East India Company ships in June and July of 1685 included 2,400 quilts among their stock, only eighty of which were silk, the rest cotton calico. Whole pieces of calico, each of twenty yards or more in length, were shipped to Europe already quilted. Accounts for several years in the late 1690s list twenty-four such pieces of quilted calico, in addition to over 1,150 yards of quilted calico, plus many thousands of printed and embroidered quilts.[42]

A 1688 English description provides further indication of the spread of this bedding. In this account quilting itself is defined as 'to put Cotton Wool of an equal thickness between two Silks or a Callicoe or other Cloth undermost, and a Silk above, which is wrought in scrolls, flowers, etc. to keep the Cotton from shifting its Place'.[43] Plate 16 depicts a room vibrant with Indian cotton, from the quilt on the bed to the calico on the walls. This rare example of late seventeenth-century décor survives from a wealthy child's doll's house: the room itself was set up for the arrival of a new 'baby'. As the seventeenth century closed, English merchants and tradesmen, great and small, from London and surrounding counties, joined other Europeans draping vibrant calicoes over walls, window and beds.[44]

Cotton quilts were becoming a staple form of bedding, valued for comfort, beauty and practicality although, as I have shown, not all celebrated this transformation. Daniel Defoe lamented this phenomenon, depicting an insidious process whereby calico furnishings 'crept into our houses, our closets and bedchambers; ... and at last the beds themselves were nothing but Callicoes or Indian stuffs'.[45] Calico quilts were characterized as invidious intruders. But the fact of the matter was that wool blankets had practical drawbacks, quite aside from any aesthetic consideration, being harder to wash. Cotton bedding offered greater potential hygiene at a time when white and light-coloured linens were culturally associated with cleanliness and when laundering was given greater cultural emphasis throughout northern Europe. The Dutch, in particular, epitomized this reverence for clean linen in bedding, throughout the house and on one's person. Weekday rituals of washing and laundering were a hallmark of seventeenth-century Dutch life. They were described as 'perfect slaves to cleanliness'; but where they led, others followed and the ideal of clean linen became the prevailing aim of more and more householders across the region.[46] Daniel Roche describes the seventeenth-century 'invention of linen', noting the new meanings inscribed in the materials of daily life. What was called in France 'great linen' (*gros linge*) included sheets and other washable bedding, tablecloths and napkins that were 'put to wash' at the laundries in and around Europe's great cities.[47] Laundering became a larger and more important trade, with elements of skill and new standards enforced within more households. Thus cotton quilts intersected with other wider cultural and material metamorphoses. This further encouraged their spread, whether ready-made from India or crafted in European workshops.

A 1696 English treatise on childbirth included instructions for the preparation of the birthing bed. What best should be provided for the woman? Why a quilt, which for functional reasons of washability and absorbency was far preferable to other options.[48] Women valued how readily Indian cottons could be laundered and how brilliant the colours remained after repeated scrubbing. Tomas Maldonado and John Cullars trace evolutions of the idea of comfort and note that 'the ideology of comfort appears closely involved with at least two parallel categories: hygiene and order'.[49] Practical and aesthetic concerns coincided perfectly in this cotton bedding and as Lady Penelope Mordaunt approached her imminent labour in 1700, she asked her husband in London to send two little pillows and a cradle quilt to their home in Warwickshire.[50] Whether for a woman in childbirth, a newborn babe or the routine bedding used by family and friends, cotton quilts added unique dimensions to domestic furnishings. Moreover, this usage was firmly in place by 1700 among all those with access to urban markets or pedlar routes. We are not surprised that six 'Indian Callicoe quilts' were bought from a London retailer for the Duke of Bedford in September 1701, prior to the onset of winter. Priced at a little more than £1 each, they would have been attractive additions to his household furnishings, selected for their looks and utility.[51] Consider as well the consolation offered to a provincial guest perhaps concerned about the rigours of a late winter journey. Writing in 1698, the host reassured the traveller: 'Your bed shall be as easy as it can be made, by putting a feather bed under the quilt.'[52] Sandwiched between these layers, their visiting kin could rest at ease.

This growing quilt culture exemplifies the heightened attention accorded comfort. John Crowley observes that 'Physical comfort – self-conscious satisfaction with the relationship between one's body and its immediate physical environment – was an innovative aspect of Anglo-American culture.'[53] Crowley puts his focus on the 1700s. But this was a long-running social project that affected many regions across Europe and the Atlantic world, extending over a longer timeframe. We need to be reminded of the singular sensual experience that new styles of bedding could represent to the user – not simply a visually enhanced sleeping environment, but warmer, lighter, sweeter-smelling washable bedcovers that were increasingly affordable. A research team led by Mark Overton assessed many thousands of probate inventories for the counties of Kent and Cornwall in England between 1600 and 1750; both are southern counties, but Kent has closer proximity to major ports in Continental Europe and London, while the western county of Cornwall is a longer distance from the metropolis. The researchers found a greater number and specialization of rooms in domestic dwellings, along with a marked increase in bedding, especially in the wealthier county of Kent. In addition, there was a slight increase in the average number of beds per household. This pattern also appears in other parts of northern Europe, marking the changing material environment enjoyed by a growing number of families.[54] While commentators and politicos debated the effects of 'luxury' on the general population, with many proposing restrictions on new commodities, more citizens happily luxuriated under quilts when the opportunity arose, slumbering in more sanitary and attractive surroundings. John Crowley notes further that: 'The language of comfort gave meaning to a consumer revolution in Anglo-American society, as more people had more money to spend on more goods.'[55] His point is well taken. However, this development extended far beyond the Anglophone world. The flood of cottons pouring into Europe, and the relative cheapness of so many of the printed cottons, brought new and dramatically demotic forms of aesthetic delight and bodily ease to a cross-cultural assortment of European men and women. Now, if we were transported back to these sleeping quarters we might find them sparse.[56] But calico quilts, sheets, bed-hangings and pillowcases represented qualitatively important accessories reshaping sleeping and waking hours (Plate 17). Moreover, their acceptance and addition to many hundreds of thousands of households reflected intentional calculations and did not take place absent-mindedly. Generations of housewives made careful reckonings, balancing newly articulated needs with income, and their collective decisions shaped new commercial and cultural agendas.

The trade in Indian cottons was a catalyst that brought changes of many kinds and reactions of many sorts, discussed in previous chapters. Most of Europe's governments resolutely banned Indian cottons. Yet the material alterations once initiated could not be restrained. Evidence of cotton quilts can be found in a range of records over the next century. In the first instance, European women easily took to quilting. By 1700, quilting was one of many needle trades followed by women, not only for bedding but for the creation of quilted petticoats, a staple of women's wardrobes. Specialist warehouses sprang up in London over the 1700s, where women could buy quilted petticoats ready-made. The size of the petticoat, like a quilt itself, required space if a frame was used and though some quilters doubtless sewed in lodgings and garret rooms, one warehouse owner advertised that his stock was 'quilted under his immediate inspection'.[57] Many women earned their living at quilting, some with exceptionally fine stitching and others showing the routine speed and basic competency that was essential to survive in the ready-made industry. Quilting was listed in a 1747 occupational guidebook as 'another Trade, performed chiefly by Women'. The author went on to state that: 'There have been some ... [who] used to buy the Materials wholesale, which they put out to be made up into Quilts, and so served the Shops ... by which Trade they got a great deal of Money.'[58] Behind these words we can glimpse the legions of women sustained by this trade.

I will focus on the English experience in particular in the further development of quilt culture, not least because it was here that the first industrialized cotton trade arose during the eighteenth century. Wills and legal records suggest how widely owned quilts became over the 1700s, as the politics of the cotton trade unfolded. Sifting through the online proceedings of the Old Bailey, London's largest and busiest court, Indian calico quilts appear from the 1680s to the 1720s, at which point Indian cottons were nominally barred from British shores. Some of these earlier quilts were valued at £1, £2, £3 or even £5 in the court records, while other more pedestrian examples had valuations of three, four or five shillings.[59] Price and quality differed widely, not just for imported Indian goods, but also for those made locally (Plate 18). One instance of theft further suggests the scope of this trade. Open warehouse doors offered an irresistible temptation to a thief, Robert Hope, who slipped into the warehouse unobserved one July day in 1713; he snatched a quilt 'from a Pile', at which point someone sounded the alarm and he was seized.[60] Warehouses selling quilts were well known in London and Amsterdam, among other European cities.

A group of London quilt-makers produced a pamphlet in 1720, as part of the debate around Indian cottons, and this offers further insights into the business of quilts. The quilt-makers of London were distressed at the proposed ban on Indian cotton. Their craft had developed as an offshoot of the printing trade, as European wood-block printers improved their skills at imitating Indian calicoes. By the early 1700s, printers in and about the English capital turned out 23,000 printed quilt tops annually, the designs applied to Indian cottons. Once the tops were printed, and in recognition of the northern climate, the eight-foot pieces were backed with locally made wool cloth and stuffed with fleece; then the whole coverlet was quilted by seamstresses hired for the purpose. This amalgam of material cultures resulted in a distinctive hybrid bedding. The quilt-makers who distributed this pamphlet defended their product and expressed their fear for 'the Destruction of . . . poor Families, that get a comfortable Livelihood by making said Quilts'. They saw little outlet for the thousands of cotton quilt tops they had in stock, made in the expectation that customers could 'quietly enjoy them'.[61] The authors had little confidence in the locally made printed linen (or linen/cotton blends); they insisted that no European fabric could match the quality of Indian cotton and the quilt-makers begged to be excluded from the forthcoming prohibition in recognition of the quantity of English wool they used. Their supplications were in vain. The ban went into effect after Christmas of 1722. Thereafter no new calico quilts could be made. In the following weeks, advertisements were printed time and again in local newspapers, urging those desirous of a new bed furnishings to act immediately as 'no Calico Furniture can be made up after Christmas next, under Penalty of 20 l. [fine]', wrote Thomas Nash of The Royal Bed on Holborn Bridge. He repeated his notice weekly then almost daily in the lead-up to the ban.[62]

MAKING MEANINGS

Did owners of cotton quilts hide them away after the ban, fearful of denunciations and fines? Did legal injunctions hobble the quilt culture developing in many parts of the Atlantic world? It appears that in England at least, quilt-owners may have received something of a dispensation from the authorities. In the spring of 1724, about sixteen months after the ban was put in place, announcements appeared in English newspapers suggesting a special status would be accorded to printed cotton quilts. 'We hear, that . . . all Furniture and Houshold [sic] stuff, that was made up before the 25th December 1722, is exempted from Seizure; but no Alteration is made . . . with Respect to Apparel'.[63] I have found no legal support for this claim. But apparently, popular sentiment supported the continued use of this bedding. Calico clothing was publicly reviled, but clothing was worn openly and quilts were used in private. Likewise, bedding represented a significant investment for most families, which may account for the continued presence of calico quilts in the public record after 1722. Calico quilts appeared in estate auctions throughout the middle decades of the century, listed openly among household wares or in auctions of stock-in-trade – 'Chints Quilts and Counterpanes'; 'Callicoe Quilts, and printed Quilts of all Sorts'; 'Chince, Calico and Linnen Quilts'; 'White Callicoe Quilts, diverse printed Quilts'.[64] There is no evidence the authorities sanctioned these owners. But essentially the legal flows of Indian cotton quilts had reached an end and the residue from earlier trade could not outfit the rising numbers eager to refurbish their beds. Calico quilts had established the model bedding for the age. A process of substitution took place thereafter. The details of common patterns of consumption are sometimes difficult to discern once goods have left the shop. However, in criminal records, in at least some of the cases, the form and context of the stolen quilt was described. Textiles and clothing of all sorts were most readily stolen and then negotiated for cash or kind through a wide range of pawnbrokers and second-hand dealers, as well as from many local taverns and shopkeepers, where few questions were asked.[65] Quilts were among the goods bought, stolen and resold, in repeating cycles.

Items described as calico, chintz and even 'India quilts' appear intermittently in the Old Bailey records throughout the 1720s and 1730s.[66] By this time quilts were widely owned and quilt-owners included a good number of lodging house keepers; other quilt owners included a woman confined to Fleet Prison for debt, and an eighteenth-century general whose bed furnishings, including the calico quilt, were bought by the Duke of Chandos in 1729. In other words, quilt owners comprised a cross-section of Londoners high and low. Among the hundreds of quilts recorded as stolen over the eighteenth century, a considerable number came from furnished lodgings, which were among the commonest types of accommodation in the capital. By the 1750s, of the cases before the Old Bailey involving bedding, John Styles notes that two-thirds involved the theft of quilts off the beds.[67] The trial accounts from the Old Bailey allow us a glimpse into the bedrooms of modest private homes, common lodging houses and more affluent residential bedchambers. The fact that so many women renting out rooms used quilts on these beds indicates how widespread this form of bedding had become. Mary Low exemplifies these metropolitan landladies. With her husband away, living on a parish pension, Mary Low rented out a room to make ends meet. Low testified in the summer of 1740 that: 'The Prisoner carried off my Goods, while I was at Market getting Bread for my Children.' After tracking down her former tenant Low demanded 'How she could be so wicked as to strip my Room?' The accused had already sold the quilt for ten shillings to a friend – the equivalent of a week's wages for a skilled male artisan at that time.[68] Quilts, then as now, elicited various reactions based on their looks or quality. The thief offered the stolen quilt to a friend for a price, presenting a false provenance, saying it had been sent by her grandmother in the country. The friend agreed to look it over. But, in the words of the friend: 'When I saw it, I told her it was too good for me.' From this simple declaration, even more than the value assigned by the court, we can get a sense of its quality and appearance.[69] Mary Low must have been relieved to have had it restored.

Many of the court transcripts provide only stark statements, listing goods lost and criminal allegations, offering few details of the circumstances or physical surroundings where the theft took place; but other court proceedings paint more intimate portraits of the relationship between people and their possessions. In May 1746, Mary White, a widow, lived in rented lodgings where she earned her living sewing 'plain work'. But Mary White's seemingly hand to mouth existence was not devoid of comforts or beauty. Along with the pair of blankets on her bed was a quilt valued at ten shillings and sixpence, and a calico cover, which gave added charm.[70] It is not clear whether this was an Indian calico or not; if it was an imported calico, it may have been some twenty years old and acquired before the ban. Still, the colours would show richly and remain bright, one of the particular advantages of this fabric. But it could also have been one of the new British-made linen/cotton 'calicoes', substitutes printed in imitation of the Indian original to growing acclaim. Whatever the truth of the matter, the simple catalogue of her bedclothes suggests the pleasure she might take in such simple luxuries. White's choice exemplifies the prevailing fashion for painted and printed fabrics bedecking the bed, a taste shared across Europe in many social settings. A 1745 Dutch doll's house vividly illustrates this trend, with a calico quilt on the bed (Plate 19).

The cultural character of quilts had evolved since the era of Indo-Portuguese quilts. But one example suggests the persistent functional role of quilts as a vehicle to celebrate imperial or dynastic achievements. The quilt in question was described as a 'curiosity' in court documents – the clerk had clearly never seen one like it. This case reveals the rare life history of a bedcover valued at £3, which had travelled through the hands of several long-term owners, interspersed with periods when it languished at pawnbrokers' as surety for loans. It was clearly an exceptional object, with features one owner believed could only be explained if it was 'made in a nunnery', thinking of no other way to account for its traits. Competing witnesses testified to the years the quilt had spent in one household or another, as personal treasure or rare oddity. The genealogy reveals the way in which quilt culture had become part of the social vernacular, with the quilts a means for social, political and emotive expression. A witness in this case, Susannah Surges, traced the first years of the contested quilt beginning with its creation by her 'first husband's wife's first husband, who was a taylor'. The tailor was inspired to make this quilt 'when the Duke of Marlborough died'. She recollected that: 'He made these two figures in the middle for the Duke and Duchess of Marlborough; and when the duke was buried, he had five guineas of a gentleman for it to lie over a balcony' – most likely for the funeral procession on 9 August 1722, which wound the mile from Marlborough House to Westminster Abbey past crowds of mourners who lined the route. With the death of the tailor and then his wife, the quilt travelled along the chain of marital connections, until such time as Susannah Surges 'married in the year [17]25 to Mr Philip Baker, who kept the Horseshoe alehouse in the Butcher-row; this quilt was his then', a legacy from his previous marriage. Susannah was pleased to keep the quilt for eleven years, pawning it only in 1737.[71]

Too few details about this exceptional quilt survive. There is no information on its colours or the fabrics used in its composition. What survives is a clear sense of its monumental scale and its extraordinary design, including the two stylized heraldic figures, echoing the devices employed in the Indo-Portuguese quilts and the underlying political ethos of those objects. The first Duke of Marlborough was a celebrated British general, with major battles to his credit and a wide popular following. And in these circumstances even the clerk at the Old Bailey felt compelled to offer an editorial comment, between parentheses: 'The Quilt was a singular laborious piece of curious workmanship'.[72] Later generations of nineteenth-century quilt-makers would produce comparable feats of needlecraft, featuring central portraits of popular figures, like the would-be Queen Caroline, wife of George IV or American heroes like George Washington. This echoes a particular tradition of material commemoration embodying political and dynastic priorities.[73] Paradoxically, a medium now associated with private and intimate comfort served intermittently as a banner for public displays of political passions.[74]

Most quilts were more modest in form. But they too could hold great importance to their owners, as markers of sentiment, tokens of affection or more opaque footnotes to a family legacy. As a result of unspecified negotiations, Thomas Stones of Mosbrough, Yorkshire, added a codicil to his will of 1731 granting his wife 'her own worked bed and quilt'.[75] Textiles like quilts, which envelop the body night after night, have many of the cultural features of clothing, as they too might hold what Jones and Stallybrass describe as 'material memories … Memories of subordination … memories of collegiality … memories of love … memories of identity'.[76] English wills of this period contain numerous references to these artefacts, material memories transferred between generations, like the bequest to a cousin in 1781 of 'a quilt that was her mother's'. Likewise, Thomas Roberts, a Bedfordshire yeoman, left to his daughter Ann Cartwright two pieces of furniture, £50 and a calico quilt in 1753. Margaret Green might have taken solace in receiving from her aunt three beds with bed-hangings in 1780, along with the aunt's 'best white bed quilt [and] two stampled bed quilts' among other housewares. Frances Mabel Sparrow bequeathed to her nephew two things of note in 1766: her gold watch and seal to be his at age eighteen and 'her white worked quilt'.[77] The bedding confirmed family connections in practical and symbolic forms.

For a time, during the middle decades of the 1700s, the actual substance of quilts changed. Those described as 'linen' appear in court and legal records in great numbers, like the 'white holland bed quilt and cradle quilt' bequeathed to a younger daughter in 1760.[78] Whiteworked quilts were another fashion of the time, harking back to the whole cloth embroidered quilts from the Indian subcontinent, now with new iterations although still employing abstracted geometric or floral patterns. However, while whole cloth quilts (in linen, worsted or satin) remained a persistent style, they were ultimately less popular than others founded on Indian calico but now made of British linen/cotton, precursors to all-cotton British calicoes. Chintz and calico quilts remained a staple. Older quilts made of Indian chintz routinely featured in estate auctions throughout the middle decades of the century, listed in dozens of advertisements in London and regional newspapers. These served as examples against which newer goods could be judged. Printed Indian cotton quilts set a standard that the British industry struggled for decades to equal and local British entrepreneurs poured their energies into furniture textiles, with growing success by mid-century. An advertisement confirms the advances made, substituting British fabrics for the Indian originals. In 1752, the owner of a 'Blanket Warehouse' in central London announced the range of goods he had on hand, including 'a great Number of Washing Beds of Checks, fine flower'd Cottons, etc. of Patterns entirely fresh and new … [and] just arrived fresh out of the Country, large Quantities of Blankets, Quilts … at Prices very low'.[79] By 1766 it was reported that 312 tons of 'Manchester wares' travelled from the hub of the British cotton industry to various national markets each week.[80] With the ban on cottons removed in France in 1759 and in England in 1774, competition intensified to create 'authentic' European-made calicoes. Ultimately, by the 1780s, many European printed goods exceeded the Indian original in price and quality.[81] Locally and internationally, the distribution of British cottons gained momentum. It is very likely then that in the court records the 'callicoe bed-quilt' valued at two shillings in 1767 was made of British fabric, likewise the number of quilts described as 'cotton' and 'callico' stolen from English beds in the 1770s. By this date the main cloth for everyday and special quilts was once again cotton, more widely and cheaply available by the century's end than in generations. The bolts of factory-made cotton filling store shelves became standard quilt fabrics, a pattern that prevailed wherever spinning mills and weaving factories arose in Europe and America.[82] The industrialization of cotton production signalled the next stage in the evolution of quilts. By the 1780s, the flood of cotton fabrics in every quality and style ensured that quilts were crafted in this cloth. The result was a flourishing of patchwork quilts, ultimately the most pervasive model of this form. Patchwork quilting and factory cottons became ineluctably connected in the industrial age. Patchwork enabled virtually infinite variations and the generations of women who worked with factory-made cottons kept their hands busy and let their imaginations run free, innovating and adapting every shade and pattern of cloth to cover family beds.

INDUSTRIAL COTTON, PATCHWORK AND CREATIVE DEMOCRACY

The advent of the patchwork cotton quilt marks the modern age of quilting, a milestone in the full flowering of quilt culture in the Western world.[83] The design influences on this form are still debated. Collections of antique quilts typically include only a few examples from the late seventeenth and early eighteenth centuries, with a much larger numbers from the late 1700s and 1800s. The cotton patchwork quilt developed as a quintessential style and reflects diverse social facets within a long-running process of material adaptation. Patches have a long history. Careful mending typified the work of housewives, negotiating between thrift and utility. Breeches, jackets and gloves are some of the garments routinely repaired to extend life and for the poor this resulted in a particoloured beggarly look distinctive of the poor – but patches were always to be preferred to ragged clothes.[84] Discrete and subtle patching was essential to maintain a respectable look. Patches were deftly applied to bedding, as well as to clothing, in virtually all classes and this ongoing domestic task was a measure of womanly skills. From 1600 there were growing volumes of cheaper light wool fabrics, fustians, linen and cotton.[85] As previously noted, the introduction of cottons (first Indian and then British) was part of this textile trajectory, bringing less costly fabrics within the grasp of common people. Cotton textiles and patchwork are inextricably linked. The stylistic use of appliqué predated widespread patchwork, though the two forms are related. But with the greater availability of printed cottons, the stage was set for a further evolution of quilt design. The 1801 patchwork quilt, Plate 20, is a robust example of the hybrid quilts devised at this time, with a handwoven linen backing, stuffed with wool. The combination of fibres, fabrics and technologies in this quilt suggests a careful use of resources at a time of industrial transition. The patchwork quilt top included twenty-one assorted cottons, printed in complementary colours. Most of the cotton fabrics were printed using wood-block techniques, although curators at the Victoria and Albert Museum speculate that some may have been decorated with the new roller printing machines that accelerated the rate of printing enormously.[86] This bedcover epitomized prudent thrift in the industrial era.

Recycling goods was the norm for virtually all households and the adroit housewife lived within this discipline. Injunctions to frugality and industry were at the heart of the 'patch', evidence of skilful needlework and deft management of resources. Patches were socially complex emblems defining thrift, prudence and economy. The patch was an acknowledgement of the inevitable exigencies of family life and the duty of a wife to be prepared. Gendered injunctions to thrift and industry animated the use of patches, a discipline enjoined on women of all ages, although enforced more sternly on the poor. It was widely agreed that for females, as one eighteenth-century author wrote, 'the Art of Oeconomy, and Household Managery [was the] most proper for their Sex … though they are never so wealthy'.[87] Another writer of that age remarked that: 'I always keep my girls at their needle. – One, perhaps, is working her a gown, another a quilt for a bed'.[88] Even young ladies from wealthy families were instructed to learn the needle arts 'to enable you to judge more perfectly of that kind of work, and to direct the execution of it in others'; as well, knowledge of stitchery could develop as an independent pleasure in order 'to fill up, in a tolerable agreeable way, some of the many solitary hours you must necessarily pass at home'.[89] There were a growing number of patterns and instruction guides available in women's magazines after 1770 to direct needlework projects. Even the least able seamstress could cobble together squares of fabric to form a patchwork. But inspiration and invention could also play a part. Thus females young and old refigured patches in complex ways that challenged simple notions of plenty or want, styling surplus or second-hand fabric into newly attractive objects that modelled ingenuity and skill in equal measure. Cotton was clearly the fabric of choice by 1800, an essential democratic textile refashioned through womanly inventiveness.[90] The pastel confection pieced and quilted by 13-year-old American, Harriet Du Bois, dated 1807, epitomizes this new form of textile labour (Figure 5.1).

Patchwork quilts did not begin in the 1770s, although they became infinitely more popular after that date, as the output of British industry soared.[91] Untold numbers of these coverlets were made by ordinary women, like the wife of John Welch, whose patchwork quilt was stolen in 1771.[92] Cotton patchwork was not peculiar to the Anglophone world. Indeed, several notable cotton patchwork quilts survive in the Netherlands from the last quarter of the eighteenth century. One, made of chintz and cotton patchwork, was signed in Dutch 'Sara Luberti, née Luydenz, 52 years old, the year 1796', reflecting the pride this older seamstress took in the fruits of her needle.[93] Another one from a museum in Dordrecht has a rare provenance and came to the Netherlands among the few belongings carried by a French refugee family fleeing to the Low Countries in the late 1700s, in a time of war. It would keep them warm on their trek to safety during politically tumultuous times.[94]

Patchwork was a vogue in the early nineteenth century, a fashionable pastime for genteel women. Jane Austen and her female relatives took part in this fad, driven less by need than creative novelty and the gendered values celebrated in such projects. Writing to her sister Cassandra in May 1811, Jane Austen chivvied her to send the pieces of cloth she had requested: 'Have you remembered

5.1 Quilt, linen and printed cotton, pieced and quilted, 1807. Made by Harriet Du Bois (b. 1794–n/a). Los Angeles County Museum of Art.

to collect peices [sic] for the Patchwork? – We are now at a standstill.'[95] Women's needlework was applauded in more self-conscious terms by nineteenth-century authors like Mary Margaret Egerton, Countess of Wilton, who employed a somewhat politicized language to describe the fruits of female industry. Wilton insisted that: 'The NEEDLE and its beautiful and useful creations hitherto remained without their due need of praise and record.' She further noted that: 'Those domestic virtues which are woman's greatest pride … find no record on pages whose chief aim and end is the blazoning of manly heroism, of royal disputations, or of trumpet-stirring records.'[96] Wilton did not set out to overturn the gender hierarchy but rather to celebrate the 'beautiful and useful creations' devised by women for the amelioration of their homes and families, their labour and inspiration defining generations. 'It is entirely of insignificant details that the sum of human life is made up', wrote Wilton, 'and any one of those details, how insignificant soever apparently in itself, as a link in the chain of human life is of definite relative value.'[97]

Inspiration, duty and necessity combined to guide the practice of housewifery and the creation of quilts. The necessary skills to succeed were outlined in an 1824 letter from Ellen Weeton Stock to her daughter, concerned that: '[You] will never be fit to be a housekeeper until you know the value of most things in daily use.'[98] That same year Ellen sent her daughter the makings for a patchwork quilt. Ellen bargained at a local market for remnants of cotton squares 'sold by weight', costing four pence, and included as well a finer piece of cotton patchwork. This example came from:

> an old Quilt I made above 20 years ago; it may serve as a pattern. The Hexagon in the middle was a shred of our best bed hangings; they were Chintz, from the East Indies, which my father brought home with him from one of his voyages. He was never in the East Indies himself, but probably purchased the Chintz in some foreign market.[99]

With the telling of this story, Ellen Weeton Stock hoped to convey 'something of the history of your mother's family', though she was physically distant from her daughter due to troubled family events. The patches bought in the marketplace had none of the resonance of chintz long worn and long used. But the creation of a new patchwork quilt could bridge past and present.[100]

Quilts entered the lexicon of North American housekeepers at various times over the eighteenth and nineteenth centuries. These were initially rare outside the Atlantic port cities, although the colonial residents of Philadelphia or Halifax, Nova Scotia had easy access to a full array of fabrics flowing through the Atlantic world. Halifax newspapers advertised 'patches', 'calico stripes', 'quiltings' and the like in 1785, selling both British and Indian cottons in ready-to-use patches in the 1780s and 1790s.[101] In British North America, as elsewhere, the abundance of textiles meant that quilt-making became common for girls, young women and their older female relatives. However, in the American colonies and early republic, the characteristics of quilt culture varied by time and place. Susan Prendergast Schoelwer traced the appearance of fabric furnishings in eighteenth-century Philadelphia, noting that bedclothes were present in nearly 90 per cent of her sample of probate inventories from that colonial community. As in England, wealth and social standing determined when comforts were secured. Schoelwer also observes that: 'By 1700 bedcoverings had clearly become indispensable to the maintenance of a self-sufficient household.'[102] Those with easy access to Atlantic ports adopted quilts early; those at greater distance owned them later in the century. Patricia Keller explored the complex quilt history of Lancaster County, Pennsylvania, an inland region fed by the Susquehanna River, with settlers including German Mennonites, English and Irish Quakers and Presbyterians. Quilting in this region was not a general feature of eighteenth-century life. Indeed, Keller notes that the shift to quilting came only after the industrialization of cotton spinning after 1800 and the associated decline of women's domestic-based spinning and textile production. Women's work was reoriented during that period as mill-spun cotton substituted for hand-spun yarn. In Lancaster County, as spinning wheels were discarded, quilting assumed greater importance.[103] Keller sees industrialization as disrupting 'an ancient gendered domestic craft tradition and an important source of women's social identity and economic authority'. Quilting, she contends, 'sought to restore cultural balance in the wake of this disruption by reinventing quilt-making as an everyday household craft'.[104] Industrialization made domestic spinning unnecessary and unprofitable, removing a chore that had once absorbed routine hours of women's lives. Factory production made cotton cloth cheaper and more affordable and offered an opportunity for Lancaster Country women to take up quilting, adding to the comforts of their homes and providing another tangible legacy of their endeavours. Industrialization reshaped domestic agendas in countless communities, changing the imperatives of women's labour to assume other forms and address other priorities. The Rhode Island quilt dated 1843 (Plate 21) demonstrates this redirection of female energies and the cotton textile employed.

The powerful affects of industrialization and large-scale migration transformed North American quilt culture over the nineteenth and early twentieth centuries. Between 1815 and 1914, tens of millions of migrants journeyed from various parts of Europe, the largest numbers arriving in North America. Immigrants often hopscotched across the country, stopping in one region only to move on to another with better prospects, carving new settlement patterns into the landscape. These families carried with them life's essentials, along with the skills to make new homes. Settlement stimulated commerce and distribution channels grew, spreading the output of factories across great distances. During the nineteenth century, printed patterns for needlework projects also circulated widely. Quilts, or the capacity to make quilts, travelled with these migrants. Nineteenth-century quilting came to epitomize the best of women's work and the essence of women's creative expression, serving as a recurring cultural metaphor and practical imperative. Countless novels of the age employed the quilting bee as a component of the plot, or quilts as a metaphor for family character.[105] More than just fictional, the quilt was an emblem of the creative industry of settler families – thrift put to practical and aesthetic purposes. Wool blankets were made in vast quantities in many regions of Europe, as well as in US and Canadian mills. But more mention is made of patchwork quilts in this era as representative of the diligence of these settlers. Thomas Hulme observed in 1818 that 'American women pride themselves' on their quilts.[106] Another mid-nineteenth-century author made the same claim for Canadians of both sexes:

> Among the home productions of Canada, the counterpane, or quilt, holds a conspicuous place … The quilts are generally made of patchwork, and the quilting, with down or wool, is done in a frame. Some of the gentlemen are not mere drones on these occasions, but make very good assistants under the superintendence of the Queen-bees.[107]

Women predominated as quilters, but men figured on occasion and were all the more notable amidst the sea of female seamstresses.

There are innumerable accounts of quilting in letters, diaries and fictional accounts from this period. Yet, needlewomen are often frustratingly anonymous. Thus despite the growing documentation of some quilters in some communities, more work remains to be done.[108] The sheer vitality and productive range of nineteenth- and early twentieth-century quilting has inspired an army of amateur and professional researchers, sifting through documents and assessing many thousands of quilts brought out for public 'quilt days' in local museums and neighbourhood centres.[109] In many instances, the commonalities of these quilts are as striking as the differences, despite the varied geographic origins. But some designs are exceptional.

This craft flourished within wide-ranging cultural communities. African American women in the American South experienced highly distinctive relationships with cotton in all its facets, as they tended this crop in the fields, spun the yarn for weaving, or made quilts for family or sale.[110] Harriett Angeline Powers was among the most distinguished nineteenth-century quilters. Born a slave in Athens, Georgia in 1837 and growing up on a cotton plantation, Powers knew at first hand the trials of the Cotton Kingdom. By the 1880s, Powers was married and worked with her husband on a small farm. Through an extraordinarily happy accident, two of the unique quilts she constructed in the late 1880s survive today in major museums. One, called the Bible Quilt, was exhibited at the Athens Cotton Fair in 1886 and attracted the notice of a female art teacher, who had never seen such original and striking design. She offered to buy. Powers refused, treasuring this quilt, and only agreed several years later following a string of bad years for her farming family (Plate 22). Powers's religious inspiration springs to life in narrative, symbolic and apocalyptic images, one depicting meteor showers in 1833 of which she had heard, as well as the biblical tale of Adam and Eve. As with so many women of her time, the quilt was her imaginative canvas and reflected the faith that sustained her. This craft offered a unique creative agency to Powers and generations of others whose lives are commemorated in the folds of these coverlets.[111] Gladys-Marie Fry contends that quilting had particular meaning for African American female slaves, offering them:

> a means of developing hidden talents and establishing a kind of emotional stability and independence. Quilting offered time for introspection and reflection, and a means of gaining perspective and control. Denied the opportunity to record their thoughts on paper, slaves left careful records of their emotional and psychological well-being on each surviving quilt.[112]

The familiar process of piecing a quilt and the infinite malleability of bits of cloth meant that some could transcend their voiceless state, inscribing with their needle what they could not in write in words.

Quilting was often shared work, a pleasurable distraction with productive ends. This pattern held true in rural Europe, as well as North America. The diary kept by a Northumberland lead miner recounts seasonal bouts of quilting over the mid-nineteenth century, with participants moving from house to house in the village over the course of years.[113] Quilts likewise served families and individuals through the money that could be earned. In poor rural areas, with some proximity to markets, instruction in quilting offered the chance of income. In nineteenth-century Ireland, for example, basic instruction was taught to tenants' children, ultimately becoming part of the curriculum for national schools. Children skilled in this craft could take finished bed quilts and exchange them for goods at the shop on the Duke of Manchester's estate in County Armagh. These were then sold to urban distributors.[114] In other British communities, bundles of cotton offcuts, sold by weight at mills or from dressmakers' back doors, became the basis of small enterprises. Quilt clubs flourished in England's northern mining regions in the late 1800s, often run by widows or the wives of injured miners, many with large families to maintain. Their neighbours were their customers, making small weekly payments until the quilt was paid for; success depended on the skill and speed of each needlewoman.[115] Necessity drove girls and women to take up quilting in many different communities, either making for the market or making for their families. Given the fashion for this bedding, it is little wonder that commercial quilt-making persisted in so many locales.[116]

In late nineteenth-century Canada, the quilt featured routinely. Mary Agnes Fitzgibbon described many quilt-covered beds in her travelogue from the 1870s as she journeyed from central

Canada to the western plains. She portrayed the room in one inn as typical of 'the "best room" of most Canadian farmhouses. A four-post bedstead stood in one corner, covered with a patchwork quilt'.[117] The 'best' room with the 'best' quilt could come in many varieties, as expressed in the reused shirting fabric employed in the example shown in Plate 23, or the miscellany of cotton patches assembled in the quilt depicted in Plate 24. The kaleidoscope of colours and prints was an emphatic assertion of individual taste and diligence. The mid-nineteenth-century recollections of a Lowell, Massachusetts millworker recount the associations of the patches of fabric, almost all of which marked family milestones or times past. One piece was 'a fragment of the first dress which baby brother wore when he left off long clothes'; another was 'a piece of the first dress which was ever earned by my own exertions!'[118] The memories of quilters animated the material archives from which they drew. In many settler families, quilting remained a necessity into the twentieth century and one elderly woman from the Canadian west recalled the role of quilting in her family life during the Depression and dust bowl years. Ruby Sills grew up in a homesteading family on the prairies and explained that home-made quilts were 'a necessity, we couldn't buy blankets'. She learned her skills from her Irish-born mother, who made 'something beautiful out of scraps and things that people might throw away'. It was a routine in the yearly cycle: 'Mother and I made a quilt every winter', she recalled, 'January was a wonderful month to quilt ... and my father used to read to us while mother and I would be quilting.' A stock of quilts could also serve a wider purpose in this setting. 'There were ... quilts in our linen closet that if there was someone burnt out, there was always a quilt to give them. It was [for] emergencies.' This craft remained a cornerstone of many communities. When Ruby reflected on the tradition of women's quilting at this time, she concludes that for the women: 'It's had a lot to do with how they survived and how frugal they were.' Ruby's first solo quilt illustrates that innovative creativity (Plate 25).

> It was made out of scraps, it's [in the pattern of] a Dresden Plate and it was [made from] washed and bleached ten-pound sugar sacks for the front of it, and the back is bleached hundred-pound sugar sacks. We sent to Eaton's, and got a yard and a half of pink broadcloth, which made the sashing, and it cost a dollar for the back. Now, that sounds very cheap. But you know we sold eggs on the farm for five cents a dozen. That was fifty dozen eggs! It was hard to get that money together ... to buy that material. However, I had joy making it ...[119]

For reluctant needlewomen, quilting might not be so appealing. One twentieth-century African American quilter, poor and with a handicapped brother to care for, already had a world of work on the southern smallholding where she lived and was reluctant to take on more. 'I didn't like to sew. Didn't want to do it', she recounted. But her grandmother had other ideas and told her flatly: 'You better make quilts. You going to need them.'[120] This account comes from Gee's Bend, Alabama, deep in the cotton belt, a community synonymous with a distinct tradition of innovative quilting extending back for generations. A long line of needlewomen paid the price of this heritage, reusing the fabrics to hand. Some came willing to the craft. And while most may have loved the products of their needle, other perhaps felt only measured satisfaction or valued the communal aspects over the work itself. But all laboured with thread and fabric to mediate needs.[121] The recycling of

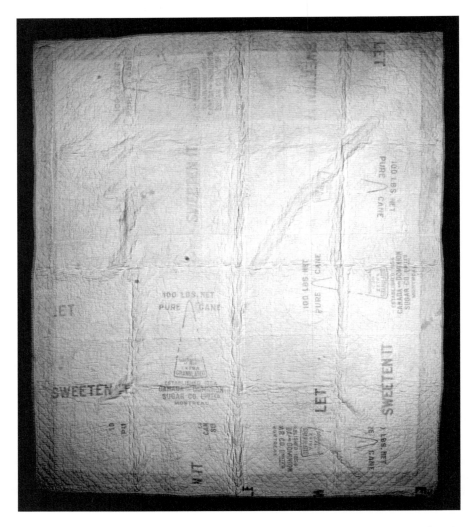

5.2 Backing of quilt made from recycled sugar sacks, with advertising in blue printing: Canada the Dominion Sugar Co. Ltd., Montreal, among other things (mirror image); c.1920s–1940s. University of Alberta, Canada.

factory-made textiles is typified in Figure 5.2, where the evidence of reused cotton sugar bags is still visible.

Quilt-making took on several different forms in the century and a half after 1800. In various parts of the Atlantic world, the making of quilts continued as a craft in homes or workshops, wholly dependent on factory-made cloth, supplying quilts to those who preferred to buy rather than to make. Remnants sold by weight or gleaned from offcuts were the basis for a growing needlework speciality. Some communities and rural regions became renowned for their quilts, as women turned long winters into essential income. At the same time, home-based quilting for family use flourished as a part of the everyday life. Necessity dictated quilting for some, while

5.3 Delectable Mountain quilt, date unknown. Hand-pieced, quilted red and white cotton. University of Alberta, Canada.

women with more resources could display fashionable needle skills using more sumptuous textiles. However, even the cheapest, plainest fabrics could result in striking designs in the hands of an adept needlewoman (Figure 5.3). The piecing of the quilt top opened vital artistic outlets for women, leaving a uniquely important cultural record. Once the top was complete, the quilting itself offered a seasonal sociability that bound together families and friends. Fundamentally, however, quilting at this scale depended on the industrial production of textiles. The flowering of this gendered craft was inextricably tied to the power of factories and mills.

CONCLUSION

Laurel Ulrich reminds us that: 'The history of textiles is fundamentally a story about international commerce in goods and ideas.'[122] The ubiquitous bed quilt mirrors a story of geopolitical ambition, industrial innovation and domestic transformation. There were three stages to the evolution of quilt culture in the West. The first began with the introduction of a uniquely masculine species of bedcovering, celebratory testaments to imperial and dynastic enterprise. The second stage of Western quilt culture saw a larger flow and wider array of quilts arrive in Europe made from Indian cloth, introducing hygienic comfort and aesthetic pleasure in equal measure. This commerce inaugurated a wider and more democratic foundation for these coverlets. Finally, the last stage witnessed the flourishing of demotic quilt culture, in all its diversity, shaped in response to the complex forces of industrialization, mass migration and settlement. The quilts assembled in our museums and private collections reflect these several stages and the skills of generations. One element did not change, however. Typically, for the amateur quilter, the creative process included some communal elements and there are early and continuing records of these endeavours. The English shopkeeper Thomas Turner noted in his 4 June 1755 diary entry: 'Dame Dallaway all day a-helping my wife quilt', a neighbour in their small village assisting with the preparation for winter.[123] Mary Price, a working woman in London, recounted in 1765 that she too 'help'd to quilt the quilt for [Ann Stanley]', an unmarried friend also living in the capital.[124]

Cottons, plain and printed, became the principal component of quilts in the industrial era. Of course, some were pieced from woollen homespun, as well as costly silks. But the mass of quilts created between the 1780s and the 1930s reflect the dominance of factory cottons, whether in whole cloth, appliqué or patchwork forms. New cloth or old, patterned chintz, worn jeans or reused sugar sacks, cotton provided the ingredients for inventive needlewomen (Figure 5.4). The

5.4 *Woman Quilting, c.*1930. Doris Ulmann, photographer. Library of Congress, Washington, DC.

profusion of factory-made cottons inspired quilters and warmed families throughout the Atlantic world. European immigrants to America, along with the grandchildren of slaves, shared a common material idiom, however diverse the circumstance of the making.[125] Moreover, the cost of the fabric did not necessarily determine the quality of the quilt. The democracy of quilt-making favoured skill over monetary resources – scraps 'left from my dresses and aprons, and my father's shift, and my brother's shirts' could as readily produce a striking bedcover as costly fabrics. The aim for those with little or no money was 'to try to make something beautiful out of [the] scraps … that people might throw away'.[126] Just as importantly, quilts 'warm[ed] … us in our beds'.[127] The evidence of this vast creative energy survives in museums around the world. The patterns of wear remind us of countless nights and the care taken to preserve their history. Each coverlet is testimony to a material world transformed. It also speaks of the long history of cross-cultural trade, the power of industry and the complex processes of material culture articulated through this medium. Comfort and culture were redefined through the spread of the cotton quilt.

6.

AFTERWORD
A World Refashioned

At one o'clock on the afternoon of 30 August 1841, Feargus O'Connor was released from prison in York Castle, England, where he had been held for over a year and a half following conviction for seditious libel for the fervour of his speeches. The Irishman was physically imposing, of enormous energy and a celebrated orator in the Chartist movement (a broad-based association demanding political reforms, including the vote for working men). A crowd had grown since daybreak, some walking for as many as forty miles to celebrate the release of their leader. On glimpsing O'Connor, the crowd burst into a joyous roar, the throng exultant at the sight of the man and his clothes, for O'Connor was dressed in heavy cotton fustian: jacket, waistcoat and trousers. And nothing gave better evidence of his political sentiments than the wearing of a fustian suit. O'Connor was born into the aristocracy and, during his rise to political prominence as a radical, he still routinely sported attire reflecting his origins. On this occasion his habit signalled his implacable alliance to working-class politics, 'the shared experiences and identity of working-class life'.[1] What were the qualities of this cloth that made it so powerful a symbol? How could it transmit such clear affiliation?

Fustian represented a cornerstone in the development of the British cotton trade and in the nineteenth century it remained a vital part of the industry: hard-wearing and sturdy, the stuff of labouring life. As discussed in Chapter 4, this cloth was now produced by fully mechanized, industrialized processes, woven by steam-powered looms in factories, the bolts of fabric rolling out at unprecedented speed. Fustians, including corduroy and jean (a twill cloth), had clothed labouring men and women for centuries. In the nineteenth-century context, fustian was now a completely cotton fabric, the output of steam-driven machinery. This fabric was linked directly to the industrial working class that produced it and wore it. Moses & Son, nineteenth-century clothes dealers, advertised a range of garments in fustian fabrics – coats made of cotton jean, 'beaverteen' and moleskin, with trousers and waistcoats in the same. Moses served London and national markets with ready-made goods, supplying provincial dealers from his London warehouses and expanding his retail outlets to the industrial cities of Sheffield and Bradford. Another London dealer in ready-made clothes emphasized 'Excellence and Cheapness' in his advertisement for 'Twilled cords', 'Thickset' and 'Velveteen', all fustians. The coal port of Newcastle likewise had retailers supplying local working families.[2] Cheapness and durability were bywords for these fabrics and a necessity for those who wore them. The scale of textile production meant that cloth was cheaper and clothes more readily affordable even for those who toiled for a living. Sweated labour in the making of garments also kept costs low for consumers; thus the legions of men and women whose footsteps echoed on the way to morning shifts were all defined by the clothing they wore. Published wits and political demagogues recognized the unifying physical features of this group and came to call them 'fustian jackets'. This fabric marked the first industrial working class. It was their emblem for generations.

On occasion, the 'fustian jackets' received insults because of what they wore. A correspondent to *Punch* magazine recounted the demands from a sitting Member of Parliament about 1840 that the keepers of St James's Park in London should not 'admit persons who wore fustian jackets'. Another member agreed that those who promenaded in the park should be spared the sight of this attire and these sorts of people – 'Men in their working-dress' could take the longer route around the park.[3] Others more sympathetic to the aspirations of the working class singled out the fustian jacket as a rallying point. O'Connor employed the language of solidarity in his speeches and writing, heading his articles in *The Northern Star* 'To the Men with Fustian Jackets, Unshorn Chins, and Blistered Hands, Their Wives and Children'. Long before he put on the garb himself, he acknowledged this visible marker as a sign of membership in the industrial proletariat. Within months, this descriptor was abbreviated to 'The Fustian Jackets', also termed in one of his essays 'the fustian army'.[4] Opponents of radical politics were less kind in interpreting O'Connor's use of fustian and the *Liverpool Mercury* mocked his 'entire costume of Fustian, as his regimental suit'. They also played with the alternate meanings of the word, quoting Dryden, who defined a colloquial meaning of fustian as a type of nonsense or 'thoughts and words ill-sorted'.[5] In sum, the adoption of fustian as a symbol of political radicalism was contentious, even as it rallied a generation of passionate militants. Paul Pickering notes that: 'Signs of this condensed symbolic nomenclature abound in radical recollections of the period.'[6] Indeed, men who espoused Chartist principles reinforced the meanings ascribed to this fabric. One supporter wrote to O'Connor while he was still in prison, having heard about his plans to wear a fustian suit on his release. The purpose of his writing 'was to know what colour of fustian or moleskin you would come out of prison in ... we would like the same colour'.[7]

The nineteenth-century cotton trade shaped the face of a new industrial society, in all its aspects. Fustian, as the fruit of this industry, was emblematic of working men. As the political temperature cooled following the last Chartist campaign in 1848, a more conciliatory tone appeared among those discussing the industrial workforce. When a new public library was opened in Manchester in 1851, an official statement was issued making it clear that this institution welcomed all who wished to improve themselves, self-improvement being a plank in the reformist agenda of this era. The author of this article insisted that 'Strength of intellect and ... moral aspiration are the exclusive birthright of no class or body ... and may be found conjoined with a toil-hardened hand and under a fustian jacket, as well as under jewels and ermine.'[8] The fustian jacket entered the wider lexicon as synonymous with working folk, a reflection of thrift and diligence and worthy of respect, no longer solely a symbol of political radicalism. In the spring of 1851, an event of national importance took place with the opening of the Great Exhibition in London's Hyde Park. This was the first world's fair, assembling industrial products and wonders of the world under one roof, while at the same time showcasing the capacities of British industry. Extensive discussions took place about whether or not to open this extraordinary exhibition to working-class visitors. Ultimately, organizers decided to admit one and all. Newspapers of the day were filled with accounts of those attending, particularly as this event allowed the mingling of classes in an entirely new context. Here, too, the industrial population was defined by its attire, using the now ubiquitous tag to describe the labouring visitors. A correspondent described 'men, with wives and daughters on their arms . . . English workmen, in their round fustian jackets and glazed caps'. The author accepted that they 'had a right to take part in the honours of the day, and to have an honest pride in the result of their own and their brethren's labours'.[9] As the second half of the century dawned, it was clear to some that broad political reforms benefiting the middle classes would be impossible 'without the moral help of the fustian jackets'.[10] The cotton trade had served as a birthing room for a new industrial workforce, later defined by the very stuff they produced and wore. The political reforms and societal shifts under way after the 1850s were inscribed on the most common industrially produced cloth. It became an iconic term and an iconic textile. In the years to come, demotic cotton textiles continued to absorb meaning and define social and political causes. Jean, one of the commonest of the fustian cloths, mirrored the aspirations of disparate peoples throughout the modern age and refashioned societies.

JEAN POLITICS AND THE MODERN AGE

Jean fabric likely had its origins in Genoa, Italy and denim is most closely associated with Nîmes, France, both of which were major textile manufacturing regions.[11] However, jeans became a quintessentially American cultural commodity, tied to the combined historical features of American cotton manufacturing and settler expansion, where hard-working fabrics were essential. In the nineteenth and twentieth centuries, jeans were equated with the frontier spirit of independence and initiative, celebrated in American popular culture and political myth. Cotton cultivation spread through southern and western regions of the US over the 1800s, ultimately becoming a major crop in California by the turn of the century. Cotton farming had been attempted in California in the eighteenth century, introduced by Spanish colonial settlers who carried the plant from Mexico. With the growth of population in California after 1850, cotton cultivation gradually came to thrive in this westerly territory. Thus, from one coast to the other, Americans became more fully entwined in the culture of cotton, as producers, labourers, industrial workers, factory owners, retailers and consumers. *The Merchants' Magazine and Commercial Review*, published in New York, illustrates in its pages the expanding capacity of American manufacturing, at a time when textile production was among the major industrial sectors. Their mid-century survey of Massachusetts cotton firms contained 144 names, although the publishers acknowledged that the list was 'not as complete as we would desire to make it'. This survey summarized the yardage produced annually in 1849 and includes dozens of firms making many millions of yards per year, like the Massachusetts Cotton Mills at Lowell who estimated their yearly production of 'Sheet'gs, Shirt'gs & Drill'gs' at 24,600,000 yards. Evidently a good portion of this was a type of heavy-duty fabric, with 'drilling' a cousin of jean and denim. This journal also noted the new cotton mills erected in Natchez, Mississippi, where local cotton growers could send some of their crop for manufacture.[12] Newspapers from the mid-nineteenth century abound with announcements for cotton products issuing from mills great and small, some like the Boston firm of Parker, Wilder & Co. named a fabric 'Kentucky Jeans' for the hinterland under development.[13] 'Kentucky Jeans' remained a standard term for some time, one of many designations, although 'cheap' jean fabric and jean trousers were perhaps the most attractive of the day.[14] The massive movement of settlers through the southern territories, the Midwest and beyond provided new markets for eastern manufacturers, even as it transformed vast tracts of land and the population of the continent. The 'age of jeans'[15] reflected the era of the hardscrabble land rush, as well as accelerating industrial production. Figure 6.1 reflects the ethos of the times in the group of men from the south-west in about 1900, dressed in jeans in a way common to hundreds of thousands of others.

Blue jeans were equated with hard labour, long hours of sweat and toil. Gentlemen wore dark wool broadcloth and white shirts, their hands were soft and smooth. Denim was impervious to thorns, abrasions, tears and the demands of long working days. Blue jeans were essential for

6.1 F. D. W. Ranch, about 1903. Cowboys pose on a tree trunk somewhere on the plains, possibly Texas or Oklahoma. Library of Congress, Washington, DC.

farmers, ranch hands and working men throughout the central and western territories and states, whose calloused hands marked their labours. The garments they wore were emblems of their lives. James Douglas Williams knew just how to use this symbol to his advantage, establishing a 'Blue Jeans Club' in 1876 prior to his run for the governorship of Indiana, where it was proposed that the wearing of blue jeans would be a rallying point for his supporters.[16] His opponents initially coined the name as a mocking reference to Williams's normal attire and his supporters took it up in defiance. Williams was from a farming family who moved from Ohio to Indiana as it was opened for settlement. He had a fifth grade education and a taste for politics; known as frugal, he habitually wore blue jeans. He rose through state politics and his style of dress appealed to rural constituents, signalling his ethical stance. Populist politics required clear signposts and nothing could be clearer than the renunciation of gentlemanly attire and the wearing of a suit made of jean. 'Blue Jeans Williams' insisted on the campaign trail that he was 'born in a corn field' and succeeded in his political ambitions despite all his decriers.[17] Later in his life, it was alleged Williams had his suits made to measure from denim and lined with silk.[18] But the visible power of jeans lay in their democratic provenance, the social affiliation of the wearers and blue jeans' malleable capacity to distil a prevailing energy. Over the next century, this fabric provided a host of material meanings.

The pedigree of American blue jeans is closely tied to the manufacturer Levi Strauss, a Bavarian immigrant who arrived in California in 1853, several years after the 1848 gold rush pulled in tens of thousands to try their luck. Levi Strauss became an outstanding exponent of jeans; his selling point was the brass rivet on the stress points of the garments, patented in 1873. He also used the best fabric he could find to make trousers and bibbed overalls for working men, in this case cloth made by Amoskeag Manufacturing Company in Manchester, New Hampshire. This company had walked away with the prize for best 'coarse cotton goods' at the 1851 Great Exhibition in Britain, to the 'surprise and chagrin of the Old World manufacturers'.[19] The plant became a world leader in production, churning out four million yards of cotton cloth per week by 1906. This expanding industrial capacity underpinned the spread of useful and fashionable consumer goods. However, the status of blue jeans as a twentieth-century North American cultural medium did not depend on one manufacturer or garment-maker, or indeed on any single designer or impresario. Blue jeans evolved through a complex intersection of forces beginning from their history as essential wear for generations of working men. The culture of hard work and self-reliance, articulated by 'Blue Jeans Williams' in Indiana, ran through the cultural fabric of American society. As the frontier gave way to settled farming, ranching and constellations of towns, the demands of industrial infrastructure brought continued opportunities for work on telegraph lines and railways. Dungarees and blue jeans epitomized the outdoor, hard-graft toil emblematic of American development and American power. Blue jeans evolved from being the perennial workwear of labouring men to a statement of political and cultural ideology, an agent of both new cultural fashions and anti-fashion, a sign of political radicalism and a malleable uniform allied to Western culture.

Hundreds of manufacturers throughout North America put their stamp on the blue jeans they made during the first fifty years of the twentieth century. Lee, Wrangler and Oshkosh are well-known US labels; GWG, or the Great Western Garment Company, is a storied Canadian company, founded in 1911, serving the ranchers, farmers, loggers and oilmen of western Canada and beyond.[20] Each manufacturer developed a loyal following through networks of distribution, regional and national, as well as through the cultural connections made between the makers and consumers of these garments. During the early decades of the 1900s, the West itself began to be marketed as a destination for city-weary adventurers, and along with the experience came the clothes with their authentic connections to this unique locale. Artists collaborated with novelists and railway hoteliers to sell the vision of mountains and plains, inviting easterners to taste a different pace of life at dude ranches or along trails in the foothills. Some artists felt a close connection with the land they memorialized and did not simply paint vistas for railway advertisements. In the 1920s a number of Santa Fe artists adopted blue jeans as a sign of their affiliation with the wider environment in which they lived and worked. Beverly Gordon points to this as the first recorded twentieth-century instance of blue jeans as consciously 'anti-fashion', a style echoed by later West Coast undergraduates at the University of California-Berkeley and at the University of Oregon in the 1930s. The unsanctioned campus style made its way to the East Coast by the 1940s. Artists and students routinely navigated the boundaries between social classes and their clothing reflected their sometimes liminal status. Jeans extended well beyond their original utilitarian uses by this date, as social groups crafted new styles and industry created new markets, each evolving independently but intersecting with the others. In 1935, Levi's launched 'Dude Ranch Duds' for its more discriminating clients and the New York retailer Abercrombie & Fitch began stocking jeans and overalls for occasions when broadcloth or tweed would not suffice.[21] The genteel classes had always worn casual clothing for sporting events like fishing, shooting and riding. The British tradition was to wear tweeds or light wools of various sorts for forays into the Scottish Highlands or Irish moors, a nineteenth-century recreational style that crossed the ocean to eastern elite society and persisted into the twentieth century.[22] Jeans represented a fully North American aesthetic in keeping with a landscape that made greater demands on its visitors. The inter-war years brought a multi-layered set of class associations with this garment, even as the underlying sensibility of jeans remained unchanged.

The twentieth-century biography of jeans is complex and contradictory. Popular culture in films, magazines and novels crafted images of jeans-clad men in heroic struggles, or in anti-hero encounters. The explosion of Hollywood movies across the continent and around the world circulated images of masculinity where resolution or defiance in the face of adversity was as common as the wearing of denim. The ethos of jeans was carried along on a wave of pre-eminent American power during and after the Second World War. At the same time, within the US, jeans spread well beyond their utilitarian and dude ranch markets and became synonymous with a post-war youth culture where casual cool was expressed in blue denim, both for males and females. America was now a predominantly urban society – by 1920, 51 per cent of the population lived in towns and cities.[23] Manufacturers and advertisers knew the value of promoting national brands through direct and indirect advertising and followed trends, even if they did not always invent them. Levi's, Wrangler and GWG designed denim for a new generation, a 'fashion revolution' as one local paper called it, employing extra shifts at mills as the social momentum of jeans got under way.[24] Youth culture embraced the wearing of jeans, even front zipper jeans for girls. The 1950s saw a growing wave of jeans-clad young women in high schools and colleges across the country, a change in attire that was not always welcomed. One suburban high school, south-east of Chicago, wrestled with the implications of 'girls' wearing of blue-jeans to school'. Teachers did not like this style and encouraged other students in the school to quash the innovation. A local newsletter reported in October 1952 that: 'On several occasions some of our high-school male athletes and other popular students have written editorials urging our girls to "be ladylike."'[25] However, material self-definition demanded jeans, at least for some defiant female high school students. The tensions surrounding established gender norms in dress, for young men and women, took various forms. Prescriptive patterns were deeply rooted and still decreed an adult-inspired wardrobe even for young teenagers, with suits and dresses as the norm. But there was increasing room for alternate youth styles. Even for a working-class young man who claimed to have no thought of fashion, the 1950s casual look required 'form-fitting jeans and a ... sports shirt with the sleeves rolled up, *à la* [movie star] James Dean'.[26]

Over the 1960s and 1970s, a range of social, cultural and political movements claimed American jeans as their emblem, as the great demographic wave of the post-war baby boom refashioned Western societies. This period coincided with the apogee of Western industrial power, including foundational sectors like textile and garment production. These sectors were still important, although no longer as central as in the 1800s. Mechanized harvesting was introduced for cotton crops in the US in the 1940s, and self-propelled cotton-pickers became more common during the 1950s and 1960s,[27] matching the capacity of spinning mills, weaving and garment factories to pour out ever larger and cheaper floods of goods. The unparalleled capacity of Western manufacturers to produce volumes of blue denim coincided with a rejection of mainstream fashions by many young women and men and the adoption of jeans as a statement – never a fully homogeneous statement, but a declaration of change that reverberated loudly through society. Those who lived through those decades have different memories as to the time and place they first wore jeans where they had never worn them before. Dress codes began to shatter, but were still enforced in schools and communities – not all schools were as relatively tolerant as the one in suburban Chicago where some girls continued in jeans despite opposition. The established rules of dress persisted well into the 1960s and 1970s, requiring women and girls to wear a dress or suit to attend church, shop in town or appear in an office or public space. Women never wore jeans in major city shopping precincts in 1960. The casual styles accepted on campus or in Santa Fe were largely restricted to those locales up to the change period later in the 1960s. Then came the migration of jeans from a peripheral space to centre stage, generating a seismic cultural impact on dress practice and social norms, as one by one dress dogmas were discarded or rebuffed. Hollywood and popular music drove this trend to the farthest corners of the world and to every neighbourhood in the Americas. To some, this seemed shocking or bewildering; to others it heralded liberation from traditional dictates. This change in the use of cotton jeans did not come about in isolation from larger social movements, but was a part of broad political and cultural forces that also included challenges to existing gender standards. Jeans mirrored, defined and recorded the generational fervour of those decades.

Demands for change fermented on American campuses and erupted more widely in conjunction with anti-war protests and campaigns against racial segregation and discrimination against African Americans. It is interesting to note, however, that the first generation of African Americans who in the 1950s and early 1960s demonstrated for racial equality in the American South, did so wearing suits or trousers with shirts and ties for the men and skirts, blouses or dresses for the women. The deadly serious venture in which they were engaged required the most serious of clothing; denim in the South was still connected to manual labour on the land or in the factory and none of the activists (whatever physical hardship they faced) would enter the political arena at a sartorial disadvantage to their opponents. Middle-class students had different options and lived amidst different social constraints. In their context, jeans ruled. Youth from later 1960s and 1970s was awash in denim. Within a generation, jeans became a uniform garb for young men and women whatever their political persuasion. In the interim, dress regulations at schools gradually fell by the wayside under local pressure, one among the many changes fomented during the jeans era. The revolution in style caught manufacturers off guard. Peter Hass, former head of Levi Strauss, recalled the years in the 1960s when business plans were thrown out of the window as sales sky-rocketed.[28] However, these shifts were not consistent across America or throughout the ethnic and social layers that comprised American society. A 16-year-old correspondent to *Ms. Magazine* wrote in 1974 of her frustration at being compelled to wear a dress whatever her date might wear when he called, and wherever they were going. 'Just once I would like to be able to wear jeans to a ball game', she wrote.[29] Strictures did not die away easily in every household, whatever *Vogue* might say about the ubiquity of jeans by the mid-1970s. Anxiety surrounding young women's dress continued as a subject of commentary. But jeans prevailed despite the anxieties expressed in many quarters. Jeans materialized a mixed set of priorities, all articulating change. Valerie Carnes recounts her analysis of the 1960s, from the distance of a single decade. 'Denim jeans became the ultimate no-fashion put-down style – a classless, cheap, unisex look that stood for, variously, frontier values, democracy, plain living, ecology and health, rebellion *à la* Brando or Dean, a new interest in the erotic import of the pelvis, or ... a deliberate rejections of the "artificial plastic-coated look" of the affluent society.'[30] The complex of meanings ascribed to jeans in American society was matched by a host of meanings in other countries.

Denim blue jeans were a transnational phenomenon, a feature of youth and political culture throughout Europe, the Americas and beyond. In the 1970s Soviet teenagers yearned for American jeans as a sign of their resistance to state-imposed standardization. Christopher Neidhart notes that, '*Apparatchiks* had their gray, ill-fitting suits ... The young rebellious urbanites longed for blue jeans to convey nonconformity with the older generation; they tried to mark a slight deviation from Soviet society.'[31] The role of jeans in the Soviet Union differed from that in the West as the Soviets denied the official existence of social hierarchies in their society; as Natalya Chernyshova notes, the Soviet state 'presented egalitarianism as one of its founding principles'.[32] Choosing a self-selected style of dress was antithetical to Soviet ideals, which made black-market jeans all the more precious to a youthful cohort disenchanted with their options. Valeria Manzano traces the different path of the jeans revolution in Buenos Aires, revealing the commonalities and unique features in this locale. Previously, cowboy or *vaquero* masculinity defined blue jeans in the post-war era. These next became a working-class style for young men in the city, leading-edge consumers who translated a rural to an inexpensive urban form. This distinctive male fashion was encouraged through advertising that emphasized that young men could now look different from their fathers, instead of adopting the same cut of suit as they reached manhood. One man who grew up in the

1950s recalls that he 'didn't go to the movies or to soccer matches in two months' in order to save up for his jeans.[33] Local manufacturers thrived with this new market. Imported American-made jeans followed, bringing a new cachet and with slightly different cloth and styling, capturing the attention of young middle-class shoppers, men and women. Class distinctions were visible in the type of jeans selected and as Manzano observes, 'Middle-class young men rejected the alternative masculinity deployed by working-class vaquero consumers.'[34] More dramatic still, in the Argentine context, was the spread of jeans to female buyers. Young women had not worn trousers to this date, a style precluded by existing dress codes for females of all social classes. Now, some young women defied local norms and embraced denim, although they were termed 'rebellious' and thought immoral. By 1975, a tango poet described the city as turning 'beautifully blue'.[35] This last wave in the Argentine jeans revolution came in combination with explosive political protests and, as one person recalled, jeans became a 'uniform for struggling'. Political activism necessitated jeans, for men and women, but increasingly the nationalist appeal of the Peronist party required that these jeans be locally made.[36]

Across the Atlantic, in Portugal, a similar scenario was played out in the 1970s. Once again, the demotic ethos of indigo jeans became the symbol of political struggle. Emilia Margarida Marques explores the shifts in material culture that accompanied the 'Carnation Revolution' in Portugal in 1974, when a long-standing totalitarian regime came to an end. Marques asked of respondents what kinds of changes in clothing they recalled from revolution times. Their answer was 'The vogue of jeans!' The men and women recollecting these events did not refer to American-made jeans, but to locally produced 'denim trousers', simple, basic, utilitarian garments that had 'new and revolutionary meaning'.[37] In Portugal, as elsewhere, jeans became the symbol of political dissent or social protest, even as at the same time they were restyled by Paris designers for a different class of clientele.[38]

I end with this brief account of jeans, tracing some of the rich history of this fabric over the modern industrial age – denim remains a potent polemical force and now attracts critics of contemporary globalization.[39] There is a long and sometimes contentious history surrounding this commodity, one of the commonest least-luxurious utility fabrics. Its story reflects a kaleidoscope of change. This cotton cloth was made to endure and was produced in industrial-scale quantities that grew with the centuries. Some present-day shoppers may choose to buy jeans priced at hundreds of dollars – there are many brands at that price point. Cashmere jeans play with the ironic juxtaposition of luxury and utility, endurance and ephemera. But the fundamental attraction of jeans lies in their proletarian provenance and the broad use, reuse and revised connotations crafted over time. Jeans have a heritage of factory production and everyday service that feeds deep wells of memory, tapped by each generation for social and political ends. True blue jeans endure because of their physical and cultural properties. The scale of cotton production, the uniformity and variability of this cross-gender style crafted a unique artefact of the industrial age that continues to resonate today. In themselves, jeans did not change the world. But they mirror the immense transformation in play from the mid-1800s through the twenty-first century. Jeans epitomize the modern industrial era of cotton. This cotton trade, in turn, generated a conspicuous material culture whose history reveals the remaking of societies across the globe.

NOTES

1. INTRODUCTION

1. Two volumes that reflect some of the more recent worldwide research on the cotton trade are: D. A. Farnie and David Jeremy (eds), *The Fibre that Changed the World: The Cotton Industry in International Perspective 1600–1999* (Oxford: Oxford University Press, 2004) and Giorgio Riello and Prasannan Parthasarathi (eds), *The Spinning World: A Global History of Cotton Textiles, 1200–1850* (Oxford: Oxford University Press, 2009).

2. Examples of North Carolina sites for the history of cotton in that region include:

   www.historync.org/NCtextilespre1860.htm
   www.learnnc.org/lp/editions/nchist-newnation/5031
   www.learnnc.org/lp/editions/nchist-newsouth/5493
   www.textileheritagemuseum.org/

3. Examples of regional Rhode Island websites that explore this history include:

   http://www.slatermill.org/museum/
   http://www.woonsocket.org/industrial.html
   http://royalmillshistory.com/rhode-island-mill-history/

4. For the living tradition of cotton printing in western India, see Eiluned Edwards, 'Cloth and Community: The Local Trade in Resist-Dyed and Block-Printed Textiles in Kachchh District, Gujarat', *Textile History* 38(2) (2007): 179–97.

5. See, for example, Beverly Lemire and Giorgio Riello, 'East and West: Textiles and Fashion in Early Modern Europe', *Journal of Social History* 41(4) (2008): 887–916; Maxine Berg, *Luxury and Pleasure In Eighteenth-Century Britain* (Oxford: Oxford University Press, 2005), pp. 46–84; Robert Finlay, 'The Pilgrim Art: The Culture of Porcelain in World History', *Journal of World History* 9(2) (1998): 141–87 and *The Pilgrim Art: Cultures of Porcelain in World History* (Berkeley: University of California Press, 2010).

6. Fustians were blends, typically including linen or flax along with another fibre such as wool or silk. Cotton/linen blends were among the commonest varieties of fustian.

7. For example, Jonathan Holstein, 'Sister Quilts from Sicily: A Pair of Renaissance Bedcovers', *Quilt Journal* 3(2) (1994).

2. BOUND UP WITH COTTON

1. This growing world system excludes consideration of the Americas pre-1500.

2. Philippe Beaujard, 'The Indian Ocean in Eurasian and African World-Systems Before the Sixteenth Century', *Journal of World History* 16(4) (2005): 430.

3. Janet L. Abu-Lughod, *Before European Hegemony: The World System A.D. 1250–1350* (New York: Oxford University Press, 1989), pp. 32–5.

4. Andrew Sherratt, 'Reviving the Grand Narrative: Archaeology and Long-Term Change', *Journal of European Archaeology* 3(1) (1995): 14.

5. S. D. Goitein, 'Portrait of a Medieval India Trader: Three Letters from the Cairo Geniza', *Bulletin of the School of Oriental and African Studies* 50(3) (1987): 449–64.

6. Abu-Lughod, *Before European Hegemony*, pp. 154–5.

7. Sherratt, 'Reviving the Grand Narrative', p. 5.

8. See, for example, from a recent British Library exhibition, Frances Wood, *The Silk Road: Two Thousand Years in the Heart of Asia* (London: The British Library, 2004); and for a wider array of sources: John Vollmer, E. J. Keall and E. Nagai-Berthrong, *Silk Roads, China Ships* (Toronto: Royal Ontario Museum, 1983); Thomas T. Allsen, *Commodity and Exchange in the Mongol Empire: A Cultural History of Islamic Textiles* (Cambridge: Cambridge University Press, 1997); Vadime Elisseef, *The Silk Roads: Highways of Culture and Commerce* (New York: Berghahn Books, 2000); Luce Boulnois, *Silk Road: Monks, Warriors & Merchants on the Silk Road*, trans. Helen Loveday with additional material by Bradley Mayhew and Angela Sheng (Hong Kong: Odyssey, 2005); Liu Xinru and Lynda Shaffer, *Connections Across Eurasia: Transportation, Communication and Cultural Exchange on the Silk Roads* (Boston: McGraw-Hill, 2007); Karen Manchester, *The Silk Road and Beyond: Travel, Trade, and Transformation* (New Haven: Yale University Press, 2007).

9. Abu-Lughod, *Before European Hegemony*, pp. 154–65.

10. Ruth Barnes has produced the most important findings employing carbon dating of Indian textile samples. See Ruth Barnes, *Indian Block-Printed Textiles in Egypt: The Newberry Collection in the Ashmolean Museum, Oxford* (Oxford: Clarendon Press, 1997), vols I and II.

11. Quoted in Abu-Lughod, *Before European Hegemony*, p. 165.

12. Angela Lakwete, *Inventing the Cotton Gin: Machine and Myth in Antebellum America* (Baltimore, MD: Johns Hopkins University Press, 2003), pp. 2–3.

13. Bernal Díaz del Castillo, *The Discovery and Conquest of Mexico* (London: Taylor & Francis, 2004), pp. 51–2, 59; Murdo J. MacLeod, *Spanish Central America, 1520–1720* (Berkeley: University of California Press, 1973), pp. 28, 124, 166; John Murra, 'Cloth and its Functions in the Inka State' in Annette B. Weiner and Jane Schneider (eds), *Cloth and Human Experience* (Washington, DC: Smithsonian Institution Press, 1989).

14. Colleen Kriger, 'Mapping the History of Cotton Textile Production in Precolonial West Africa', *African Economic History* 33 (2005): 95–9 and '"Guinea Cloth": Production and Consumption of Cotton Textiles in West Africa Before and During the Atlantic Slave Trade', in Giorgio Riello and Prasannan Parthasarathi (eds), *The Spinning World: A Global History of Cotton Textiles, 1200–1850* (Oxford: Oxford University Press, 2009), pp. 105–26.

15. D. Schlingloff, 'Cotton Manufacture in Ancient India', *Journal of the Economic and Social History of the Orient* 17 (1974): 81–90.

16. William A. Green, 'Periodizing World History', *History & Theory* 34(2) (1995): 99–111; Abu-Lughod, *Before European Hegemony*; William H. McNeill, 'The Changing Shape of World History', *History & Theory* 34(2) (1995): 2–26; Andre Gunder Frank, *ReOrient: Global Economy in the Asian Age* (Berkeley: University of California Press, 1998); Prasannan Parthasarathi, 'Rethinking Wages and Competitiveness in the Eighteenth Century: Britain and South India', *Past & Present* 158 (1998): 79–109.

17. Jack Goody, *The East in the West* (Cambridge: Cambridge University Press, 1996), p. 7.

18. Antonia Finnane, *Changing Clothes in China: Fashion, History, Nation* (New York: Columbia University Press, 2008), p. 7.

19. In the classic study, A. P. Wadsworth and Julia de Lacy Mann, *The Cotton Trade and Industrial Lancashire, 1600–1780* (Manchester: Manchester University Press, 1931), pp. 116–19.

20. Lynda Shaffer, 'Southernization', *Journal of World History* 5(1) (1994): 1.

21. Lakwete, *Inventing the Cotton Gin*, p. 2.

22. Mattiebelle Gittinger, *Master Dyers to the World: Technique and Trade in Early Indian Dyed Cotton Textiles* (Washington, DC: The Textile Museum, 1982), pp. 20–2.

23. Lakwete, p. 5.

24. Shaffer, 'Southernization', p. 2; Grant Parker, 'Topographies of Taste: Indian Textiles and Mediterranean Contexts', *Ars Orientalis* 34 (2004): 19–37 and Grant Parker, '*Ex Oriente Luxuria*: Indian Commodities and Roman Experience', *Journal of the Economic and Social History of the Orient* 45(1) (2002): 40–95; the Berenike Project, http://www.archbase.com/

berenike/english1.html accessed 4 December 2009.

25. Robert Finlay, 'The Pilgrim Art: The Culture of Porcelain in World History', *Journal of World History* 9(2) (1998): 143. See also, Finlay, *The Pilgrim Art: Cultures of Porcelain in World History* (Berkeley: University of California Press, 2010).

26. For an earlier treatment of Persian and Indian textile cultures, some of whose conclusions have been superseded, see: R. M. Riefstahl, *Persian and Indian Textile from the Late Sixteenth to the Early Nineteenth Century* (New York: E. Weyhe, 1923).

27. Gittinger, *Master Dyers to the World*, pp. 16–7.

28. K. N. Chaudhuri, 'Trade as a Cultural Phenomenon', in Jens Christian V. Johansen, Erling Ladewig Petersen and Henrik Stevnborg (eds), *Clashes of Cultures: Essays in Honour of Niels Steensgaard* (Odense: Odense University Press, 1992), p. 210.

29. Sherratt, 'Reviving the Grand Narrative', p. 14.

30. S. D. Goitein, 'From the Mediterranean to India: Documents on the Trade to India, South Arabia, and East Africa from the Eleventh and Twelfth Centuries', *Speculum* 29(2) (1954): 185–90.

31. Abu-Lughod, *Before European Hegemony*, p. 13. The phrase was coined by Richard Haëpke and also adopted by Fernand Braudel. See also Scott Levi, 'India, Russia and the Eighteenth-Century Transformation of the Central Asian Caravan Trade', *Journal of the Economic and Social History of the Orient* 42(4) (1999): 522–24.

32. Warmington, *The Commerce Between the Roman Empire and India*, pp. 212–3; Parker, '*Ex Oriente Luxuria*', p. 48 and note 10; Michael Loewe, 'Spices and Silk: Aspects of World Trade in the First Seven Centuries of the Christian Era', *Journal of the Royal Asiatic Society* (1971): 166–79; S. D. Goitein, *A Mediterranean Society: The Jewish Communities of the Arab World as Portrayed in the Documents of the Cairo Geniza, Vol. IV, Daily Life* (Berkeley: University of California Press, 1983), p. 170; Abu-Lughod, *Before European Hegemony*, pp. 269–72; Lotika Varadarajan, *South Indian Traditions of Kalamkari* (Bombay: Perennial Press, 1982).

33. Gittinger, *Master Dyers to the World*, p. 153.

34. John Guy, *Woven Cargoes: Indian Textiles in the East* (London: Thames and Hudson, 1998), pp.

14–18; K. N. Chaudhuri, *Asia Before Europe: Economy and Civilisation of the Indian Ocean from the Rise of Islam to 1750* (Cambridge: Cambridge University Press, 1990).

35. Gittinger, *Master Dyers to the World*, p. 153. See also, Mattiebelle Gittinger, *Splendid Symbols: Textiles and Tradition in Indonesia* (Washington, DC: The Textile Museum, 1979, reprinted Singapore, 1991), p. 15.

36. Gittinger, *Splendid Symbols*, pp. 27, 45.

37. John Guy, *Woven Cargoes*, p. 10.

38. Michel Aghassian, 'The Armenian Merchant Network: Overall Autonomy and Local Integration', in Sushil Chaudhury and Michel Morineau (eds), *Merchants, Companies and Trade: Europe and Asia in the Early Modern Era* (Cambridge: Cambridge University Press, 1999), p. 75. For early modern Armenian commerce see: Sebouh Aslanian, '"The Salt in a Merchant's Letter": The Culture of Julfan Correspondence in the Indian Ocean and the Mediterranean', *Journal of World History* 19(2) (2008): 127–88; and Sushil Chaudhury and Kéram Kévonian, *Les Arméniens dans le commerce asiatique au début de l'ère moderne* (Paris: Édition de la Maison des sciences de l'homme, 2008).

39. Abu-Lughod, *Before European Hegemony*, p. 137.

40. For example, Gittinger, *Master Dyers to the World*, pp. 31, 33, 52.

41. Ruth Barnes, 'Indian Trade Textiles', *Hali: The International Magazine of Antique Carpet and Textile Art*, 87 (July 1996): 80–1.

42. Barnes, 'Indian Trade Textiles', p. 80.

43. Among the other museums that hold cottons excavated from Fustat, Old Cairo are the Victoria and Albert Museum, the Royal Ontario Museum, Toronto, the Museum of Fine Arts, Boston, the Textile Museum, Washington, DC, the Calico Museum, Ahmedabad and the National Museum, New Delhi.

44. Goitein, *Mediterranean Society*, pp. 170, 332–3.

45. Barnes, *Indian Textiles in Egypt*, vol. 1, p. 1.

46. Barnes, *Indian Textiles in Egypt*, vol. 1, p. 47.

47. Abu-Lughod, *Before European Hegemony*, pp. 236–44.

48. Finlay, 'Pilgrim Art', p. 158.

49. Goitein, *Mediterranean Society*, pp. 170, 332–3.

50. Barnes, *Indian Textiles in Egypt*, vol. 1, p. 1.

51. Yedida Stillman points out that Muslim and Jewish women dress alike in certain medieval periods, noting as well the signal importance of textiles in family budgets. Yedida K. Stillman, 'The Importance of the Cairo Geniza Manuscripts for the History of Medieval Female Attire', *International Journal of Middle East Studies* 7(4) (1976): 582–5.

52. Barnes, *Indian Textiles in Egypt*, vol. I, plate 13, plate 40; fragment 6.134, thought to arise from the fifteenth century. Gittinger, *Master Dyers to the World*, p. 52; accession number 48.1081, Museum of Fine Arts, Boston. Deepika Shah, *Masters of the Cloth: Indian Textiles Traded to Distant Shores* (New Delhi: Garden Silk Mills, 2005), pp. 8–9.

53. Abu-Lughod, *Before European Hegemony*, pp. 239–41. For the impact of the medieval cotton trade in Europe see Maureen F. Mazzaoui, *The Italian Cotton Industry in the Later Middle Ages* (Cambridge: Cambridge University Press, 1981).

54. Mazzaoui, *Italian Cotton Industry in the Later Middle Ages*.

55. Shaffer, 'Southernization', p. 20.

56. *A Discourse Written by a Faithfull Subject to His Christian Majesty, Concerning the Establishment of a French Company for the Commerce of the East-Indies* (London, 1664), in Beverly Lemire (ed.), *The British Cotton Trade*, vol. 1 (London: Pickering and Chatto, 2009), p. 153.

57. For example, the classic W. R. Scott, *Constitution and Finance of English, Scottish and Irish Joint-Stock Companies to 1720* (Cambridge: Cambridge University Press, 1912, reprinted New York, 1951); and Chaudhuri, *The Trading World of Asia and the English East India Company, 1660–1760* (Cambridge: Cambridge University Press, 1978); Desai Tripta, *The East India Company: A Brief Survey from 1599–1857* (New Delhi: Kanak Publications, 1984). For the Dutch East India Company (VOC) see Charles R. Boxer, *The Dutch Seaborne Empire* (London: Hutchinson, 1965); Om Prakash, *The Dutch East India Company and the Economy of Bengal, 1630–1720* (Princeton: Princeton University Press, 1985). And for Portugal see James C. Boyajian, *Portuguese Trade in Asia under the Habsburgs, 1580–1640* (Baltimore: Johns Hopkins University Press, 1993); Anthony R. Disney, *Twilight of the Pepper Empire: Portuguese Trade in Southwest India in the Early Seventeenth Century* (Cambridge, MA: Harvard University Press, 1978).

58. Boyajian, *Portuguese Trade*, p. 14.

59. The process of reception is discussed in greater detail for specific commodities. See Chapters 3 and 5.

60. For a discussion of silk imports and the resultant sumptuary laws in Europe see Beverly Lemire and Giorgio Riello, 'East and West: Textiles and Fashion in Early Modern Europe', *Journal of Social History* 41(4) (2008): 887–916.

61. Jan De Vries, *The Industrious Revolution: Consumer Behavior and the Household Economy, 1650 to the Present* (Cambridge: Cambridge University Press, 2008), p. 155.

62. Guy, *Woven Cargo*, p. 9.

63. Boyajian, *Portuguese Trade*, p. 141.

64. Boyajian, *Portuguese Trade*, p. 140. Robert DuPlessis is currently researching the Atlantic trade in textiles to Argentina, a project which will provide further insights into this sector of the global traffic. See also Marta V. Vicente, *Clothing the Spanish Empire: Families and the Calico Trade in the Atlantic World, 1700–1815* (Basingstoke: Palgrave, 2007).

65. Examples on this subject include: Boxer, *Dutch Seaborne Empire*; K. N. Chaudhuri, *The English East India Company: The Study of an Early Joint-Stock Company* (London: Frank Cass & Co., 1965) and *Trading World of Asia*; Om Prakash, *The Dutch Factories in India: A Collection of Dutch East India Company Documents Pertaining to India* (New Delhi: Munshirma Manohariai, 1984).

66. The collection of quilts by monarchs and nobles is discussed in Chapter 5.

67. Laurence Fontaine, *History of Pedlars in Europe* (Cambridge: Polity Press, 1996), p. 20.

68. Fontaine, *History of Pedlars*, pp. 8–9, 11–12.

69. L. M. Diez de Salazar Fernandez and M. R. Ayerbe Iribar, *Juntas y Diputaciones de Gipuzkoa* [1554–1557] (San Sebastián: Juntas Generales de Gipuzkoa, Diputación Foral de Gipuzkoa, 1990), vol. 2, pp. 477, 487, 498. My sincere thanks to Renato Barahona for providing this information and to Prasannan Parthasarathi for facilitating our introduction. Thanks also to Ehud Ben Zvi for translation.

70. Boyajian, *Portuguese Trade in Asia under the Habsburgs*, p. 139.

71. See Chapter 3 for a discussion of the low price of Indian cottons during the 1600s.

72. Mukerji observes that: 'The expansion of trade in early modern Europe constituted a revolution in communications as well as a commercial revolution.' Mukerji, *From Graven Images: Patterns of Modern Materialism* (New York: Columbia University Press, 1983), p. 11. Printed cottons had a very particular role as a medium of non-literate, iconic communication.

73. *Letters and Papers, Foreign and Domestic, of the Reign of Henry VIII* (London: Public Record Office, 1898), vol. 16, p. 241.

74. *Letters and Papers ... of the Reign of Henry VIII*, vol. 16, p. 491.

75. 'A speciall direction for divers trades of marchaundize to be used for soundrie placis upon advertisements, as well for the chusinge of the time and wares for every of those placis ...' Transcribed in Conyers Read, 'English Foreign Trade under Elizabeth', *English Historical Review* 29 (1914): 519.

76. Read, 'English Foreign Trade under Elizabeth', p. 521.

77. Anthony Disney, 'Smugglers and Smuggling in the Western Half of the Estado Da India in the Late Sixteenth and Early Seventeenth Centuries' *Indica* 26: 1 and 2 (1989): 67–9.

78. For example, East India Company servants were forbidden to trade privately in the most desirable commodities, which in the 1630s included diamonds and calicoes. Neville Williams, *Contraband Cargoes: Seven Centuries of Smuggling* (London: Longmans, 1959), p. 69; *A Letter to a Member of Parliament Concerning Clandestine Trade. Shewing how far the Evil Practices at the Custom-house at London tend to the Encouragement of such a Trade.* Written by a Fair Merchant (London, 1700).

79. T. S. Willan (ed.), *A Tudor Book of Rates* (Manchester: Manchester University Press, 1962), p. 38.

80. Quoted in Edward Roberts and Karen Parker (eds), *Southampton Probate Inventories, 1447–1575* (Southampton: Southampton University Press, 1992), vol. 1, p. xvii.

81. Roberts and Parker, *Southampton Probate Inventories*, vol. 1, pp. 65–70; 150–2; 159–62; 165–7; vol. II, pp. 244–52; 346–7; 358–9.

82. F. W. Weaver (ed.), *Somerset Medieval Wills (3rd series) 1531–1558* (London: Somerset Record Society, 1905), pp. 86, 157.

83. Joan Thirsk, *Food in Early Modern England: Phases, Fads, Fashions 1500–1760* (London: Hambledon Continuum, 2007), especially Chapters 3 and 4.

84. The persistence of the Portuguese terminology suggests their continuing role in this trade.

85. John S. Moore (ed.), *The Goods and Chattels of Our Forefathers: Frampton Cotterell and District Probate Inventories 1539–1804* (London: Phillimore, 1976), p. 52.

86. Armenian merchants were another dynamic commercial group, bringing printed cottons to Italy and southern France – goods carried along caravan routes. See Olivier Raveux, 'Armenian Networks in the Trade and Production of Calicoes in the Mediterranean During the Last Third of the Seventeenth Century', unpublished paper presented at the American Historical Association's conference, San Diego, January 2010. My thanks to Olivier Raveux for allowing me to see a copy of his paper.

87. Roberts and Parker, *Southampton Probate Inventories*, vol. 1, pp. 70, 152, 159.

88. Alfred Gell, *Art and Agency: An Anthropological Theory* (Oxford: Oxford University Press, 1998), pp. 17–21. I thank Marko Zivkovic for this reference.

89. Gell, *Art and Agency*, p. 20.

90. The anti-calico campaign discussed in Chapter 3 is at least as significant as the ready adoption of calicoes across Atlantic world markets.

91. *Calendar of State Papers Colonial*, 1617–21, p. 312, quoted in A. M. Millard, 'The Import Trade of London, 1600–1640', Unpublished Ph.D. (University of London, 1956), p. 142.

92. *Calendar of State Papers Colonial*, 1617–21, p. 110, quoted in Millard, 'Import Trade of London', p. 144.

93. See Chapter 3 for several instances of the excitement generated by the seizure of Portuguese cargoes.

94. Glamann, *Dutch-Asiatic Trade*, pp. 133–51; G. V. Scammel, 'England, Portugal and the *Estado da India, c.*1500–1635', *Modern Asian Studies* 16(2) (1982): 177–92; Boyijian, *Portuguese Trade*, Appendix A, pp. 247–57. For the expansion of exports from the Coromandel Coast see Sanjay Subrahmanyam, *The Political Economy of Commerce. Southern India 1500–1650* (Cambridge: Cambridge University Press, 1990), p. 171.

95. For a further discussion see Lemire and Riello, 'East and West'.

96. Therle Hughes, *English Domestic Needlework, 1660–1860* (London: Lutterworth Press, 1961).

97. An active trade in plants was also under way over this era. Jack Goody, *The Culture of Flowers* (Cambridge, 1993), Chapters 6 and 7 and Beverly Lemire, 'Domesticating the Exotic: Floral Culture and the East India Calico Trade with England, *c.*1600–1800', *Textile: Journal of Cloth and Culture*, 1(1) (2003): 82.

98. Trading companies later provided further assistance by sending examples of patterns to be interpreted by inventive Indian artisans.

99. Hughes, *English Domestic Needlework*, p. 34. On the arrival of Indian embroiderers in sixteenth-century Portugal, see Maria Jose de Mendonça, 'Some Kinds of Indo-Portuguese Quilts in the Collection of the Museu de Arte Antiga' in *Embroidered Quilts From the Museu Nacional de Arte Antiga, Lisboa* (London: Kensington Palace, 1978), pp. 13–14.

100. See, for example, Maria Alice Beaumont, *Embroidered Quilts From the Museu Nacional de Arte Antiga, Lisboa* (London: Kensington Palace, 1978), figures 19–21; Fernando Antonio Baptista Pereira, 'Cuatro Notas Sobre el Arte en Portugal en el Tiempo de los Felipes' in *Las Sociedades Ibericas ye el Mar a finales de siglo XVI* (Lisbon: Exposición de Lisboa, 1998), p. 78.

101. Hughes, *English Domestic Needlework*, p. 36. María Angeles González Mena, *Colección Pedagógico Textil de la Universidad Complutense de Madrid. Estudio e Inventario* (Madrid: Consejo Social de la Universidad Complutense de Madrid, 1994), pp. 20, 30–31. I thank Ana Cabrera, Museo Nacional de Artes Decorativas, Madrid, for bringing this book to my attention.

102. Quoted in Joan Evans, *Pattern: A Study of Ornament in Western Europe, 1180–1900*, vol. II (Oxford: Oxford University Press, 1931), p. 61.

103. Department of Textiles, Art Institute of Chicago, 1997.197a-e. My thanks to Ryan Paveza for arranging this study tour.

104. Department of Textiles, Philadelphia Museum of Art, 1996-107-3. My thanks to Dilys Blum for allowing me to study this example.

105. Ann Rosalind Jones and Peter Stallybrass, *Renaissance Clothing and the Materials of Memory* (Cambridge: Cambridge University Press, 2000), p. 134.

106. Natalie Zemon Davis, *Trickster Travels: A Sixteenth-Century Muslim Between Worlds* (New York: Hill and Wang, 2006), p. 224.

107. For discussion of the early efforts to replicate Indian printing techniques and their significance, see, for example, Lemire and Riello, 'East and West'; Olivier Raveux 'Space and Technologies in the Cotton Industry in the Seventeenth and Eighteenth Centuries: The Example of Printed Calicoes in Marseilles', *Textile History* 36(2) (2005): 131–45.

108. Willan, *Tudor Book of Rates*, p. 45. A Somerset will from 1554 also includes a bequest of 'a pece of paynted clothe'. Weaver, *Somerset Medieval Wills*, p. 157. And for examples from Oxfordshire, see selected examples in M. A. Havinden (ed.), *Household and Farm Inventories in Oxfordshire, 1550–1590* (London: Her Majesty's Stationery Office, 1965), pp. 48, 53, 55, 57, 59, 60. For Devon, see Margaret Cash, *Devon Inventories of the Sixteenth and Seventeenth Centuries* (Exeter: Devonshire Press for the Exeter Diocesan Record Office, 1966), pp. 3, 4, 7.

109. Victoria and Albert Museum, Textile Department, 75A 1880.

110. Willan, *Tudor Book of Rates*, p. 45.

111. Lien Bich Luu, *Immigrants and the Industries of London 1500–1700* (Aldershot: Ashgate Publishers, 2005), p. 186.

112. See Chapter 3.

113. Daniel Defoe, *The Just Complaint of the Poor Weavers Truly Represented, with as much Answer as it deserves, to a Pamphlet Lately written against them Entitled The Weavers Pretences examin'd, etc.* (London, 1719), p. 31.

114. Joan Thirsk, *Economic Policy and Projects: The Development of a Consumer Society in Early Modern England* (Oxford: Clarendon Press, 1978), pp. 15–16.

115. De Vries, *Industrious Revolution*.

116. See, for example, Maxine Berg, *Luxury and Pleasure in Eighteenth-Century Britain* (Oxford: Oxford University Press, 2005).

117. Mary Douglas, *Thought Styles: Critical Essays on Good Taste* (London: Sage Publications, 1996); Georg Simmel, 'Fashion', *International Quarterly* 10 (1904): 136.

118. Prasannan Parthasarathi makes the important point that the European market was one of many served by India in the eighteenth century. 'Cotton Textile Exports from the Indian Subcontinent, 1680–1780', unpublished paper presented at the 'Global Economic History Network, Cotton Textiles as Global Industry Conference', University of Padua, November 2005.

119. Braudel, *Structures of Everyday Life*, p. 324.

120. K. N. Chaudhuri states that one million pieces of cotton were imported in 1684 by the English East India Company, making up 84 per cent of English trade. *Trading World of Asia*, pp. 96–7 and 282. Private trade and smuggling make absolute precision impossible. See Chapter 4 for further discussion of the social and economic impact of cotton's growth.

121. Lemire, 'Domesticating the Exotic'. For the impact of the prohibition of Indian cottons in France see Olivier Raveux, 'Space and Technology'.

122. Stanley D. Chapman and Serge Chassagne, *European Textile Printers in the Eighteenth Century* (London: Heinemann Educational Books, 1981); Wadsworth and Mann, *The Cotton Trade and Industrial Lancashire*, pp. 111–44.

123. *The Voyage of François Pyrard of Laval to the East Indies, the Maldives, the Moluccas and Brazil*, translated into English from the Third French Edition of 1619, and edited with notes by Albert Gray … (London: Hakluyt Society, 1888), p. 246.

124. Giovanni Andrea Vavassore, *Esemplario di lavori: che insegna alle donne il modo e l'ordine di lavorare* (1540).

125. Shaffer, 'Southernization'.

3. FASHION'S FAVOURITE

1. Fashion was unquestionably a social force in parts of the world, such as some of the coastal and urban regions of China, for example, as well as in Renaissance Europe. See, for example, Craig Clunas, *Superfluous Things: Material Culture and Social Status in Early Modern China* (Cambridge: Cambridge University Press, 1991) and Tim Brook, *The Confusions of Pleasure: Commerce and Culture in Ming China* (Berkeley: University of California Press, 1998).

2. Francis Bacon, *The essays, or councils, civil and moral, of Sir Francis Bacon, Lord Verulam, Viscount St. Alban with a table of the colours of good and evil, and a discourse of The wisdom of the ancients: to this edition is added The character of Queen Elizabeth, never before printed in English* (London, 1696), p. 38.

3. Hubert Hall, *History of the Customs Revenue*, vol. II (London: Elliot Stock, 1885), pp. 236–42.

4. Alan Hunt, *Governance of the Consuming Passions: A History of Sumptuary Law* (Basingstoke: Macmillan, 1996). Hunt observes that: 'In both the cases of China and Japan, with the passage of time the key target of sumptuary regulation became the merchant classes whose irresistible rise was eating away at the very possibility of a stable system of social closure required by the bureaucratic regimes' (p. 23).

5. Wilfrid Hooper, 'The Tudor Sumptuary Laws', *English Historical Review* 30 (1915): 438.

6. Aside from the rationing that accompanied the two world wars, various communist governments retained close control of general consumption through many decades of the twentieth century.

7. Susan Vincent, *Dressing the Elite: Clothes in Early Modern England* (Oxford: Berg, 2003), p. 119.

8. Phyliss G. Tortora and Keith Eubank, *Survey of Historic Costume: A History of Western Dress*, 5th edition (New York: Fairchild Books, 2010), pp. 187, 193; Vincent, *Dressing the Elite*, pp. 14–19.

9. Joan Thirsk, 'The Fantastical Folly of Fashion: The English Stocking Knitting Industry, 1500–1700' in N. B. Harte and K. G. Ponting (eds), *Textile History and Economic History: Essays in Honour of Miss Julia de Lacy Mann* (Manchester: Manchester University Press, 1973), p. 51.

10. Hooper, 'Tudor Sumptuary Laws', pp. 439–40.

11. Hooper, 'Tudor Sumptuary Laws', p. 441.

12. Quoted in Hunt, *Consuming Passions*, p. 28.

13. Kent Roberts Greenfield, *Sumptuary Law in Nürnberg: A Study in Paternal Government* (Baltimore: Johns Hopkins Press, 1918), pp. 7–9; Catherine Kovesi Killerby, *Sumptuary Law in Italy, 1200–1500* (Oxford: Oxford University Press, 2002), pp. 17–47.

14. Hunt, *Consuming Passions*, pp. 29–33, 46–7; Killerby, *Sumptuary Law in Italy*, pp. 46–7.

15. Frances Elizabeth Baldwin, *Sumptuary Legislation and Personal Regulation in England* (Baltimore: Johns Hopkins Press, 1926), pp. 157–61.

16. Hunt, *Consuming Passions*, pp. 29, 33.

17. Proceedings of the Court with View of Frankpledge, Mancath/2/A1/8, 8 November 1585, Manchester Cathedral Archives.

18. *The order of my Lord Mayor, the Aldermen, and the sheriffs, for their meetings and wearing of their apparel throughout the whole year …* (London, 1669), pp. 29, 31. This volume was republished into the mid-eighteenth century.

19. Vincent, *Dressing the Elite*, pp. 139–43.

20. Edward Chamberlayne, *Englands wants, or, Several Proposals beneficial for England humbly offered to the Consideration of all good Patriots in both Houses of Parliament by a true lover of his Country* (London, 1667), p. 29.

21. Jeremy Collier, *Miscellanies in Five Essays … the four last by way of dialogue* (London, 1694), p. 7.

22. Collier, *Miscellanies in Five Essays*, p. 9.

23. Alan Hunt observes that this was also the case for China and Japan, where sumptuary legislation targeted the merchant classes. Much the same could be said of Europe, though the timing and context of sumptuary legislation varied from region to region. Hunt, *Governance of the Consuming Passions*, p. 23.

24. Quoted in Vincent, *Dressing the Elite*, p. 125.

25. Gilles Lipovetsky notes the pivotal role of fashion in the transformation of society when 'no longer is some specific form of dress imposed from the outside'. Gilles Lipovetsky, *The Empire of Fashion: Dressing Modern Democracy*, trans. Catherine Porter (Princeton: Princeton University Press, 1994), p. 24.

26. The Spanish Netherlands, part of the powerful Hapsburg Empire, revolted against Spain in 1568, inspired by Protestant beliefs, as well as political grievances. The conflict ebbed and flowed over generations, with the ultimate establishment of the Dutch Republic (1581) in the seven northern provinces of the Netherlands. The formerly great entrepôt of Antwerp lost its commercial pre-eminence, to be succeeded by Amsterdam, in the Dutch Republic, in a region that became a commercial powerhouse in the seventeenth century.

27. Lawrence Stone, 'Elizabethan Overseas Trade', *Economic History Review*, 2nd series, 2 (1949): 36–9.

28. Worsted fabrics are those made with long-staple wool, combed instead of carded, to produce a lighter, smooth-surfaced cloth. This type of wool fibre can be easily combined with silk, linen or cotton to produce a variety of textiles, often at lower cost. The New Draperies represented one of the momentous changes in a sector that was the principal industrial employer in England.

29. The golden fleece has a rich symbolic tradition. For example, the Order of the Golden Fleece was established in 1431 by Philip the Good, Duke of Burgundy, an order that carried immense prestige and included among its members the Holy Roman Emperor. The symbol was employed in portraits and heraldic symbols and can be found in royal and noble portraits. The fleece was also used by guilds in European towns, both for its Christian symbolism and for its connection to the wool and weaving trades.

30. N. B. Harte (ed.), *The New Draperies in the Low Countries and England, 1300–1800* (Oxford: Oxford University Press, 1997).

31. Phillip Stubbes, *Anatomie of abuses* (London, 1595).

32. Lipovetsky, *Empire of Fashion*, p. 18.

33. Daniel Roche, *A History of Everyday Things: The Birth of Consumption in France, 1600–1800*, trans. B. Pearce (Cambridge: Cambridge University Press, 2000). See also Joan Thirsk, *Economic Policy and Projects: The Development of a Consumer Society in Early Modern England* (Oxford: Clarendon Press, 1978).

34. Thirsk, *Economic Policy and Projects*, p. 120.

35. Ann Rosalind Jones and Peter Stallybrass, *Renaissance Clothes and the Materials of Memory* (Cambridge: Cambridge University Press, 2000), p. 22.

36. Lipovetsky, *Empire of Fashion*, p. 18.

37. T. Dekker, *The Seven Deadly Sins of London* (London: Edward Allde, 1606), quoted in Jones and Stallybrass, *Renaissance Clothing*, p. 1.

38. Stubbes, *Anatomie of abuses*, p. 28.

39. Jones and Stallybrass, *Renaissance Clothes and the Materials of Memory*, p. 2.

40. *The Journal of William Schellinks' Travels in England, 1661–1663*, trans. M. Exwood and H. L. Lehmann (London: Royal Historical Society, 1993) pp. 76–7, 169.

41. *The order of my Lord Mayor, the Aldermen, and the sheriffs, for their meetings and wearing of their apparel throughout the whole year* (London, 1655). Other editions were published throughout the rest of the 1600s and well into the eighteenth century.

42. Ann Buck, *Dress in Eighteenth-Century England* (London: Batsford, 1979), p. 106.

43. *The golden fleece, wherein is related the riches of the English wools in its manufacturers ...* (London: printed by I. Grismond, 1656), reprinted in J. Smith, *Chronicon rusticum-commerciale; or, memoirs of wool, etc ...* (London: 1747; reprinted New York: Augustus M. Kelley, 1969), vol. 1, p. 197.

44. Roze Hentschell, *The Culture of Cloth in Early Modern England: Textual Construction of a National Identity* (Aldershot: Ashgate, 2008), p. 158; Vivienne Aldous, 'Cokayne, Sir William (1559/60–1626)', in H. C. G. Matthew and Brian Harrison (eds), *Oxford Dictionary of National Biography* (Oxford: Oxford University Press, 2004); online edn (ed.) Lawrence Goldman, January 2009, http://www.oxforddnb.com.login.ezproxy.library.ualberta.ca/view/article/5824 (accessed 12 October 2009).

45. Playwright Thomas Dekker opined: 'An English-mans suite is like a traitors bodie that hath beene hanged, drawne, and quartered, and is set up in several places: his Cod-peece is in *Denmark*, the coller of his Duble[doublet] and the belly in *France*: the wing and narrow sleeve in Italy: the short waste hangs over a *Dutch* Botchers stall in *Utrich*: his huge slopes [loose jacket] speakes *Spanish*: *Polonia* gives him the Bootes: the blocke for his heade alters faster than the Feltmaker can fitte him ... And thus we that mocke every Nation, for keeping one fashion, yet steale patches from every one of them, to peece out our pride.' Thomas Dekker, *The Seven Deadly Sins of London* (London, 1606), p. 32.

46. Beverly Lemire, 'Domesticating the Exotic: Floral Culture and the East India Calico Trade with England, *c*.1600–1800', *Textile: The Journal of Cloth and Culture* 1(1) (2003): 65–85.

47. James Boyajian, *Portuguese Trade in Asia under the Habsburgs, 1580–1640* (Baltimore: Johns Hopkins University Press, 1993), p. 140.

48. D. R. Starkey (ed.), *The Inventory of King Henry VIII*, vol. 1 (London: Harvey Miller, 1998), entry number 11390. I would like to thank Maria Hayward for this information; Janet Arnold, *Queen Elizabeth's Wardrobe Unlock'd* (Leeds: Maney Publishing, 1988) p. 185.

49. Lien Bich Luu, *Immigrants and the Industries of London 1500–1700* (Aldershot: Ashgate, 2005), p. 186.

50. Stone, 'Elizabethan Overseas Trade', p. 48.

51. Pepper constituted just 5 per cent of the value of these same cargoes. Boyajian, *Portuguese Trade in Asia under the Habsburgs*, pp. 249, 205–6.

52. There was no specific designation for painted as opposed to printed cottons in English. Both were called calicoes, though there were many varieties typically identified by regional variants of Indian words, illustrated in guides to textiles such as J. F., *The Merchant's Ware-House Laid Open: or, The Plain Dealing Linnen Draper ...* (London, 1696).

53. CR1886/Cupboard4/Third Shelf/BB832; Talbot Papers MS.3203 1583–1612, Lambeth Palace Library, London, Folio 75. Bess of Hardwick's Indian quilts have been well documented. See Chapter 5.

54. Thomas Campion, A *Relation of the Late Royall Entertainment Given by the Right Honorable the Lord Knowles, at Cawsome-House neere Redding ...* (London, 1613), p. 1.

55. Thomas Dekker, *The Honest Whore, with the Humours of the Patient Man, and the Longing Wife* (London, 1615), Act 1, Scene 1.

56. K. N. Chaudhuri, *The English East India Company: The Study of an Early Joint-Stock Company, 1600–1640* (London: Frank Cass & Co., 1965), pp. 192–3. A 'piece' of cotton might vary from about twelve to thirty metres in length, depending on variety.

57. Chaudhuri, *English East India Company*, pp. 192–4.

58. Chaudhuri, *English East India Company*, p. 195.

59. Chaudhuri, *English East India Company*, pp. 201–3.

60. SP 46/76 Bayning Papers, National Archives, Kew, London.

61. William Wood, *New Englands Prospect: A True, Lively, and Experimentall Description of that part of America, commonly called New England* ... (London, 1634), reprinted in Beverly Lemire (ed.), *The British Cotton Trade* (London: Pickering & Chatto, 2009), vol. 1, p. 127.

62. SP 46/130, National Archives, Kew, London.

63. E101.527.17, f.46r., National Archives, Kew, London. Calico is also noted in the same document in at least a dozen other instances, with descriptors like fine, narrow, broad and stripe.

64. W. Petyt, *Britannia Languens: or, A Discourse of Trade: Shewing that the Present Management of Trade in England, is the True Reason of the Decay of our Manufactures, and the late Great Fall of Land-Rents ... wherein is particularly Demonstrated, that the East-India Company, as now Managed, has already Near Destroyed our Trade ... humbly offered to the Consideration of this present Parliament* (London, 1689), p. 132.

65. ZA/B/2/103–105, 15 August 1654, Cheshire and Chester Archives and Local Studies Service.

66. Robert Latham and William Matthews (eds), *The Diary of Samuel Pepys*, vol. 1 (London: G. Bell and Sons Ltd, 1970), p. 158.

67. *Diary of Samuel Pepys*, vol. 4, p. 358.

68. Neil McKendrick, 'The Commercialization of Fashion' in Neil McKendrick, John Brewer and J. H. Plumb, *The Birth of a Consumer Society: The Commercialization of Eighteenth-Century England* (London: Hutchinson & Co., 1983).

69. For a discussion of various new luxuries, see Maxine Berg and Helen Clifford (eds), *Consumers and Luxury: Consumer Culture in Europe 1650–1850* (Manchester: Manchester University Press, 1999).

70. Jan de Vries, *The Industrious Revolution: Consumer Behavior and the Household Economy, 1650 to the Present* (Cambridge: Cambridge University Press, 2008), pp. 40–58.

71. Lorna Weatherill, *Consumer Behaviour & Material Culture in Britain, 1660–1760* (London: Routledge, 1988), p. 185.

72. Herbert Blumer, 'Fashion: From Class Differentiation to Collective Selection', *Sociological Quarterly* 10(3) (1969): 282, 283.

73. C. S. Knighton, 'Pepys, Samuel (1633–1703)', *Oxford Dictionary of National Biography* (Oxford: Oxford University Press, 2004); online edn, Jan 2008, http://www.oxforddnb.com/view/article/21906, accessed 5 November 2009.

74. *Diary of Samuel Pepys*, vol. 4, p. 358.

75. For a study of the Venetian case see Stella Mary Newton, *The Dress of the Venetians, 1495–1525* (Aldershot: Scolar Press, 1988), pp. 9–47. Over this period gentlemen's legs became visible and were celebrated and eroticized through the new forms of male dress.

76. Bianca M. du Mortier, *Aristocratic Attire: The Donation of the Six Family* (Amsterdam: Rijksmuseum, 2000), p. 35. See also A. M. Lubberhuizen-van Gelder, 'Japonsche Rocken', *Oud-Holland* 64 (1949): 137–51.

77. Blumer, 'Fashion: From Class to Collective', p. 280.

78. *The Book of Duarte Barbosa. An Account of the Countries Bordering on the Indian Ocean and their Inhabitants, Written by Duarte Barbosa, and Completed about the Year 1518 A.D.* Translated from the Portuguese text, first published in 1812 by the Royal Academy of Sciences at Lisbon in vol. II of its *Collection of Documents Regarding the History and Geography of the Nations Beyond the Seas*, and edited and annotated by Mansel Longworth Dames. Vol. II (London: Hakluyt Society, 1921), p. 73 and note 2.

79. Jean Baptiste Bonnart, *Recueil des modes de la cour de France* (Paris, 1676), described as 'robe d'Armenien'.

80. Ebeltje Hartkamp-Jonxis, *Sitsen uit India* (Amsterdam: Rijksmuseum, 1994), p. 70.

81. R. W. Connell, 'The Big Picture: Masculinity in Recent World History', *Theory and Society* 22(5) (1993): 608, 609.

82. Quoted in Leonard Blussé, *Visible Cities: Canton, Nagasaki, and Batavia and the Coming of the Americans* (Cambridge, MA: Harvard University Press, 2008), p. 35.

83. François-Hubert Drouais painted an informal family portrait of a prosperous bourgeois family in 1756, with the husband swathed in a banyan of this sort. 1946.7.4, National Gallery of Art,

Washington, DC. See http://www.nga.gov/collection/gallery/gg55/gg55-32698.0.html, accessed 23 August 2007.

84. Margot Finn, 'Men's Things: Masculine Possession in the Consumer Revolution', *Social History* 25(2) (2000): 142; Du Mortier, *Aristocratic Attire*, p. 35.

85. See, for example, Mark A. Meadow, 'Merchants and Marvels: Hans Jacob Fugger and the Origins of the *Wunderkammer*', in Pamela H. Smith and Paula Findlen (eds), *Merchants and Marvels: Commerce, Science, and Art in Early Modern Europe* (London: Routledge, 2002), pp. 182–200.

86. As Brian Cowan observes, the virtuosi's interests were practical and utilitarian and they 'led the way in spurring consumer interest [as with] … coffee'. Brian Cowan, *The Social Life of Coffee: The Emergence of the British Coffeehouse* (New Haven: Yale University Press, 2005) p. 14.

87. For a further commentary on this evocative play see Daniel Roche, *The Culture of Clothing: Dress and Fashion in the Ancient Régime*, trans. Jean Birrell (Cambridge: Cambridge University Press, 1989), pp. 91–3.

88. Brandon Brame Fortune with Deborah J. Warner, *Franklin and His Friends: Portraying the Man of Science in Eighteenth-Century America* (Philadelphia: University of Philadelphia Press, 1999), p. 53.

89. Inv. 7510, Inv. 7511, R.F. 2885, Louvre, Paris. See http://www.louvre.fr/llv/commun/home.jsp?bmLocale=en, accessed 22 August 2007.

90. N.P.G. 2890. National Portrait Gallery, London.

91. *The History of the Lives and Actions of Jonathan Wild, Thief-taker …* (London, 1725), p. 61. Jonathan Wild amassed a fortune during his reign as chief thief-taker of London, at the same time running much of the organized property crime in the city.

92. Denis Diderot, 'Regrets on Parting with my Old Dressing Gown: Or, a Warning to Those Who Have More Taste than Money', 1772, reprinted in Jacques Barzun and Ralph H. Bowen (trans.), *Rameau's Nephew and Other Works* (Indianapolis IN: Hackett Publishing Co., 1956), p. 309.

93. Brandon Brame Fortune, 'Studious Men are Always Painted in Gowns', *Dress* 29 (2002): 27–41; Susan Rather, 'Benjamin West's Profession

Endgame and the Historical Conundrum of William Williams', *The William and Mary Quarterly* 59(4) (2002): 13, 16 and Figures IV and V. Additional portraits of men in banyans can be found in the National Portrait Gallery collection online at www.npg.org.uk/live/search/portraits. For example, NPG: 11, 278, 299, 550, 558, 562, 1045, 1167, 1179, 1323, 1920, 2106, 2890, 3230, 3228, 5188, 5932, 6063 and 6143. Website accessed 21 July 2007. Portraits reflecting this style produced for French and Low Countries men held in the Louvre, Paris, include R. F. 2169, Inv. 27-622, Inv. 4306, R. F. 1991-4, R. F. 1972-14, R. F. 1982-66, r. F. 2002-5. See http://www.louvre.fr/llv/commun/home.jsp?bmLocale=en, accessed 22 August 2007. The portrait of a geographer, school of Caravaggio from the seventeenth century, offers another example of this form of dress. F. 1968.11.03.P, Norton Simon Museum, Pasadena. See http://www.nortonsimon.org/collections/browse_title.asp?id=F.1968.11.03.P, accessed 23 August 2007.

94. For a full summary of trade volumes to England, see K. N. Chaudhuri, *The Trading World of Asia and the English East India Company, 1660–1760* (Cambridge: Cambridge University Press, 1979).

95. AM/P1 (1) 1672/33, London Metropolitan Archives.

96. Hartkamp-Jonxis, *Sitsen uit India*, p. 78.

97. Trade Cards Box 13, John Johnson Collection, Bodleian Library, Oxford. A later eighteenth-century bill head with reference to Indian as well as French textile novelties is noted in Natacha Coquery, 'The Language of Success: Marketing and Distributing Semi-Luxury Goods in Eighteenth-Century Paris', *Journal of Design History* 17(1) (2004): 79, Figure 4.

98. *Oracle and Public Advertiser*, 16 January 1797, in Beverly Lemire (ed.), *The British Cotton Trade*, vol. 4 (London: Pickering & Chatto, 2009), p. 106.

99. Chaudhuri, *Trading World of Asia*, p. 282.

100. P175/11/1 1662-78, Centre for Kentish Studies; MS 3312/395094 1668, Birmingham City Archives.

101. *London Gazette*, 11 January 1693, in Lemire (ed.), *British Cotton Trade*, vol. 1, (London: Pickering & Chatto, 2009), p. 19.

102. P. O'Brien, T. Griffiths and P. Hunt, 'Political Components of the Industrial Revolution: Parliament and the English Cotton Textile Industry, 1660–1774', *Economic History Review* 44(3) (1991): 396.

103. D. C. Coleman, 'Textile Growth', in N. B. Harte and K. G. Ponting (eds), *Textile History and Economic History: Essays in Honour of Miss Julia de Lacy Mann* (Manchester: Manchester University Press, 1973), pp. 1–21.

104. C. W. Willet and P. Cunnington, *A History of Underclothes* (London: Michael Joseph, 1951), p. 55.

105. *The Good-wives lamentation, or, The womens complaint on the account of their being to be buried in woollen* (London, 1678), p. 6.

106. Although wealthy families might happily pay fines for non-compliance, ensuring that their dead were buried in fine silk and lace. R. Houlbrooke, *Death, Religion and the Family in England, 1480–1750* (Oxford: Clarendon Press, 1998), p. 341.

107. N. B. Harte, 'The Rise of Protection and the English Linen Trade, 1690–1790' in N. B. Harte and K. G. Ponting (eds), *Textile History and Economic History: Essays in Honour of Miss Julia de Lacy Mann* (Manchester: Manchester University Press, 1973), pp. 74–112.

108. Josiah Child, *A Treatise: Wherein is Demonstrated that the East-India Trade is the most Nation of all the Foreign Trades* ... (London, 1681), in Lemire (ed.), *British Cotton Trade*, vol. 1, p. 246.

109. Olivier Raveux, 'Armenian Networks in the Trade and Production of Calicoes in the Mediterranean During the Last Third of the Seventeenth Century', unpublished paper presented at the American Historical Association's conference, San Diego, 8 January 2010.

110. Fernand Braudel, *Civilization and Capitalism 15th–18th Century, The Wheels of Commerce*, vol. 2, translated from the French by Siân Reynolds (New York: Harper & Row, 1982), p. 178.

111. Jan de Vries offers an insightful account of women's prominence in consumer markets over the course of the long eighteenth century, in new patterns of activity of equal importance to plebeian women's revised patterns of work.

112. Roche, *The Culture of Clothing*, p. 504.

113. Laura Gowing, 'Women, Status and the Popular Culture of Dishonour', *Transactions of the Royal Historical Society*, 6th Series, vol. 6 (1996), p. 225.

114. *Prince Butler's Tale: Representing the State of the Wool-Case, or the East-India Case Truly Stated* (London, 1699) reprinted in Lemire (ed.), *The British Cotton Trade*, vol. 1, pp. 433–4.

115. Quoted in O'Brien, Griffiths and Hunt, 'Political Components of the Industrial Revolution', p. 405. For the spread of textile printing knowledge in Europe, see Giorgio Riello, 'Asian Knowledge and the Development of Calico Printing in Europe in the Seventeenth and Eighteenth Centuries', *Journal of Global History* 5(1) (2010): 1–28.

116. R. L., *Pride's Exchange Broke Up: or Indian Calicoes and Silks Expos'd* (London, 1703), in Beverly Lemire (ed.), *The British Cotton Trade* (London: Pickering & Chatto, 2009), vol. 2, p. 37.

117. Ibid., p. 38.

118. Thomas Baker, *Tunbridge-Walks: or, the yeoman of Kent; a comedy. As it is acted at the Theatre Royal by Her Majesty's servants* (London, 1703), p. 19.

119. See, for example, Sara Mendelson and Patricia Crawford, *Women in Early Modern England* (Oxford: Oxford University Press, 2000), pp. 203–4.

120. Beverly Lemire, *Dress, Culture and Commerce: The English Clothing Trade Before the Factory* (Basingstoke: Macmillan, 1997), Chapters 1, 2, 4; Elizabeth Sanderson, *Women and Work in Eighteenth-Century Edinburgh* (Basingstoke: Macmillan, 1996).

121. De Vries, *Industrious Revolution*, p. 179. For discussion of the involvement of women and girls in key consumer industries, see Maxine Berg, *The Age of Manufactures, 1700–1820*, 2nd edition (London: Routledge, 1994), Chapter 7.

122. Quoted in Ilja Van Damme, 'Middlemen and the Creation of a "Fashion Revolution": The Experience of Antwerp in the Late Seventeenth and Eighteenth Centuries', in Beverly Lemire

(ed.), *The Force of Fashion in Politics and Society: Global Perspectives from Early Modern to Contemporary Times* (Aldershot: Ashgate, 2010), p. 29.

123. Quoted in Chloe Wigston Smith, '"Calico Madams": Servants, Consumption, and the Calico Crisis', *Eighteenth-Century Life* 31(2) (2007): 32; *The Just Complaints of the Poor Weavers Truly Represented* ... (London: W. Boreham, 1719), p. 6.

124. Hentschell, 'Treasonous Textile', p. 544.

125. Daniel Defoe wrote that: 'Ladies converted their Carpets and Quilts into Gowns and Petticoats, and made the broad and uncouth Bordures of the former, serve instead of the rich Laces and Embroideries they were used to wear, and dress'd more like the Merry-Andrews of Bartholomew-Fair, than like Ladies and the Wives of trading People.' Daniel Defoe, *A Brief State of the Question Between the Printed and Painted Callicoes, and the Woollen and Silk Manufacture ...*, 2nd edition (London, 1719), p. 11.

126. The numbers represent a contemporary's estimate and may well be inflated, though there is no doubt of the considerable numbers employed in the worsted and silk industries. Lemire, *British Cotton Trade*, vol. 2, p. 289.

127. *Weekly Journal or Saturday's Post*, 13 June 1719.

128. Quoted in Wigston Smith, 'Calico Madam', p. 33.

129. *Weekly Journal or British Gazetteer*, 20 June 1719.

130. Lemire, *Fashion's Favourite*, p. 36.

131. *Weekly Journal or Saturday's Post*, 27 June 1719; 8 July 1719, Old Bailey online, ref. no. t17190708-59, accessed 10 November 2009.

132. E. P. Thompson, 'The Moral Economy of the English Crowd', in *Customs in Common: Studies in Traditional Popular Culture* (New York: W. W. Norton & Co., 1993), p. 188.

133. *Daily Courant*, 9 July 1719.

134. Lemire, *British Cotton Trade*, vol. 2, pp. 281–4, 291–2.

135. *Weekly Journal of Saturday's Post*, 11 July 1719.

136. Lemire, *Fashion's Favourite*, pp. 35–7.

137. *A Collection of Miscellany Letters, Selected Out of Mist's Weekly Journal* ... (London, 1722–27), vol. 1, p. 132.

138. *Weekly Journal or Saturday's Post*, 12 September 1719.

139. Defoe, *Just Complaint*, p. 102.

140. *Weekly Journal or Saturday's Post*, 12 September 1719; *Original Weekly Journal*, 2 January 1720; *Daily Post*, 5 May 1720; *Weekly Journal or Saturday's Post*, 7 May 1720, 14 May 1720, 21 May 1720.

141. *Weekly Packet*, 16 July 1720; *Applebee's Original Weekly Journal*, 13 August 1720.

142. *Weekly Journal or British Gazetteer*, 11 June 1720, 12 July 1720, 20 August 1720; Old Bailey online, ref. no. t17200712-28, accessed 10 November 2009.

143. *The Female Manufacturers Complaints: Being the Humble Petition of Dorothy Distaff ...* (London, 1720), quoted in Lemire, *British Cotton Trade*, vol. 2, p. 247.

144. *The Linen Spinster, in Defence of the Linen Manufactures, etc.* (London, 1720), in Lemire, *The British Cotton Trade*, vol. 2, p. 255.

145. De Vries, *Industrious Revolution*, p. 139.

146. Thirsk, *Economic Policy and Projects*, pp. 106–32. The expansion of ready-made clothes production over this period, for military and civilian markets, employed tens of thousands of seamstresses in a decentralized system of subcontracting. For the expansion of this type of female employment, see Lemire, *Dress, Culture and Commerce*, Chapter 1, pp. 9–41 and Chapter 2, pp. 43–74, and for the second-hand trade, Chapter 4, pp. 95–120.

147. For information on eighteenth-century shopping see, for example, Nancy Cox, *The Complete Tradesman: A Study of Retailing, 1550–1820* (Aldershot: Ashgate, 2000); Helen Berry, 'Polite Consumption: Shopping in Eighteenth-Century England', *Transactions of the Royal Historical Society* 12 (2002), pp. 375–94; Patrick Wallis, 'Consumption, Retailing, and Medicine in Early Modern London', *Economic History Review* 61(1) (2008): 26–53; Claire Walsh, 'Shops, Shopping and the Art of Decision-Making in Eighteenth-Century England', in John Styles and Amanda Vickery (eds), *Gender, Taste, and Material Culture in Britain and North America, 1700–1830* (New Haven: Yale University Press, 2006), pp. 151–77.

148. *The Female Manufacturers Complaints: Being the Humble Petition of Dorothy Distaff* ... (London, 1720) quoted in Lemire, *British Cotton Trade*, vol. 2, p. 247.

149. *Weekly Journal or Saturday's Post*, 1 April 1721.

150. *Weekly Journal or Saturday's Post*, 21 July 1721.

151. He penned an acidic verse some years earlier, in which he concluded 'Females of all Sizes, Go in the Devils new Disguises'. Daniel Defoe, *The London Ladies Dressing-Room: Or the Shop-keepers Wives Inventory* (London, 1705), in Lemire, *British Cotton Trade*, vol. 2, p. 264. For a full discussion of Defoe's perspective on female consumption and the calico controversy, see Wigston Smith, 'Calico Madams'.

152. Daniel Defoe, 'The Women's Complaint against the Weavers' in Lemire, *British Cotton Trade*, vol. 2, p. 273.

153. Paula R. Backscheider, 'Defoe, Daniel (1660?–1731)', *Oxford Dictionary of National Biography*, Oxford University Press, Sept 2004; online edn, Jan 2008, http://www.oxforddnb.com/view/article/7421, accessed 11 Jan 2010.

154. *A Further Examination of the Weavers Pretences* (London, 1719) in Lemire, *British Cotton Trade*, vol. 2, p. 151.

155. See Chapter 4. In fact, Manchester fustian (linen/cotton) manufacturers joined the wool industry in petitioning for the ban on Indian cottons. But the Lancashire manufacturers wanted permission for 'all cloths and stuff s manufactured in this Kingdom of Cotton Wooll of the produce of his majesties plantations in America may be allowed to be printed, painted, stained or dyed and wore in Great Britaine'. Lemire, *British Cotton Trade*, vol. 2, p. 59.

156. *Daily Journal*, 1 January 1723, 3 January 1723, 24 January 1723.

157. *Post Boy*, 27 December 1722.

158. *Post Boy*, 27 December 1722.

159. *British Journal*, 18 May 1723; *London Journal*, 18 May 1723.

160. *Country Journal for the Craftsman*, 3 August 1728, in Lemire, *British Cotton Trade*, vol. 2, p. 314.

161. Carole Shammas, 'The Decline of Textile Prices in England and British America Prior to Industrialization', *Economic History Review* 57(3) (1994): 504.

162. *London Journal*, 5 September 1730, in Lemire, *British Cotton Trade*, vol. 3, p. 7.

163. Lemire, *British Cotton Trade*, vol. 3, pp. 8–11; *General Evening Post*, 31 May 1735.

164. *The Case of the Worsted and Silk Manufacturers* (1735?).

165. *Journal of the House of Commons*, February 1735/6, in Lemire, *British Cotton Trade*, vol. 3, p. 39.

166. *Read's Weekly Journal or British Gazetteer*, 17 April 1736.

167. Lemire, *British Cotton Trade*, vol. 3, pp. 9–11.

168. Gilles Lipovetsky, *The Empire of Fashion: Dressing Modern Democracy*, trans. Catherine Porter (Princeton: Princeton University Press, 1994), p. 47.

169. *Report from the Committee Relating to Chequed and Striped Linens*, in Lemire, *British Cotton Trade*, vol. 3, pp. 93, 95.

170. 'Pretty Poll', in *A Complete Collection of Old and New English and Scotch Songs, with their Respective Tunes Prefixed* ... (London, 1736), p. 66.

4. COTTAGE, MILL, FACTORY, PLANTATION

1. Karl Polyani, *The Great Transformation: The Political and Economic Origins of Our Time* (Boston: Beacon Press, 1944), p. 33.

2. For a full discussion of the road to Whitney's innovation and its full context, see Angela Lakwete, *Inventing the Cotton Gin: Machine and Myth in Antebellum America* (Baltimore: Johns Hopkins University Press, 2003).

3. For further information on medieval guilds, see Steven A. Epstein, *Wage Labor and Guilds in Medieval Europe* (Chapel Hill, NC: University of North Carolina Press, 1991).

4. Richard Goldthwaite, *The Economy of Renaissance Florence* (Baltimore: Johns Hopkins University Press, 2009), pp. 3–10.

5. Goldthwaite, *The Economy of Renaissance Florence*, pp. 417.

6. Anthony Lejeune (ed.), *The Concise Dictionary of Foreign Quotations* (London: Stacey, 1998), p. 207.

7. Fernand Braudel, *Civilization and Capitalism 15ᵗʰ–18ᵗʰ Century: The Perspective of the World*, vol. 3, trans. Siân Reynolds (New York: Harper & Row, 1984), p. 112.

8. Epstein, *Wage Labor and Guilds in Medieval Europe*, p. 180.

9. For further information on the medieval cloth trade, see: Braudel, *Civilization and Capitalism 15th–18th Century: The Perspective of the World*; E. M. Carus-Wilson, 'An Industrial Revolution of the Thirteenth Century', *Economic History Review* 11 (1941): 41–60; C. M. Cipolla, *Before the Industrial Revolution: European Society and Economy, 1000–1700* (New York: Norton, 1976); Raymond de Roover, 'The Organization of Trade', in *Cambridge Economic History of Europe* (Cambridge: Cambridge University Press, 1963).

10. Janet Abu Lughod, *Before European Hegemony: The World System A.D. 1250–1350* (New York: Oxford University Press, 1989), p. 98, notes 2 and 3.

11. Constance Hoffman Berman, 'Women's Work in Family, Village, and Town After 1000 CE: Contributions to Economic Growth?', *Journal of Women's History* 19(3) (2007): 10–32.

12. John Fitzherbert, *The Boke of Husbandry* (London: Thomas Berthelet, *c.*1540), p. 61. Spelling has been modernized.

13. William Bullein, *Bulleins bulwarke of defence against all sicknesse, soarenesse, and woundes that doe daily assaulte mankinde: which bulwarke is kept with Hilarius the gardener, [and] Health the phisicion, with the chirurgian, to helpe the wounded soldiours. Gathered and practised from the most worthy learned, both olde and new: to the great comfort of mankinde: by William Bullein, Doctor of Phisicke* (London: Thomas Marshe, 1579), p. 28. Spelling has been modernized.

14. Walter Simons, *Cities of Ladies: Beguine Communities in the Medieval Low Countries, 1200–1565* (Philadelphia: University of Pennsylvania Press, 2001), p. 86.

15. Simons, *Cities of Ladies*, p. 86.

16. The stages of fibre preparation are described in more detail in Adrienne Hood, *The Weaver's Craft: Cloth, Commerce, and Industry in Early Pennsylvania* (Philadelphia: University of Pennsylvania Press, 2003), pp. 48–55.

17. See Chapter 2 for discussion of the spread of cotton textiles from Asia to the eastern Mediterranean.

18. Maureen Fennell Mazzaoui, *The Italian Cotton Industry in the Later Middle Ages, 1100–1600* (Cambridge: Cambridge University Press, 1981), pp. 67, 68.

19. Mazzaoui, *The Italian Cotton Industry*, p. 74.

20. Mazzaoui, *The Italian Cotton Industry*, pp. 75–85.

21. A. P. Wadsworth and Julia de Lacy Mann, *The Cotton Trade and Industrial Lancashire, 1600–1780* (Manchester: Manchester University Press, 1965 [1931]), p. 21.

22. John May, *A Declaration of the Estate of Clothing now Used within this Realm of England …* (London: A. Islip, 1613), in Beverly Lemire (ed.), *The British Cotton Industry*, vol. 1 (London: Pickering & Chatto, 2009), p. 125.

23. Quoted in Joan Thirsk, *Economic Policy and Projects: The Development of a Consumer Society in Early Modern England* (Oxford: Clarendon Press, 1978), p. 132. For an analysis of the textile trades throughout the north-west of England see Jon Stobart, *The First Industrial Region: North-West England, c.1700–1760* (Manchester: Manchester University Press, 2004), pp. 66–74.

24. Carole Shammas, 'The Decline of Textile Prices in England and British America Prior to Industrialization', *Economic History Review* 47(3) (1994): 483–507, on p. 484, Table 1, and p. 493, Table 4.

25. Stobart, *The First Industrial Region*, p. 74.

26. Arthur Trevor to the Marquis of Ormonde, 21 December 1642, quoted in Wadsworth and Mann, *Cotton Trade and Industrial Lancashire*, p. 25.

27. Negley Harte, 'The Rise of Protection and the English Linen Trade, 1690–1790' in N. B. Harte and K. G. Ponting (eds), *Textile History and Economic History: Essays in Honour of Miss Julia de Lacy Mann* (Manchester: Manchester University Press, 1973), pp. 74–80.

28. *The Case of the Printed Linnens of North Britain* (London, 1720?), in Lemire, *British Cotton Trade*, vol. 2, p. 235.

29. HL/PO/JO/10/3/213/34, Parliamentary Archives, in Lemire, *British Cotton Trade*, vol. 2, pp. 58, 59.

30. Wadsworth and Mann, *Cotton Trade and Industrial Lancashire*, pp. 69, 54–70.

31. Harte, 'Rise of Protectionism', pp. 75–6.

32. *Report from the Committee Related to Chequed and Striped Linens* (1751), in Lemire, *British Cotton Trade*, vol. 3, pp. 87–96.

33. *The Life and Times of Samuel Crompton, Inventor of the Spinning Machine Called The Mule*

(London: Simpkin, Marshall & Co., 1859), pp. 264–5.

34. John Harris, 'Law, Espionage, and the Transfer of Technology from Eighteenth-Century Britain', in Robert Fox (ed.), *Technology Change: Methods and Themes in the History of Technology* (Amsterdam: Harwood Academic Publishers, 1996), pp. 125–6.

35. Beverly Lemire, *Fashion's Favourite: The Cotton Trade and the Consumer in Britain, 1660–1800* (Oxford: Oxford University Press, 1991), pp. 79–86.

36. Wadsworth and Mann, *Cotton Trade and Industrial Lancashire*, p. 201.

37. Wadsworth and Mann, *Cotton Trade and Industrial Lancashire*, p. 176.

38. Anon. [John Collier], *Dialect of South Lancashire, or Tim Bobbin's Tummus and Meary: Revised and Corrected ... and Enlarged and Amended ... by Samuel Bamford*, in Lemire, *British Cotton Trade*, vol. 4, p. 92.

39. Wadsworth and Mann, *Cotton Trade and Industrial Lancashire*, pp. 274–5.

40. Wadsworth and Mann, *Cotton Trade and Industrial Lancashire*, pp. 284–303.

41. For more on hosiery manufacture and the framework-knitting trade, see S. D. Chapman, *Hosiery and Knitwear: Four Centuries of Small-Scale Industry in Britain c.1589–2000* (Oxford: Oxford University Press, 2002); see also Maxine Berg, *The Age of Manufactures, 1700–1820: Industry, Innovation and Work in Britain*, 2nd edition (London: Routledge, 1994), pp. 242–3.

42. Wadsworth and Mann, *Cotton Trade and Industrial Lancashire*, pp. 304–5; R. B. Prosser and Susan Christian, 'Lombe, Sir Thomas (1685–1739)', rev. Maxwell Craven and Susan Christian, *Oxford Dictionary of National Biography* (Oxford: Oxford University Press, 2004), online edn, Jan 2008, http://www.oxforddnb.com.login.ezproxy.library.ualberta.ca/view/article/16956, accessed 8 Feb 2010.

43. Thomas Bentley, *Letters on the Utility and Policy of Employing Machines to Shorten Labour ...* (London, 1780), in Lemire, *British Cotton Trade*, vol. 4, p. 162.

44. Quoted in Lemire, *Fashion's Favourite*, p. 81.

45. Patrick O'Brien, Trevor Griffiths and Philip Hunt, 'Political Components of the Industrial Revolution: Parliament and the English Cotton Textile Industry, 1660–1774', *Economic History Review* 44(3) (1991): 411.

46. Quoted in Trevor Griffiths, Philip A. Hunt and Patrick O'Brien, 'Inventive Activity in the British Textile Industry, 1700–1800', *Journal of Economic History* 52(4) (1992): 886.

47. Wadsworth and Mann, *Cotton Trade and Industrial Lancashire*, pp. 447–8. For examples of other abortive spinning inventions, see also pages 472–6.

48. James A. Mann, *The Cotton Trade of Great Britain: Its Rise, Progress, & Present Extent ...* (London: Simpkin, Marshall & Co., 1860), p. 20.

49. Quoted in Christopher Aspin, 'Hargreaves, James (*bap.* 1721, *d.* 1778)', *Oxford Dictionary of National Biography* (Oxford: Oxford University Press, 2004), http://www.oxforddnb.com/view/article/12316, accessed 10 February 2010.

50. Berg, *The Age of Manufactures*, p. 239.

51. Berg, *The Age of Manufactures*, p. 241; J. J. Mason, 'Arkwright, Sir Richard (1732–1792)', *Oxford Dictionary of National Biography* (Oxford: Oxford University Press, 2004), http://www.oxforddnb.com/view/article/645, accessed 10 February 2010.

52. Mason, 'Arkwright'. See also R. S. Fitton, *The Arkwrights: Spinners of Fortune* (Manchester: Manchester University Press, 1989), pp. 1–50.

53. Wadsworth and Mann, *Cotton Trade and Industrial Lancashire*, pp. 448–9.

54. Fitton, *The Arkwrights: Spinners of Fortune*, p. 28.

55. Wadsworth and Mann, *Cotton Trade and Industrial Lancashire*, pp. 496–7.

56. *Journal of the House of Commons* (1780) in Lemire, *British Cotton Trade*, vol. 4, p. 123.

57. *Journal of the House of Commons* (1780) in Lemire, *British Cotton Trade*, vol. 4, p. 124.

58. There is an extensive literature on machine-breaking, its causes and consequences. See, for example, Malcolm I. Thomis, *The Luddites: Machine-Breaking in Regency England* (Newton Abbot: David & Charles, 1970); Adrian Randall, *Before the Luddites: Custom, Community and Machinery in the English Woollen Industry, 1776–1809* (Cambridge: Cambridge University Press, 1991); Adrian Randall and A. Charlesworth (eds), *Moral Economy and Popular Protest: Crowds, Conflict and Authority* (New

York: St Martin's, 1999); John E. Archer, *Social Unrest and Popular Protest in England, 1780–1840* (Cambridge: Cambridge University Press, 2000), pp. 52–56.

59. *Journal of the House of Commons* (1780) in Lemire, *British Cotton Trade*, vol. 4, p. 127.

60. *Journal of the House of Commons* (1780) in Lemire, *British Cotton Trade*, vol. 4, p. 128.

61. Anon. [Dorning Rasbotham], *Thoughts on the Use of Machines in the Cotton Manufacture. Addressed to the Working People in that Manufacture and to the Poor in General* (Manchester: J. Harrop, 1780), in Lemire, *British Cotton Trade*, vol. 4, pp. 135, 137.

62. D. A. Farnie, 'Crompton, Samuel (1753–1827)', *Oxford Dictionary of National Biography* (Oxford: Oxford University Press, Sept 2004), online edn, Oct 2007, http://www.oxforddnb.com/view/article/6760, accessed 11 Feb 2010; Michael M. Edwards, *The Growth of the British Cotton Trade, 1780–1815* (Manchester: Manchester University Press, 1967), pp. 7–49.

63. Quoted in Ivy Pinchbeck, *Women Workers and the Industrial Revolution 1750–1850* (London: Virago Books 1981 [1930]), p. 148.

64. Katrina Honeyman, *Child Workers in England, 1780–1820: Parish Apprentices and the Making of the Early Industrial Labour Force* (Aldershot: Ashgate Publishing, 2007), p. 1.

65. David Eltis, 'The Volume and Structure of the Transatlantic Slave Trade: A Reassessment', *William and Mary Quarterly* 55 (2001): 45; see also James A. Rawley and Stephen D. Behrendt, *The Transatlantic Slave Trade: A History*, revised edition (Lincoln, NE: University of Nebraska Press, 2005).

66. Sidney M. Greenfield, 'Slavery and the Plantation in the New World: The Development and Diffusion of a Social Form', *Journal of Inter-American Studies* 11(1) (1969): 44–57; Kenneth Morgan, *Slavery and the British Empire: From Africa to America* (Oxford: Oxford University Press, 2007), pp. 3–4.

67. Colleen Kriger, '"Guinea Cloth": Production and Consumption of Cotton Textiles in West Africa Before and During the Atlantic Slave Trade', in Giorgio Riello and Prasannan Parthasarathi (eds), *The Spinning World: A Global History of Cotton Textiles, 1200–1850* (Oxford: Oxford University Press, 2009), p. 112.

68. Wadsworth and Mann, *Cotton Trade and Industrial Lancashire*, p. 151.

69. *Report from the Committee Related to Chequed and Striped Linens* (1751) in Lemire, *British Cotton Trade*, vol. 3, p. 91.

70. Wadsworth and Mann, *Cotton Trade and Industrial Lancashire*, p. 153.

71. Ann Smart Martin, *Buying into the World of Goods: Early Consumers in Backcountry Virginia* (Baltimore: Johns Hopkins University Press, 2008), pp. 81–2, 173–93.

72. Shane White and Graham White, 'Slave Clothing and African-American Culture in the Eighteenth and Nineteenth Centuries', *Past and Present* no. 148 (1995): 154.

73. The political context of growth in the cotton trade is discussed in O'Brien, Griffiths and Hunt, 'Political Components of the Industrial Revolution' and Patrick O'Brien, 'The Geopolitics of Global Industry: Eurasian Divergence and the Mechanization of Cotton Textile Production in England', in Giorgio Riello and Prasannan Parthasarathi (eds), *The Spinning World: A Global History of Cotton Textiles, 1200–1850* (Oxford: Oxford University Press, 2009), pp. 351–65.

74. Robert S. DuPlessis, 'Cottons Consumption in the Seventeenth- and Eighteenth-Century North Atlantic', in Giorgio Riello and Prasannan Parthasarathi (eds), *The Spinning World: A Global History of Cotton Textiles, 1200–1850* (Oxford: Oxford University Press, 2009), p. 227.

75. The argument was made most forcefully by Eric Williams, *Capitalism and Slavery* (Chapel Hill, NC: University of North Carolina Press, 1944) and has been re-articulated with new emphases by Joseph Inikori, 'Slavery and the Development of Industrial Capitalism in England', in Barbara Solow and Stanley E. Engerman (eds), *British Capitalism and Caribbean Slavery: The Legacy of Eric Williams* (Cambridge: Cambridge University Press, 1987), pp. 79–101 and *Africans and the Industrial Revolution in England: A Study in International Trade and Economic Development* (New York: Cambridge University Press, 2002); see also Ronald Bailey, 'The Other Side of Slavery: Black Labor, Cotton, and Textile Industrialization in Great Britain and the United States', *Agricultural History* 68(2) (1994): 35–50.

76. Eltis, 'Volume and Structure of the Transatlantic Slave Trade', p. 42.

77. For a synthesis of issues and perspectives see Morgan, *Slavery and the British Empire: From Africa to America*.

78. David Eltis and Stanley Engerman, 'The Importance of Slavery and the Slave Trade to Industrializing Britain', *Journal of Economic History* 60(1) (2000): 130.

79. Eltis and Engerman, 'Importance of Slavery and the Slave Trade', pp. 123–41.

80. More on this debate can be found in John Brooke, 'Ecology', in Daniel Vickers (ed.), *A Companion to Colonial America* (Oxford: Blackwell Publishing, 2003), p. 66.

81. Slavery would be abolished throughout the British Empire in 1833.

82. Lakwete, *Inventing the Cotton Gin*, pp. 24–5.

83. Philip D. Morgan, 'Task and Gang Systems: The Organization of Labor on New World Plantations', in Stephen Innes (ed.), *Work and Labor in Early America* (Chapel Hill, NC: University of North Carolina Press, 1988).

84. See, for example, Martin, *Buying into the World of Goods*, pp. 173–93; White and White, 'Slave Clothing and African-American Culture'; Sophie White, '"Wearing Two or Three Handkerchiefs About Him": Slaves' Constructions of Masculinity and Ethnicity in French New Orleans', *Gender and History* 15(3) (2004): 528–49; James Oliver Horton and Lois E. Horton, *Slavery and the Making of America* (Oxford: Oxford University Press, 2005), pp. 50–54.

85. Lakwete, *Inventing the Cotton Gin*, pp. 2–3

86. Edwards, *Growth of the British Cotton Trade*, pp. 90–91.

87. Angela Lakwete shows, however, that Eli Whitney was not the unique inventive genius so long presented. Cotton gins of various sorts had been widely used in Asia and the Americas. Whitney improved the roller mechanism by adding wire teeth that pulled the fibre from the seeds. Planters later adapted the mechanism further, substituting fine-toothed circular saws for the wire teeth. Lakwete, *Inventing the Cotton Gin*.

88. Edwards, *Growth of the British Cotton Trade*, p. 91.

89. Stanley Engerman, 'Slavery and its Consequences for the South', in Stanley Engerman and Robert E. Gallman (eds), *The Cambridge Economic History of the United States*, vol. 1 (Cambridge: Cambridge University Press, 2000), p. 335.

90. Gavin Wright, 'Slavery and American Agricultural History', *Agricultural History* 77(4) (2003): 342.

91. Edward Baptist, *Creating an Old South* (Chapel Hill, NC: University of North Carolina Press, 2002), p. 28.

92. Quoted in Baptist, *Creating an Old South*, p. 33.

93. Susan Dabney Smedes, 'Memorials of a Southern Planter', in Stuart Bruchey (ed.), *Cotton and the Growth of the American Economy: 1790–1860. Sources and Readings* (New York: Harcourt, Brace & World, Inc., 1967), p. 214.

94. Solomon Northup, *Twelve Years a Slave* (New York: C. M. Saxton, 1859, reprinted Bedford, MA: Applewood Books, 2008), pp. 167–8.

95. Engerman, 'Slavery and its Consequences', pp. 337–9.

96. Engerman, 'Slavery and its Consequences', p. 338.

97. Edward Baines, *History of the Cotton Manufacture in Great Britain ...* (London: H. Fisher, R. Fisher and P. Jackson, 1835), p. 378.

98. Katrina Honeyman, *The Origins of Enterprise: Business Leadership in the Industrial Revolution* (Manchester: Manchester University Press, 1982), pp. 77–83.

99. William Radcliffe, *Origin of the New System of Manufacture, Commonly Called 'Power-Loom Weaving' ...* (Stockport: J. Lomax, 1828), p. 10.

100. Radcliffe, *Origin of Power-Loom Weaving*, p. 67.

101. Radcliffe, *Origin of Power-Loom Weaving*, p. 12.

102. Pinchbeck, *Women Workers*, p. 164.

103. Sydney Pollard, 'Labour in Great Britain', in Peter Mathias and M. M. Postan (eds), *The Cambridge Economic History of Europe. The Industrial Economies: Capital, Labour and Enterprise*, vol. 7, part 2 (Cambridge: Cambridge University Press, 1978), p. 131.

104. There is a voluminous literature on trade unionism in nineteenth-century Britain, including the textile trades. More recently, studies of this sort have come to incorporate

gender analysis in the assessment of trade union activities for both male and female activists. See, for example, E. P. Thompson, *The Making of the English Working Class* (Harmondsworth: Penguin Books, 1963); Anna Clark, *The Struggle for the Breeches: Gender and the Making of the British Working Class* (Berkeley: University of California Press, 1995); Alastair J. Reid, *United We Stand: A History of Britain's Trade Unions* (London: Penguin Group, 2004); Patrick Joyce, *The Historical Meanings of Work* (Cambridge: Cambridge University Press, 1987); S. S. Chapman, *The Cotton Industry in the Industrial Revolution*, 2nd edition (Basingstoke: Macmillan, 1987).

105. This attitude was reflected by William Pitt, who wrote in 1796 that 'Experience has already shown how much could be done by the industry of children, and the advantage of early employing them in such branches of manufacture as they were capable to execute.' Quoted in Honeyman, *Child Workers in England*, p. 5.

106. E. A. Wrigley and R. S. Schofield, *The Population History of England and Wales, 1541–1871* (Cambridge: Cambridge University Press, 1989), p. 217; M. J. Daunton, *Progress and Poverty: An Economic and Social History of Britain 1700–1850* (Oxford: Oxford University Press, 1995), p. 574.

107. Honeyman, *Child Workers in England*, p. 69.

108. Honeyman, *Child Workers in England*, pp. 71–89.

109. Frances Trollope, *The Life and Adventures of Michael Armstrong, the Factory Boy* (London: Henry Colburn, 1840). This novel exemplifies these sort of melodramatic tales.

110. This Act was a virtual dead letter from its inception, as enforcement depended on activist Justices of the Peace in each community. Still, it did articulate the minimum standards acceptable for male and female apprentices in this era.

111. Honeyman, *Child Workers in England*, p. 89.

112. Honeyman, *Child Workers in England*, p. 261.

113. Jane Humphries, *Childhood and Child Labour in the British Industrial Revolution* (Cambridge: Cambridge University Press, 2010), p. 30.

114. Baines, *History of the Cotton Manufacture*, p. 6.

115. François Crouzet, *The Victorian Economy* (London: Routledge, 1982), p. 199.

116. James Walvin, *English Urban Life, 1776–1851* (London: Hutchinson, 1984), pp. 11–18.

117. Quoted in Walvin, *English Urban Life*, p. 19.

118. Frances Collier notes the 'glowing reports' in the 1830s given to the housing of mill owner Thomas Ashton, who built 300 homes for his workforce, each comprised of a sitting room, kitchen, pantry, several bedrooms and a walled garden area. 'The women appear to have taken pride in these model dwellings, for the cleanliness and comfort of their homes made this factory colony an object of wonder and admiration.' Exceptional conditions brought significant attention. Frances Collier, *The Family Economy of the Working Classes in the Cotton Industry, 1784–1833* (Manchester: Manchester University Press, 1964), p. 50.

119. See, for example, the plan of industrial development implemented in northern Italy. Giovanni Luigi Fontana and Giorgio Riello, 'Seamless Industrialization: The Lanificio Rossi and the Modernization of the Wool Textile Industry in Nineteenth-Century Italy', *Textile History* 36(2) (2005): 168–95.

120. For example, French machine-makers brought the spinning jenny to the textile town of Barcelona in 1784. See K. J. Thomson, 'Transferring the Spinning Jenny to Barcelona: An Apprenticeship in the Technology of the Industrial Revolution', *Textile History* 34(1) (2003): 21–46; the subject is also widely addressed in Douglas A. Farnie and David Jeremy (eds), *The Fibre That Changed the World: The Cotton Industry in International Perspective, 1600–1900s* (Oxford: Oxford University Press, 2004).

121. David Jeremy, *Transatlantic Industrial Revolution: The Diffusion of Textile Technologies Between Britain and America, 1790–1830s* (Cambridge, MA: Massachusetts Institute of Technology Press, 1981).

122. Sara E. Wermiel, 'Major Entrepreneurs and Companies', in Kevin Hillstrom and Laurie Collier Hillstrom (eds), *The Industrial Revolution in America: Textiles*, vol. 6 (Santa Barbara, CA: ABC-CLIO, 2006), pp. 53–4.

123. Hood, *The Weaver's Craft*, p. 153.

124. Quoted in Thomas Dublin, *Transforming Women's Work: New England Lives in the Industrial Revolution* (Ithaca, NY: Cornell University Press, 1994), pp. 77–8.

125. Dublin, *Transforming Women's Work*, pp. 79–89.

126. Dublin, *Transforming Women's Work*, p. 95.

127. Harriet H. Robinson, 'Early Factory Labor in New England', in *Fourteenth Annual Report of the Bureau of Statistics of Labor* (Boston: Wright & Potter, 1883), p. 387.

128. E. J. Hobsbawm, *Industry and Empire: The Making of Modern English Society, vol. 2 1750 to the Present Day* (New York: Pantheon, 1968), p. 40.

129. For a contemporary perspective on cotton and globalization, see Pietra Rivoli, *The Travels of a T-Shirt in the Global Economy: An Economist Examines the Markets, Power, and Politics of World Trade*, 2nd edition (Hoboken, NJ: John Wiley & Sons Inc., 2009).

130. Ruth Barnes, *Indian Block-Printed Textiles in Egypt: The Newberry Collection in the Ashmolean Museum, Oxford*, vol. 1 (Oxford: Clarendon Press, 1997), p. 107.

131. Prasannan Parthasarathi and Ian Wendt, 'Decline in Three Keys: Indian Cotton Manufacturing from the Late Eighteenth Century', in Giorgio Riello and Prasannan Parthasarathi (eds), *The Spinning World: A Global History of Cotton Textiles, 1200–1850* (Oxford: Oxford University Press, 2009), pp. 397–407.

132. Quoted in Parthasarathi and Wendt, 'Decline in Three Keys', p. 399.

133. See, for example, Kaoru Sugihara, 'The Resurgence of Intra-Asian Trade, 1800–1850', in Giorgio Riello and Tirthankar Roy (eds), *How India Clothes the World: The World of South Asian Textiles, 1500–1850* (Leiden: Brill, 2009), pp. 139–69. Sugihara states that: 'The survival and revitalization of regional trade in Asia suggest the need for a fundamental rethinking of our understanding of the prime movers of world trade' (169).

134. Parthasarathi and Wendt, 'Decline in Three Keys', p. 405.

135. See Chapter 5 for the connection between the decline in spinning and rise of quilting as illustrated among Pennsylvania residents, following the industrialization of spinning.

136. Sven Beckert, 'Emancipation and Empire: Reconstructing the Worldwide Web of Cotton Production in the Age of the American Civil War', *American Historical Review* 109(5) (2004): 1408–9.

137. Sven Beckert assesses the global implications of these events. 'The struggles that resulted in abolition were drawn out and often violent. Labor lords throughout the world resisted the emancipation of their workers, but faced with the determined resistance of slaves, declining support from metropolitan elites, diminishing influence over national governments, and a growing abolitionist movement, they gave way.' Sven Beckert, 'Reconstructing the Empire of Cotton: A Global Story', in Manisha Sinha and Penny Marie Von Eschen (eds), *Contested Democracy: Freedom, Race, and Power in American History* (New York: Columbia University Press, 2007), p. 164.

5. CRAFTING COMFORT, CRAFTING CULTURE

1. Ralli quilts (appliquéd cotton quilts), for example, were widely made in the north-west Indus River region, where the geometric patterns found on many of the quilts can be found on surviving ancient ceramics. Patricia Ormsby Stoddard, *Ralli Quilts: Traditional Textiles from Pakistan and India* (Atglen, PA: Schiffer Publishing, 2003), pp. 103–9.

2. Jonathan Holstein, 'Sister Quilts from Sicily: A Pair of Renaissance Bedcovers', *Quilt Journal* 3(2) (1994) and Margaret Renner Lidz, 'Mystery of Seventeenth-Century Quilts', *Antiques* (December 1998): 834–43.

3. Averil Colby, *Quilting* (New York: Charles Scribner's Sons, 1971); Kathryn Berenson, *Quilts of Provence: The Art and Craft of French Quiltmaking* (New York: H. Holt, 1996).

4. 'The Itinerary of Ludovico de Varthema of Bologna from 1502 to 1508', trans. John Winter Jones, *SOAS Bulletin of Burma Research* 2(2) (2004): 125, 121.

5. *The Book of Duarte Barbosa. An Account of the Countries Bordering on the Indian Ocean and their Inhabitants, Written by Duarte Barbosa, and Completed about the Year 1518 A.D.* Translated from the Portuguese text, first published in 1812 by

the Royal Academy of Sciences at Lisbon, in vol. II of its *Collection of Documents Regarding the History and Geography of the Nations Beyond the Seas*. Vol. II (London: Hakluyt Society, 1921), pp. 75–6.

6. *The Voyage of François Pyrard of Laval to the East Indies, the Maldives, the Moluccas and Brazil,* translated into English from the Third French Edition of 1619, and edited with notes by Albert Gray ... (London: Hakluyt Society, 1888), p. 246.

7. Pyrard, *Voyage*, p. 246.

8. Pyrard, *Voyage*, p. 328.

9. James C. Boyajian, *Portuguese Trade in Asia under the Habsburgs, 1580–1640* (Baltimore: Johns Hopkins University Press, 1993), p. 14; see also Geneviève Bouchon, 'Glimpses of the Beginnings of the "Carreira Da India" (1500–1518)' in Teotonio R. de Souza (ed.), *Indo-Portuguese History. Old Issues, New Questions* (New Delhi: Concept Publishing, 1985), pp. 41–2; K. S. Mathew, *Indo-Portuguese Trade and the Fuggers of Germany: Sixteenth Century* (New Delhi: Manohar, 1997), especially Chapter 5.

10. The first English ambassador in the Indian court brought with him miniatures and portraits of royal subjects, which were subsequently copied by Indian artists. Such visual exchanges were commonplace in this era. Frances Morris, 'An Indian Hanging', *The Metropolitan Museum of Art Bulletin* 20(6) (June 1925): 150.

11. Maria Jose de Mendoça, 'Some Kinds of Indo-Portuguese Quilts in the Collection of the Museu de Arte Antiga', in *Embroidered Quilts From the Museu Nacional de Arte Antiga, Lisboa* (London: Kensington Palace, 1978), pp. 13–14.

12. Di Varthema, 'Itinerary of Ludovico di Varthema of Bologna', pp. 119–21.

13. *The Suma Oriental of Tomé Pires: An Account of the East, from the Red Sea to Japan, Written in Malacca and India in 1512–1515 and The Book of Francisco Rodrigues Rutter of a Voyage in the Red Sea, Nautical Rules, Almanack and Maps, Written and Drawn in the East before 1515*. Translated from the Portuguese MS in the Bibliothèque de la Chambre des Députés, Paris, and edited by Armando Cortesão (London, Hakluyt Society, 1944), vol. 1, pp. 19, 48.

14. See, for example, Figures 8, 9, 10, and 11 in Rosemary Crill, 'The Earliest Surviving Example? The Indian Embroideries at Hardwick Hall', in Rosemary Crill (ed.), *Textiles from India: The Global Trade* (Calcutta: Seagull Press, 2006), pp. 256–9.

15. John Irwin, 'Indian Textile Trade in the Seventeenth Century: Bengal', *Journal of Indian Textile History* 3 (1957): 63.

16. R. W. Connell, 'The Big Picture: Masculinity in Recent World History', *Theory and Society* 22(5) (1993): 608 and also R. W. Connell, *Masculinities*, 2nd edition (Cambridge: Polity Press, 2005), Chapter 8. For examples of Indo-Portuguese quilt motifs, see Maria Alice Beaumont, *Fábulas Bordadas: Uma colcha indo-portuguese do séc. XVII* (Lisbon: Museu Nacional de Arte Antiga, 1988); Mendoça, *Embroidered*; Jasleen Dhamija, *Asian Embroidery* (New Delhi: Abhinav Publications, 2004), pp. 67–84. See also Fernando Antonio Baptista Pereira, 'Cuatro Notas Sobre el Arte en Portugal en el Tiempo de los Felipes', in *Las Sociedades Ibericas y el Mar a finales de siglo XVI* (Lisbon: Exposición Mundial de Lisboa, 1998), pp. 76, 78.

17. T 438-1882, Victoria and Albert Museum, London.

18. I50-1869, Victoria and Albert Museum, London. A similar embroidered coverlet, depicting European maritime vessels, is held at the Museum of Fine Arts, Boston.

19. Thierry-Nicolas Tschaloff, *La Route des Indes. Les Indes et l'Europe: Échanges artistiques et Héritage Común 1650–1850*. Musée des Arts Décoratifs, Musée d'Aquitaine, Bordeaux. (Paris: Somogy éditions d'art, 1998), pp. 104–5, 120–21.

20. Boyajian, *Portuguese Trade in Asia*, p. 140. Four Indian quilts were included among the objects sent to Morocco in thanks for the return of the body of King Sebastião on his ill-fated crusade against that country in 1578. Mendoça, *Embroidered Quilts*, p. 15.

21. Janet Rae, *Quilts of the British Isles* (New York: E. P. Dutton Inc., 1987), p. 13.

22. Angela Delaforce, 'The Collection of Antonio Pérez, Secretary of State to Philip II', *The Burlington Magazine* 124: 957 (Dec 1982): 742, 747; Angela Delaforce, Review: 'Lisbon. Artes Decorativas Portuguesas', *The Burlington Magazine* 123: 945 (Dec 1981): 770; Martin A. S. Hume, 'Antonio Perez in Exile', *Transactions of the Royal Historical Society* 8 (1894): 71–107.

23. An Moonen, *'t is al Beddegoet: Nederlandse Antieke Quilts 1650–1900* (Uitgeverij Terra: Warnsveld, 1986), p. 7. I thank Marijke Kerkhoven for translating notes from this text for me.

24. Por Maria Paz Aguilo Alonso, 'El Coleccionism de Objetos Procendentes de Ultramar a Travers de los Inventario de los Siglos XVI y XVII', *Relaciones Artisticas Entre Espana y America* (Madrid: Consejo Sperior de Investigaciones Científicas, 1990), pp. 118, 128–9.

25. James Boyajian finds that: 'By the 1580s no wealthy household of the Iberian overseas colonies would be without the finest cloths for furnishings, *cochas* (Indian bedspreads) and suitable wall hangings of various colours embroidered with silk …' Boyajian, *Portuguese Trade in Asia*, pp. 141–2.

26. 44'28/404, 25 Sept 1567, Leicestershire, Leicester and Rutland Record Office.

27. James Orchard Halliwell (ed.), *Ancient Inventories of Furniture, Pictures, Tapestry, Plate, etc. illustrative of the Domestic Manners of the English in the Sixteenth and Seventeenth Centuries …* (London, 1854), pp. 122, 123, 125–6, 129, 131.

28. A 1610 inventory from that family included a cupboard cloth of 'Indyan stuff', along with cushions, and 'fower newe curteans, never used' of the same. Halliwell, *Ancient*, p. 78.

29. Santina M. Levy, *Elizabethan Treasures: The Hardwick Hall Textiles* (London: National Trust, 1999), pp. 9–15, and 28–9; Crill, 'The Earliest Survivors? The Indian Embroideries at Hardwick Hall', pp. 245–58.

30. 6729/7/119, 21 Dec 1594, Surrey History Centre.

31. S. W. A. Drossaers and T. H. Lunsingh Scheurleer, *Inventarissen van de Inboedels in de Verblijven van de Oranjes en daarmede gelijk te stellen stukken 1567–1795* ('s-Gravenhage: Verkrijgbaar bij Martinus Nijhoff, 1974), vol. I.

32. Quilts were understood by literate consumers to be exotic commodities, routinely described in travel literature or in foreign depictions of Ottoman, Indian or other South East Asian domestic settings. A popular 1623 Spanish novel, translated into English, mentioned a quilt or *colcha* in such a manner, as Spain was among the first regions to enthusiastically adopt Indian goods. See, for example, William Davies, *A true relation of the travailes and most miserable captivitie of William Davies, … Wherein is try set downe the manner of his taking, the long time of his slaverie and means of his deliverie …* (London, 1614) n.p.; Pierre d'Avity, *The Estates, Empires and Principalities of the World … The Estage of the Emperor of Morocco …* (1615), p. 1125; Adam Olearius, *The voyages and travels of the ambassadors sent by Frederick, Duke of Holstein, to the Great Duke of Muscovy and the King of Persia …* (1669), p. 114; Mateo Alemán, *The Rogue: or the Life of Guzman de Alfarche …* (1623), p. 19.

33. *English Factories in India, 1622–1621*, quoted in Alice Baldwin Beer, *Trade Goods: A Study of Indian Chintz in the Collection of the Cooper-Hewitt Museum of Decorative Arts and Design, Smithsonian Institution* (Washington, DC: Smithsonian Institution, 1970), p. 26.

34. Quoted in Margaret Renner Lidz, 'The Mystery of Seventeenth-Century Quilts', *The Magazine Antiques* 154(6) (Dec 1998): 836.

35. A 1628 royal proclamation attempted to end all private trade, without success. Robert Steele, *A Bibliography of Royal Proclamations of the Tudor and Stuart Sovereigns … 1485–1714* (1910, reprinted New York: Burt Franklin, 1967), vol. 1, p. 181, no. 1535.

36. Lynne Bassett and Jack Larkin, *Northern Comfort: New England's Early Quilts 1780–1850* (Nashville, TN: Rutledge Hill Press, 1998), p. 12; Philip Carter, 'Fairfax, Thomas, Sixth Lord Fairfax of Cameron (1693–1781)', *Oxford Dictionary of National Biography*, Oxford University Press, 2004, online edn, http://www.oxforddnb.com/view/article/9094, accessed 4 Dec 2009.

37. Unfortunately, the monochromatic face of this object makes it exceedingly difficult to reproduce effectively.

38. John Irwin and Margaret Hall, *Indian Embroideries: Historic Textiles of India at the Calico Museum* (Ahmedabad: Calico Museum of Textiles, 1973), pp. 2, 29–30, 35–6. Agnes Geijer, *Oriental Textiles in Sweden* (Copenhagen: Rosenkilde and Bagger, 1951), pp. 73–5, 119–20; Baldwin Beer, *Trade Goods*, p. 27.

39. Olivier Raveux, 'Armenian Networks in the Trade and Production of Calicoes in the

Mediterranean During the Last Third of the Seventeenth Century', unpublished paper presented at the conference of the American Historical Association, San Diego, 8 January 2010.

40. Giorgio Riello, 'Fabricating the Domestic: The Material Culture of Textiles and Social Life of the Home in Early Modern Europe', in Beverly Lemire (ed.), *The Force of Fashion in Politics and Society: Global Perspectives from Early Modern to Contemporary Times* (Aldershot: Ashgate, 2010).

41. Quoted in G. P. Baker, *Calico Printing and Painting in the East Indies in the XVIIth and XVIIIth Centuries* (London, Edward Arnold, 1921), p. 33.

42. 'A Particular of Goods'; *Cargoe, of two Ships Arrived from India the 19th and 20th of June 1685. viz. The Henry and William from the Bay of Bengal, and the East-India Merchant, from Surrat* (London, 1685); and *Cargoe, of two Ships from Surrat, Arrived the 25th of July, 1685. viz. Charles the 2d. and the Asia* (London, 1685); *Journal of the House of Commons*, 5 February 1699/1700, in Beverly Lemire (ed.), *The British Cotton Trade* (London: Pickering & Chatto, 2009), vol. 1, pp. 185–204, 325–33.

43. Randle Holme, *The Academy of Armoury* (1688), quoted in Clare Browne, 'Making and Using Quilts in Eighteenth-Century Britain', in Sue Pritchard (ed.), *Quilts 1700–2010: Hidden Histories, Untold Stories* (London: V&A Publishing, 2010), p. 25.

44. TNA, PROB 5, 2268, 3731, 3790, 3961; GL, Ms 9174/28; OA, W P 25 May 1704, City of London Corporation, London Metropolitan Archives. See also Beverly Lemire, *Fashion's Favourite: The Cotton Trade and the Consumer in Britain, 1660–1800* (Oxford: Oxford University Press, 1991), Chapter 1.

45. Quoted in Lemire, *Fashion's Favourite*, p. 16.

46. Simon Schama, *The Embarrassment of Riches: An Interpretation of Dutch Culture in the Golden Age* (Berkeley: University of California Press, 1988), pp. 377, 375–97.

47. Daniel Roche, *The Culture of Clothing: Dress and Fashion in the Ancient Regime*, trans. Jean Birrell (Cambridge: Cambridge University Press, 1994), pp. 152–3; see also Georges Vigarello, *Concepts of Cleanliness: Changing Attitudes in France Since the Middle Ages*, trans. Jean Birrell

(Cambridge: Cambridge University Press, 1988).

48. John Pechey, *The general treatise of the diseases of maids, bigbellied women, child-bed-women, and widows . . .* (London, 1696), p. 126.

49. Tomas Maldonado and John Cullars, 'The Idea of Comfort', *Design Issues* 8(1) (1991): 39.

50. Cr1368 vol. 1/29, 22 October 1700, Warwickshire County Record Office.

51. Baldwin Beer, *Trade Goods*, p. 33.

52. AR/25/86/1, 2, 8 March 1697/8. Cornwall Record Office.

53. John E. Crowley, 'The Sensibility of Comfort', *American Historical Review* 104(3) (1999): 750.

54. Mark Overton, Jane Whittle, Darron Dean and Andrew Hann, *Production and Consumption in English Households, 1600–1750* (London: Routledge, 2004), pp. 110–13, 125; Lorna Weatherill, *Consumer Behaviour and Material Culture in Britain, 1660–1760* (London: Routledge, 1988) pp. 159–61; see also H. Dibbits, 'Between Society and Family Values: The Linen Cupboard in Early Modern Households', in A. Schuurman and P. Spierenburg (eds), *Private Domain, Public Enquiry: Families and Life-Styles in the Netherlands and Europe, 1550 to the Present* (Hilversum, NL: Verloren, 1996), pp. 125–45.

55. Crowley, 'Sensibility of Comfort', p. 752.

56. 'Sparse' is the relative term Lorna Weatherill applies. Weatherill, *Consumer Behaviour and Material Culture*, p. 6.

57. Beverly Lemire, *Dress, Culture and Commerce: The English Clothing Trade Before the Factory, 1660–1800* (Basingstoke: Macmillan, 1997), pp. 68–9.

58. *A general description of all trades, digested in alphabetical order: by which parents, guardians, and trustees, may, with greater ease and certainty, make choice of trades agreeable to the capacity, education, inclination, strength, and fortune of the youth under their care* (London, 1747), pp. 178–9.

59. For examples of more highly valued calico quilts, see: 2 July 1685 ref. tl6840702-38, 9 October 1689 ref. tl6891009-7, 8 May 1695 ref. tl6950508-26, 11 October 1699 ref. tl6991011-2, 7 December 1709 ref. tl7091207-41, 8 July 1718 ref. tl7130708-18, 12 October 1715 ref. tl7151012-36, 13 January 1716 ref.

tl7160113-37. And for cheaper examples of calico quilts, see also: 8 December 1697 ref. tl6971208-16, 13 October 1708 ref. tl7081013-27, 18 April 1710 ref. tl7100418-18, 17 May 1716 ref. tl7160517-35. Old Bailey Online, http://www.oldbaileyonline.org/, accessed 4 October 2007.

60. 8 July 1713 ref. tl7130708-18. Old Bailey Online, http://www.oldbaileyonline.org/, accessed 4 October 2007.

61. *The Case of the Quilt-Makers* (London, 1720?).

62. *Weekly Journal or Saturday's Post*, 24 November 1722, 1 December 1722, 8 December 1722, 22 December 1722. *Daily Courant*, 24 December 1722.

63. *Daily Journal*, 30 April 1724; *Weekly Journal or British Gazetteer*, 2 May 1724.

64. For example: *Daily Courant*, 16 April 1729; *Daily Post*, 1 February 1731; *London Evening Post*, 1 June 1732; *Daily Post*, 3 July 1733; *Daily Advertiser*, 18 February 1743.

65. This important pattern of theft was first identified by John Beattie. Later histories of theft and the second-hand trade further contextualized this phenomenon. J. M. Beattie, *Crime and the Courts in England, 1660–1800* (Princeton: Princeton University Press, 1986); Beverly Lemire, 'Consumerism in Preindustrial and Early Industrial England: The Trade in Second-hand Clothes', *Journal of British Studies* 27(1) (1988): 1–24; Lemire, *Fashion's Favourite*, Chapter 3; Lemire, *Dress, Culture and Commerce*, Chapters 4 and 5; Beverly Lemire, *The Business of Everyday Life: Gender, Practice and Social Politics in England, c.1600–1900* (Manchester: Manchester University Press, 2005), Chapter 4; Garthine Walker, 'Women, Theft and the World of Stolen Goods', in Jenny Kermode and Garthine Walker (eds), *Women, Crime and the Courts in Early Modern England* (London: University College of London Press, 1994); Laurence Fontaine, 'Women's Economic Sphere and Credit in Pre-Industrial Europe', in B. Lemire, R. Pearson and G. Campbell (eds), *Women and Credit: Researching the Past, Refiguring the Future* (Oxford: Berg, 2002); Elizabeth M. Sanderson, '"Nearly New": The Second-Hand Clothing Trade in Eighteenth-Century Edinburgh', *Costume* 21 (1997): 38–48; Patricia Allerston, 'Reconstructing the Second-Hand

Clothes Trade in Sixteenth- and Seventeenth-Century Venice', *Costume*, 33 (1999): 46–56; Harald Deceulaer, 'Entrepreneurs in the Guilds: Ready-to-Wear Clothing and Subcontracting in Late Sixteenth and Early Seventeenth-Century Antwerp', *Textile History* 31(2) (2000): 133–49; Miles Lambert, '"Cast-Off Wearing Apparel": The Consumption and Distribution of Second-Hand Clothing in Northern England During the Long Eighteenth Century', *Textile History* 35(1) (2004): 1–26; Carole Collier Frick, 'The Florentine Arigattieri: Second-Hand Clothing Dealers and the Circulation of Goods in the Renaissance', in Alexandra Palmer and Hazel Clark (eds), *Old Clothes, New Looks: Second-Hand Fashion* (Oxford: Berg, 2004).

66. 25 April 1726 ref. tl7260425-2; 21 July 1736 ref. tl7360721-28; 13 October 1736 ref. tl7361013-3; 14 January 1737 ref. tl7370114-30; Old Bailey Online, http://www.oldbaileyonline.org/, accessed 4 October 2007.

67. John Styles, 'Lodging at the Old Bailey. Lodgings and their Furnishing in Eighteenth-Century London', in John Styles and Amanda Vickery (eds), *Gender, Taste and Material Culture in Britain and North America* (New Haven: Yale Center for British Art, 2006), p. 74.

68. 9 July 1740, ref. tl7400709-41, Old Bailey Online, http://www.oldbaileyonline.org/, accessed 4 October 2007.

69. 9 July 1740, ref. t17400709-41, Old Bailey Online, http://www.oldbaileyonline.org/, accessed 4 October 2007.

70. 15 May 1746, Proceedings of the Old Bailey ref: tl7460515-23, Old Bailey Online, http://www.oldbaileyonline.org/, accessed 4 October 2007.

71. 23 May 1751, ref. tl7510523-37, Old Bailey Online, http://www.oldbaileyonline.org/, accessed 4 October 2007.

72. 23 May 1751, ref. tl7510523-37, Old Bailey Online, http://www.oldbaileyonline.org/, accessed 4 October 2007.

73. For an illustration of a British-made quilt featuring Queen Caroline, a figure of wide popular appeal from 1815–20, see Rae, *Quilts of the British Isles*, pp. 32–3. For American examples, see Linda Eaton, *Quilts in the Material World: Selections from the Winterthur Collection* (New York: Abrams in association with The Henry Francis du Pont Winterthur Museum,

2007), pp. 140–61; Lynne Zacek Bassett (ed.), *Massachusetts Quilts* (Hanover, NH: University Press of New England, 2009), pp. 194–5.

74. The multi-faceted associations of quilts were explored by twentieth-century artists like Joyce Wieland in *Reason Over Passion* (quilt 1968) and David McDairmid. See Iris Nowell, *Joyce Wieland: A Life in Art* (Toronto: ECW Press, 2001); Sally Gray, 'Reinterpreting a Textile Tradition: David McDairmid's Ecstatic and Utopian *Klub Kwilt*', *Textile History* 38(2) (2007): 198–210.

75. OD/691, 6 November 1731, Sheffield Archives.

76. Ann Rosalind Jones and Peter Stallybrass, *Renaissance Clothing and the Materials of Memory* (Cambridge: Cambridge University Press, 2000), p. 2.

77. D1296, 1781, Dorset Record Office; P95/28/1, Bedfordshire and Luton Archives and Record Services; 1326/5, Shropshire Archives; 665/5925, Shropshire Archives.

78. 2868/2, 29 May 1760, Shropshire Archives.

79. *General Advertiser*, 1 September 1752, quoted in Browne, 'Making and Using Quilts', p. 24.

80. Lemire, *Fashion's Favourite*, p. 126.

81. Giorgio Riello, 'Asian Knowledge and the Development of Calico Printing in Europe in the Seventeenth and Eighteenth Centuries', *Journal of Global History* 5(1) (2010): 1–28.

82. For the example of US connections between factory cotton production and the spread of cotton quilt-making, see Rachel Maines, 'Paradigms of Scarcity and Abundance: The Quilt as an Artifact of the Industrial Revolution', *In the Heart of Pennsylvania: Symposium Papers* (Lewisburg, PA: Oral Traditions Project of the Union County Historical Society, 1986), p. 84.

83. Patchwork quilts were traditionally made in other parts of the world and this tradition continues. In India, Ralli patchworks were typically produced in the north-west border regions of what is now India and Pakistan. However, Western patchwork takes different forms than the Ralli quilts. See, for example, Stoddard, *Ralli Quilts*.

84. Vagabonds were described according to their looks, as in this 1566 example, which termed them 'rowsey, ragged rabblement of rakehells'. Thomas Harman, *A Caveat or Warning for Common Cursetors, Vulgarly Called Vagabonds ...*

For the Utility and Profit of his Natural Country ... (1566, reprinted London, T. Bensley, 1814), p.i.

85. Carole Shammas, 'The Decline of Textile Prices in England and British America Prior to Industrialization', *Economic History Review* 47 (1994): 483–507.

86. See http://collections.vam.ac.uk/item/ O165092/bed-cover/, accessed 3 August 2010.

87. James Bland, *An Essay in Praise of Women: Or, a Looking-glass for Ladies To see their PERFECTIONS in ...* (London, 1733), p. 189.

88. *The Female Spectator*, vol. 3, book 15, (1744–6), p. 158.

89. *The New Lady's Magazine; Or, Polite Entertaining Companion for the Fair Sex: Entirely Devoted to their Use and Amusement ...* (London, May 1787), p. 232.

90. 20 February 1771, ref. t17710220-63, Old Bailey Online, http://www.oldbaileyonline.org/, accessed 4 October 2007.

91. This quilt, composed of silk, linen and cotton elements, found its way to Montreal and is described as 'the second-oldest silk patchwork quilt known to exist in the Western world'. McCord Museum, Montreal. See http://www. mccord-museum.qc.ca/en/collection/artifacts/ M972.3.1&section=196?Lang=1&accessnumbe r=M972.3.1&section=196, accessed 22 October 2007.

92. 20 February 1771, ref. t17710220-63, Old Bailey Online, http://www.oldbaileyonline.org/, accessed 4 October 2007. Also, DD/1499/2, Nottinghamshire Archives; D96/53, Herefordshire Record Office.

93. Moonen, *'t is al Beddegoet*, Figures 18 and 19.

94. An Moonen, *Quilts, een Nederlandse traditie* (Quilts, the Dutch Tradition) (Arnhem: Nederlands Openluchtmuseum, 1992) pp. 136, 152.

95. Letter from Jane Austen to Cassandra Austen, 31 May 1811, in R. W. Chapman (ed.), *Jane Austen's Letters to her Sister Cassandra and Others*, 2nd ed., (Oxford: Oxford University Press, 1952), p. 286.

96. Countess of Wilton (ed.), *The Illuminated Book of Needlework: Comprising Knitting, Netting, Crochet, and Embroidery ... Preceded by a History of Needlework, Including An Account of the Ancient Historical Tapestries* (London: Henry G. Bohn,

1847), pp.v, 1. Mrs Owen is the designer of the patterns included in this volume and Countess Wilton the author of the text.

97. *Illuminated Book of Needlework*, p. 5.

98. *Miss Weeton's Journal of a Governess*, revised epilogue by Edward Hall (New York, 1969), vol. 2, p. 331.

99. *Miss Weeton's Journal*, vol. 2, p. 325.

100. *Miss Weeton's Journal*, vol. 2, p. 325.

101. Scott Robson and Sharon MacDonald, *Old Nova Scotia Quilts* (Halifax: Nimbus Publishing, 1995), p. 15. My thanks to Sharon MacDonald for this reference.

102. Susan Prendergast Schoelwer, 'Form, Function, and Meaning in the Use of Fabric Furnishings: A Philadelphia Case Study', *Winterthur Portfolio* 14(1) (1979): 27. Note that this form of furnishing assumed importance over a century later than in the Spanish colonies.

103. Patricia J. Keller, 'Spinning Quilt History: Household Textile Production and Quilt-making in Lancaster County, Pennsylvania, 1750–1884' unpublished paper presented in the 'Object Centered History' seminar, 14th Berkshire Conference, Minneapolis, June 2008. This is part of a larger project on Pennsylvania quilts on which Keller is working.

104. Patricia Keller, 'Taking Inventory: Quilts and Quiltmaking in Chester County, Pennsylvania, 1725–1860', in Catherine E. Hutchins (ed.), *Layers: Unfolding the Stories of Chester County Quilts* (Philadelphia, PA: Pearl Pressman Liberty and Chester County Historical Society, 2009), p. 70. For discussion of the textile composition of Chester County quilts over time, see also Adrienne Hood, 'Cloth and Color: Fabrics in Chester County Quilts' in Hutchins, *Layers*, pp. 79–104.

105. For American examples, Catherine Maria Sedgewick, *Home* (1835), p. 139; Catherine Maria Sedgewick, *The Poor Rich Man and the Rich Poor Man* (1836), pp. 104–5; Mary Jane Holmes, *Millibank; or, Roger Irving's Ward. A Novel* (1871), p. 364; Harriet Beecher Stowe, *Oldtown Fireside Stories* (1872), p. 184; and for Canadian examples, Susanna Moodie, *Roughing it in the Bush, or, Life in Canada* (1871), pp. 126, 155–6; Mary Agnes FitzGibbon, *A Trip to Manitoba* (London, 1880), p. 78; Lily Douglas, *What Necessity Knows* (New York,

1893), p. 131; Katherine A. Clarke, *Lyrical Echoes* (1899), pp. 150–51.

106. Thomas Hulme, *Early Western Travels, Vol. 10: Julme's Journal, 1818–1819 …* (Cleveland, OH, 1904), p. 300.

107. Samuel Strickland, *Twenty-Seven Years in Canada West, or, The Experience of an Early Settler* (London, 1853), p. 295. This is far from the only mention of male quilting prowess. Karen Hansen explores the practice of Brigham Nims, without whose diary we would have less evidence of the circumstances in which at least some men would engage in quilting. Karen V. Hansen, '"Helped Put in a Quilt": Men's Work and Male Intimacy in Nineteenth-Century New England', *Gender and Society* 3(3) (1989).

108. In the Metropolitan Museum of Art, New York, for example, see the honeycomb quilt, circa 1830, made by Elizabeth Van Horne Clarkson, possibly for a wedding present for her son. Ref. 23.80.75, Metropolitan Museum of Art, New York. See also the sunburst quilt, cotton, attributed to Rebecca Scattergood Savery, Philadelphia, 1835–45, held in the American Folk Art Museum, New York, 1979.26.2. Or of the published examples of women's quilt production, see Amelia Peck, '"A Marvel of Woman's Ingenious and Intellectual Industry": The Adeline Harris Sears Autograph Quilt', *Metropolitan Museum Journal* 33 (1998): 263–90.

109. Campaigns to document and preserve regional quilt histories have multiplied in the last thirty years throughout the Atlantic world, though also in New Zealand and Australia. These campaigns represent an important movement to recover and preserve material history, as well as the social context for the production and use of quilts. Design history has also benefited from this broad project. Collectively, great strides have been made in quilt history. See the Quilt Index for further discussion of this initiative and in particular, the essay under the heading 'Exhibition Hall', http://www.quiltindex.org/index.php, accessed 17 July 2008. The University of Nebraska is the site of an exceptional research centre on this subject: the International Quilt Study Center and Museum.

110. Ann Smart Martin, *Buying into the World of Goods: Early Consumers in Backcountry Virginia* (Baltimore: Johns Hopkins University Press, 2008), p. 176.

111. See, for example, Darlene Clark Hine and Kathleen Thompson, *A Shining Thread of Hope: The History of Black Women in America* (New York: Broadway Books, 1998), p. 187; Mary E. Lyons, *Stitching Stars: The Story Quilts of Harriet Powers* (New York: Atheneum, 1993); and Anita Zaleski Weinraub (ed.), *Georgia Quilts: Piecing Together a History* (Athens, GA: University of Georgia Press, 2007), Chapter 1; and more generally, Maude Wahlman, *Signs and Symbols: African Images in African-American Quilts*, 2nd edition (New York: Tinwood Books, 2001). Catherine Holmes is currently completing a detailed study of this quilt as part of her doctoral dissertation. See '"God's Hand Staid the Stars": Reading the Second Bible Quilt of Harriet Powers', unpublished paper presented in the 'Object Centered History' seminar, 14th Berkshire Conference on the History of Women, Minneapolis, MN, June 2008.

112. Gladys-Marie Fry, *Stitched from the Past: Slave Quilts from the Antebellum South* (New York: Dutton Studio Books, 1990), p. 1.

113. Dorothy Osler, *North Country Quilts: Legend and Living Tradition* (Bowes Museum, Barnard Castle, 2000), p. 9.

114. Laura Jones, *Irish Patchwork* (Kilkenny, Ireland: Kilkenny Design Workshop, 1979). Quilting was taught to schoolgirls in many regions, including New England. See the extracts of the diary of Lucy Larcom, *A New England Girlhood* (1889) in Mirra Bank, *Anonymous Was a Woman* (New York: St. Martin's Press, 1979), p. 20.

115. Osler, *North Country Quilts*, p. 27.

116. Osler, *North Country Quilts*, pp. 5, 8–9; *Liverpool Mercury*, 5 December 1834; *The Manchester Times and Gazette*, 3 April 1841; *The Preston Guardian*, 7 April 1855; *The Leeds Mercury*, 20 August 1869; *The Leeds Mercury*, 12 July 1876; *Liverpool Mercury*, 14 September 1878.

117. Mary Agnes FitzGibbon, *A Trip to Manitoba* (London: Richard Bentley and Son, 1880), pp. 89–90.

118. 'The Patchwork Quilt', in Benita Eisler (ed.), *The Lowell Offering: Writings by New England Mill Women 1840–1845* (New York: W. W. Norton, 1977), p. 153.

119. Quilting Practice Research Project, Department of Human Ecology, University of Alberta, July 2007. My thanks to Elysia Donald for her assistance.

120. For the interview with Loretta Pettway (b. 1942), see John Beardsley, William Arnett, Paul Arnett and Jane Livingston, *Gee's Bend, The Women and Their Quilts* (Atlanta, GA: Tinwood Books, 2002), p. 80.

121. For an example of the unique results of necessity and industry, see *Gee's Bend, The Women and Their Quilts*. And for another description of a quilt made by Allie Pettway, see Christa C. Mayer Thurman and Jessica Batty, 'Two-Sided Bedcover', *Art Institute of Chicago Museum Studies*, 29(2) (2003): 30–31.

122. Laurel Thatcher Ulrich, *Age of Homespun: Objects and Stories in the Creation of an American Myth* (New York: Vintage Books, 2001), p. 414.

123. David Vaisey (ed.), *The Diary of Thomas Turner 1754–1765* (Oxford: Oxford University Press, 1985), p. 9.

124. 10 July 1765, ref. tl7650710-26, Old Bailey Online, http://www.oldbaileyonline.org/, accessed 4 October 2007.

125. Jennie Chinn, 'African American Quiltmaking Traditions: Some Assumptions Reviewed', in Barbara Brackman, *Kansas Quilts and Quilters* (Lawrence, KS: University Press of Kansas, 1993), pp. 157–75; Nancy Callahan, *The Freedom Quilting Bee* (Tuscaloosa, AL: University of Alabama Press, 1987).

126. Interview in 2007 with Ruby Sills. Quilting Practice Research Project, Department of Human Ecology, University of Alberta.

127. Interview in 2007 with Ada Moyles, born in Newfoundland and quilting for thirty years. Quilting Practice Research Project, Department of Human Ecology, University of Alberta.

6. AFTERWORD

1. Paul Pickering, 'Class Without Words: Symbolic Communication in the Chartist Movement', *Past and Present* 112 (1986): 160.

2. 'Whitsuntide Holiday', Men's Clothes, Box 2 (12); 'John Heydon, Woollen Draper, Man's-Mercer, Tailor', Men's Clothes, Box 1 (58); 'B. Johnson & Co., Temple of Fashion', Men's Clothes, Box 4 (12); 'The minion of the millions', Men's Clothes, Box 4 (23); John Johnson Collection, Bodleian Library. Moses & Son had also set up shop in Melbourne Australia by 1851.

3. 'Fustian Jackets', *Punch*, or the *London Charivari* (1841), p. 74.

4. *The Northern Star and Leeds General Advertiser* (Leeds, England), 6 February 1841, 10 July 1841.

5. *Liverpool Mercury*, 29 October 1841. This usage was widely employed in North America as well during the nineteenth century. See references to *The Globe* (Washington, DC) Thursday, 18 October 1832, issue 109, col. F; *The New York Herald* (New York, NY) Tuesday, 11 January 1848, col. B.

6. Pickering, 'Class Without Words', p. 155.

7. Quoted in Pickering, 'Class Without Words', p. 161.

8. *Manchester Times*, 11 January 1851.

9. *Manchester Times*, 3 May 1851.

10. *Reynold's Newspaper*, 16 February 1851.

11. The fustian twill cloth called jean was given that name in English from the port of Genoa, a major source of supply for fustian fabrics in the early modern period. Similarly, the town of Nîmes in France is associated with the English term 'denim', coming from the phrase *de Nîmes*, 'from Nîmes'.

12. Freeman Hunt, *The Merchants' Magazine and Commercial Review*, vol. 22 (New York, 1850), pp. 234–7.

13. *The Boston Daily Atlas* (Boston, MA), Thursday, 11 November 1852, issue 114, col. H. The Montgomery Ward & Co. catalogue listed 'Kentucky Jeans' in 1895 and jeans and jean fabric with this designation continue to be marketed today regionally. *Montgomery Ward & Co. Catalogue & Buyers' Guide 1895* (reprinted New York: Skyhorse Publishing, 2008), p. 31, col. A.

14. *The Ripley Bee* (Ripley, OH), 25 September 1867, issue 5, col. A.

15. Hambleton Tapp and James C. Klotter, *Kentucky: Decades of Discord, 1865–1900* (Frankfort, KY: Kentucky Historical Society, 1977), p. 68.

16. *St. Louis Globe-Democrat* (St Louis, MO), Sunday, 23 April 1876, p. 7, issue 340, col. B.

17. *St. Louis Globe-Democrat* (St Louis, MO), Monday, 25 September 1876, p. 4, issue 128, col. A.

18. William Wesley Woollen, *Biographical and Historical Sketches of Early Indiana* (Indianapolis: Hammond & Co., 1883), pp. 147–60.

19. James Sullivan, *Jeans: A Cultural History of an American Icon* (New York: Gotham Books, 2006), pp. 29–30.

20. The recovering of the history of the Great Western Garment Company has been spearheaded by Catherine C. Cole. For a virtual exhibition of GWG, see http://www.royalalbertamuseum.ca/virtualExhibit/GWG/.

21. Beverly Gordon, 'American Denim: Blue Jeans and their Multiple Layers of Meaning', in Patricia A. Cunningham and Susan Voso Lab (eds), *Dress and Popular Culture* (Madison: University of Wisconsin Press, 1991), pp. 31–2; Sullivan, *Jeans*, pp. 50–55, 73–4. For an example of the marketing of the West see, for example, Colleen Skidmore, *This Wild Spirit: Women in the Rocky Mountains of Canada* (Edmonton, AB: University of Alberta Press, 2006); Ian MacLaren (ed.), *Culturing Wilderness in Jasper National Park: Studies in Two Centuries of Human History in the Upper Athabasca River Watershed* (Edmonton: University of Alberta Press, 2007).

22. See, for example, Fiona Anderson, 'This Sporting Cloth: Tweed, Gender and Fashion 1860–1900', *Textile History* 37(2) (2006): 166–86; Lou Taylor, '"To Attract the Attention of Fishes as Little as Possible": An Object-Led Discussion of Three Garments for Country Wear for Women, Made of Scottish Woollen Cloth … 1883–1908', *Textile History* 38(1) (2007): 92–105.

23. Regina Lee Blaszczyk, *American Consumer Society, 1865–2005: From Hearth to HDTV* (Wheeling, IL: Harlan Davidson, 2009), p. 95.

24. Sullivan, *Jeans*, pp. 77–8.

25. Virgil Henry, 'Orland Park High Handles a Problem: Should High-School Girls Wear Blue-Jeans to School?', *The Clearing House* 27(2) (1952): 107.

26. Blaszczyk, *American Consumer Society*, p. 219.

27. Willard Wesley Cochrane, *The Development of American Agriculture: An Historical Analysis* (Minneapolis: University of Minnesota Press, 1993), p. 126.
28. Sullivan, *Jeans*, p. 109.
29. Harriet Sigerman (ed.), *The Columbia Documentary History of American Women Since 1941* (New York: Columbia University Press, 2003), p. 285.
30. Quoted in Gordon, 'American Denim', p. 34.
31. Christopher Neidhart, *Russia's Carnival: The Smells, Sights, and Sounds of Transition* (Lanham, ML: Rowman & Littlefield, 2003), p. 34.
32. Natalya Chernyshova, '"Even the Most Backward Segments of Society Have Put on Jeans": Consumption and Social Status Under Late Soviet Socialism, 1964–1985', unpublished paper presented at the 'Seventh European Social Science History Conference', Lisbon, 2008.
33. Valeria Manzano, 'The Blue Jean Generation: Youth, Gender, and Sexuality in Buenos Aires, 1958–1975', *Journal of Social History* 42(3) (2009): 660.
34. Manzano, 'Blue Jean Generation', p. 662.
35. Manzano, 'Blue Jean Generation', p. 657.
36. Manzano, 'Blue Jean Generation', pp. 657–76.
37. Emilia Margarida Marques, 'Material Culture and Social Conflict: Distinction and Counter-Distinction in the Portuguese Carnation Revolution', unpublished paper presented at the 'Seventh European Social Science History Conference', Lisbon, 2008.
38. Illustrated in the exhibition catalogue *Stories of Jeans* (Paris: Musée de la Mode et du Costume, 1994).
39. For a detailed contemporary investigation of denim politics, see Rachel Louise Snyder, *Fugitive Denim: A Moving Story of People and Pants in the Borderless World of Global Trade* (New York: W. W. Norton & Co. Ltd., 2008).

SELECTED BIBLIOGRAPHY

Abu Lughod, Janet (1989), *Before European Hegemony: The World System A.D. 1250–1350*, New York: Oxford University Press.

Bailey, Ronald (1994), 'The Other Side of Slavery: Black Labor, Cotton, and Textile Industrialization in Great Britain and the United States', *Agricultural History*, 68: 35–50.

Baker, G. P. (1921), *Calico Printing and Painting in the East Indies in the XVIIth and XVIIIth Centuries*, London: Edward Arnold.

Baptist, Edward (2002), *Creating an Old South*, Chapel Hill, NC: University of North Carolina Press.

Barnes, Ruth (1997), *Indian Block-Printed Textiles in Egypt: The Newberry Collection in the Ashmolean Museum, Oxford*, Oxford: Clarendon Press, vols. I and II.

Beckert, Sven (2004), 'Emancipation and Empire: Reconstructing the Worldwide Web of Cotton Production in the Age of the American Civil War', *American Historical Review*, 109: 1405–38.

Beckert, Sven (2007), 'Reconstructing the Empire of Cotton: A Global Story', in Manisha Sinha and Penny Marie Von Eschen (eds), *Contested Democracy: Freedom, Race, and Power in American History*, New York: Columbia University Press.

Beer, Alice Baldwin (1970), *Trade Goods: A Study of Indian Chintz in the Collection of the Cooper-Hewitt Museum of Decorative Arts and Design, Smithsonian Institution*, Washington, DC: Smithsonian Institution.

Berg, Maxine (1994), *The Age of Manufactures, 1700–1820*, 2nd edition, London: Routledge.

Berg, Maxine (2005), *Luxury and Pleasure in Eighteenth-Century Britain*, Oxford: Oxford University Press.

Berg, Maxine and Helen Clifford (eds) (1999), *Consumers and Luxury: Consumer Culture in Europe 1650–1850*, Manchester: Manchester University Press.

Berry, Helen (2002), 'Polite Consumption: Shopping in Eighteenth-Century England', *Transactions of the Royal Historical Society*, 12: 375–94.

Blaszczyk, Regina Lee (2009), *American Consumer Society, 1865–2005: From Hearth to HDTV*, Wheeling, IL: Harlan Davidson.

Blumer, Herbert (1969), 'Fashion: From Class Differentiation to Collective Selection', *Sociological Quarterly*, 10: 275–91.

Boyajian, James (1993), *Portuguese Trade in Asia under the Habsburgs, 1580–1640*, Baltimore: Johns Hopkins University Press.

Braudel, Fernand (1984), *Civilization and Capitalism 15ᵗʰ–18ᵗʰ Century: The Perspective of the World*, vol. 3, trans. Siân Reynolds, New York: Harper & Row.

Carus-Wilson, E. M. (1941), 'An Industrial Revolution of the Thirteenth Century', *Economic History Review*, 11 (1941): 41–60.

Chapman, Stanley D. and Serge Chassagne (1981), *European Textile Printers in the Eighteenth Century*, London: Heinemann Educational Books.

Chapman, S. D. (2002), *Hosiery and Knitwear: Four Centuries of Small-Scale Industry in Britain c.1589–2000*, Oxford: Oxford University Press.

Chaudhuri, K. N. (1965), *The English East India Company: The Study of an Early Joint-Stock Company, 1600–1640*, London: Frank Cass & Co. Ltd.

Chaudhuri, K. N. (1978), *The Trading World of Asia and the English East India Company, 1660–1760*, Cambridge: Cambridge University Press.

Chaudhuri, K. N. (1990), *Asia Before Europe: Economy and Civilisation of the Indian Ocean from the Rise of Islam to 1750*, Cambridge: Cambridge University Press.

Clark, Anna (1995), *The Struggle for the Breeches: Gender and the Making of the British Working Class*, Berkeley: University of California Press.

Coleman, D. C. (1973), 'Textile Growth', in N. B. Harte and K. G. Ponting (eds), *Textile History and Economic History: Essays in Honour of Miss Julia de Lacy Mann*, Manchester: Manchester University Press.

Connell, R. W. (1993), 'The Big Picture: Masculinity in Recent World History', *Theory and Society*, 22: 597–623.

Coquery, Natacha (2004), 'The Language of Success: Marketing and Distributing Semi-Luxury Goods in Eighteenth-Century Paris', *Journal of Design History*, 17: 71–89.

Cox, Nancy (2000), *The Complete Tradesman: A Study of Retailing, 1550–1820*, Aldershot: Ashgate.

Crill, Rosemary (2006), 'The Earliest Surviving Example? The Indian Embroideries at Hardwick Hall', in Rosemary Crill (ed.), *Textiles from India: The Global Trade*, Calcutta: Seagull Press.

Crowley, John E. (1999), 'The Sensibility of Comfort', *American Historical Review*, 104: 749–82.

Daunton, M. J. (1995), *Progress and Poverty: An Economic and Social History of Britain 1700–1850*, Oxford: Oxford University Press.

De Mendoça, Maria Jose (1978), 'Some Kinds of Indo-Portuguese Quilts in the Collection of the Museu de Arte Antiga' in *Embroidered Quilts from the Museu Nacional de Arte Antiga, Lisboa*, London: Kensington Palace.

De Roover, Raymond (1963), 'The Organization of Trade', in *Cambridge Economic History of Europe*, Cambridge: Cambridge University Press.

De Vries, Jan (2008), *The Industrious Revolution: Consumer Behavior and the Household Economy, 1650 to the Present*, Cambridge, MA: Cambridge University Press.

Dibbits, H. (1996), 'Between Society and Family Values: The Linen Cupboard in Early Modern Households', in A. Schuurman and P. Spierenburg (eds), *Private Domain, Public Enquiry: Families and Life-Styles in the Netherlands and Europe, 1550 to the Present*, Hilversum, Netherlands: Verloren.

Dublin, Thomas (1994), *Transforming Women's Work: New England Lives in the Industrial Revolution*, Ithaca, NY: Cornell University Press.

Du Mortier, Bianca M. (2000), *Aristocratic Attire: The Donation of the Six Family*, Amsterdam: Rijksmuseum.

DuPlessis, Robert S. (2009), 'Cottons Consumption in the Seventeenth- and Eighteenth-Century North Atlantic', in Giorgio Riello and Prasannan Parthasarathi (eds), *The Spinning World: A Global History of Cotton Textiles, 1200–1850*, Oxford: Oxford University Press.

Eaton, Linda (2007), *Quilts in the Material World: Selections from the Winterthur Collection*, New York: Abrams in association with The Henry Francis du Pont Winterthur Museum.

Eltis, David (2001), 'The Volume and Structure of the Transatlantic Slave Trade: A Reassessment', *William and Mary Quarterly*, 55: 17–46.

Eltis, David and Stanley Engerman (2000), 'The Importance of Slavery and the Slave Trade to Industrializing Britain', *Journal of Economic History*, 60: 123–44.

Engerman, Stanley (2000), 'Slavery and its Consequences for the South', in Stanley Engerman and Robert E. Gallman (eds), *The Cambridge Economic History of the United States*, vol. 1, Cambridge, MA: Cambridge University Press.

Epstein, Steven A. (1991), *Wage Labor and Guilds in Medieval Europe*, Chapel Hill, NC: University of North Carolina Press.

Edwards, Michael M. (1967), *The Growth of the British Cotton Trade, 1780–1815*, Manchester: Manchester University Press.

Farnie, D. A. and David Jeremy (eds) (2004), *The Fibre that Changed the World: The Cotton Industry in International Perspective 1600–1999*, Oxford: Oxford University Press.

Finn, Margot (2000), 'Men's Things: Masculine Possessions in the Consumer Revolution', *Social History* 25:2.

Fitton, R. S. (1989), *The Arkwrights: Spinners of Fortune*, Manchester: Manchester University Press.

Fontana, Giovanni Luigi and Giorgio Riello (2005), 'Seamless Industrialization: The Lanificio Rossi and the Modernization of the Wool Textile Industry in Nineteenth-Century Italy', *Textile History*, 36: 168–95.

Fortune, Brandon Brame (2002), 'Studious Men Are Always Painted in Gowns', *Dress*, 29: 27–41.

Fry, Gladys-Marie (1990), *Stitched from the Past: Slave Quilts from the Ante-Bellum South*, New York: Dutton Studio Books.

Gittinger, Mattiebelle (1982), *Master Dyers to the World: Technique and Trade in Early Indian Dyed Cotton Textiles*, Washington, DC: The Textile Museum.

Goldthwaite, Richard (2009), *The Economy of Renaissance Florence*, Baltimore: Johns Hopkins University Press.

Gordon, Beverly (1991), 'American Denim: Blue Jeans and their Multiple Layers of Meaning' in Patricia A. Cunningham and Susan Voso Lab (eds), *Dress and Popular Culture*, Madison: University of Wisconsin Press.

Greenfield, Sidney M. (1969), 'Slavery and the Plantation in the New World: The Development and Diffusion of a Social Form', *Journal of Inter-American Studies*, 11: 44–57.

Griffiths, Trevor, Philip A. Hunt and Patrick O'Brien (1992), 'Inventive Activity in the British Textile Industry, 1700–1800', *Journal of Economic History*, 52: 881–906.

Guy, John (1998), *Woven Cargoes: Indian Textiles in the East*, London: Thames and Hudson.

Harte, N. B. (1973), 'The Rise of Protection and the English Linen Trade, 1690–1790' in N. B. Harte and K. G. Ponting (eds), *Textile History and Economic History: Essays in Honour of Miss Julia de Lacy Mann*, Manchester: Manchester University Press.

Harris, John (1996), 'Law, Espionage, and the Transfer of Technology from Eighteenth-Century Britain', in Robert Fox (ed.),

Technology Change: Methods and Themes in the History of Technology, Amsterdam: Harwood Academic Publishers.

Hoffman Berman, Constance (2007), 'Women's Work in Family, Village, and Town after 1000 CE: Contributions to Economic Growth?', *Journal of Women's History*, 19: 10–32.

Honeyman, Katrina (1982), *The Origins of Enterprise: Business Leadership in the Industrial Revolution*, Manchester: Manchester University Press.

Honeyman, Katrina (2007), *Child Workers in England, 1780–1820: Parish Apprentices and the Making of the Early Industrial Labour Force*, Aldershot: Ashgate Publishing.

Hood, Adrienne (2003), *The Weaver's Craft: Cloth, Commerce, and Industry in Early Pennsylvania*, Philadelphia: University of Pennsylvania Press.

Hood, Adrienne (2009), 'Cloth and Color: Fabrics in Chester County Quilts' in Catherine E. Hutchins (ed.), *Layers: Unfolding the Stories of Chester County Quilts*, Philadelphia: Pearl Pressman Liberty and Chester County Historical Society.

Hunt, Alan (1996), *Governance of the Consuming Passions: A History of Sumptuary Law*, Basingstoke: Macmillan.

Inikori, Joseph (1987), 'Slavery and the Development of Industrial Capitalism in England', in Barbara Solow and Stanley E. Engerman (eds), *British Capitalism and Caribbean Slavery: The Legacy of Eric Williams*, Cambridge: Cambridge University Press.

Irwin, John and Margaret Hall (1973), *Indian Embroideries: Historic Textiles of India at the Calico Museum*, Ahmedabad: Calico Museum of Textiles.

Jeremy, David (1981), *Transatlantic Industrial Revolution: The Diffusion of Textile Technologies Between Britain and America, 1790–1830s*, Cambridge, MA: Massachusetts Institute of Technology Press.

Jones, Ann Rosalind and Peter Stallybrass (2000), *Renaissance Clothing and the Materials of Memory*, Cambridge: Cambridge University Press.

Keller, Patricia (2009), 'Taking Inventory: Quilts and Quiltmaking in Chester County, Pennsylvania, 1725–1860', in Catherine E. Hutchins (ed.), *Layers: Unfolding the Stories of Chester County Quilts*, Philadelphia: Pearl Pressman Liberty and Chester County Historical Society.

Kovesi Killerby, Catherine (2002), *Sumptuary Law in Italy, 1200–1500*, Oxford: Oxford University Press.

Kriger, Colleen (2009), '"Guinea Cloth": Production and Consumption of Cotton Textiles in West Africa Before and During the Atlantic Slave Trade', in Giorgio Riello and Prasannan Parthasarathi (eds), *The Spinning World: A Global History of Cotton Textiles, 1200–1850*, Oxford: Oxford University Press.

Lakwete, Angela (2003), *Inventing the Cotton Gin: Machine and Myth in Antebellum America*, Baltimore: Johns Hopkins University Press.

Lemire, Beverly (1991), *Fashion's Favourite: The Cotton Trade and the Consumer in Britain, 1660–1800*, Oxford: Oxford University Press.

Lemire, Beverly (1997), *Dress, Culture and Commerce: The English Clothing Trade Before the Factory*, Basingstoke: Macmillan.

Lemire, Beverly (2003), 'Domesticating the Exotic: Floral Culture and the East India Calico Trade with England, c.1600–1800', *Textile: The Journal of Cloth and Culture*, 1: 65–85.

Lemire, Beverly (ed.) (2009), *The British Cotton Trade*, London: Pickering & Chatto, vols. 1–4.

Lemire, Beverly and Giorgio Riello (2008), 'East and West: Textiles and Fashion in Early Modern Europe', *Journal of Social History*, 41(4): 887–916.

Lipovetsky, Gilles (1994), *The Empire of Fashion: Dressing Modern Democracy*, trans. Catherine Porter, Princeton: Princeton University Press.

Manzano, Valeria (2009), 'The Blue Jean Generation: Youth, Gender, and Sexuality in Buenos Aires, 1958–1975', *Journal of Social History* 42: 657–76.

Mazzaoui, Maureen F. (1981), *The Italian Cotton Industry in the Later Middle Ages*, Cambridge: Cambridge University Press.

McKendrick, Neil, John Brewer and J. H. Plumb (1983), *The Birth of a Consumer Society: The Commercialization of Eighteenth-Century England*, London: Hutchinson & Co.

Mendelson, Sara and Patricia Crawford (2000), *Women in Early Modern England*, Oxford: Oxford University Press.

O'Brien, Patrick (2009), 'The Geopolitics of Global Industry: Eurasian Divergence and the Mechanization of Cotton Textile Production in England', in Giorgio Riello and Prasannan Parthasarathi (eds), *The Spinning World: A Global History of Cotton Textiles, 1200–1850*, Oxford: Oxford University Press.

O'Brien, Patrick, T. Griffiths and P. Hunt (1991), 'Political Components of the Industrial Revolution: Parliament and the English Cotton Textile Industry, 1660–1774', *Economic History Review*, 44: 395–423.

Overton, Mark, Jane Whittle, Darron Dean and Andrew Hann (2004), *Production and Consumption in English Households, 1600–1750*, London: Routledge.

Parthasarathi, Prasannan and Ian Wendt (2009), 'Decline in Three Keys: Indian Cotton Manufacturing from the Late Eighteenth Century', in Giorgio Riello and Prasannan Parthasarathi (eds), *The Spinning World: A Global History of Cotton Textiles, 1200–1850*, Oxford: Oxford University Press.

Pickering, Paul (1986), 'Class with Words: Symbolic Communication in the Chartist Movement', *Past and Present*, 112: 144–62.

Pinchbeck, Ivy (1981 [1930]), *Women Workers and the Industrial Revolution 1750–1850*, London: Virago Books.

Randall, Adrian and A. Charlesworth (eds.,) (1999), *Moral Economy and Popular Protest: Crowds, Conflict and Authority*, New York: St Martin's Press, 1999.

Raveux, Olivier (2005), 'Space and Technologies in the Cotton Industry in the Seventeenth and Eighteenth Centuries: The Example of Printed Calicoes in Marseilles', *Textile History*, 36(2): 131–45.

Riello, Giorgio (2010), 'Fabricating the Domestic: The Material Culture of Textiles and Social Life of the Home in Early Modern Europe' in Beverly Lemire (ed.), *The Force of Fashion in Politics and Society: Global Perspectives from Early Modern to Contemporary Times*, Aldershot: Ashgate.

Riello, Giorgio and Prasannan Parthasarathi (eds) (2009), *The Spinning World: A Global History of Cotton Textiles, 1200–1850*, Oxford: Oxford University Press.

Roche, Daniel (1989), *The Culture of Clothing: Dress and Fashion in the Ancient Régime*, trans. Jean Birrell, Cambridge: Cambridge University Press.

Sanderson, Elizabeth (1996), *Women and Work in Eighteenth-Century Edinburgh*, Basingstoke: Macmillan.

Shah, Deepika (2005), *Masters of the Cloth: Indian Textiles Traded to Distant Shores*, New Delhi: Garden Silk Mills.

Shammas, Carole (1994), 'The Decline of Textile Prices in England and British America

Prior to Industrialization', *Economic History Review*, 57: 483–507.

Simons, Walter (2001), *Cities of Ladies: Beguine Communities in the Medieval Low Countries, 1200–1565*, Philadelphia: University of Pennsylvania Press.

Smart Martin, Ann (2008), *Buying into the World of Goods: Early Consumers in Backcountry Virginia*, Baltimore: Johns Hopkins University Press.

Stobart, Jon (2004), *The First Industrial Region: North-West England, c.1700–1760*, Manchester: Manchester University Press.

Styles, John (2006), 'Lodging at the Old Bailey. Lodgings and their Furnishing in Eighteenth-Century London', in John Styles and Amanda Vickery (eds), *Gender, Taste and Material Culture in Britain and North America*, New Haven: Yale Center for British Art.

Sugihara, Kaoru (2009), 'The Resurgence of Intra-Asian Trade, 1800–1850', in Giorgio Riello and Roy Tirthankar (eds), *How India Clothes the World: The World of South Asian Textiles, 1500–1850*, Leiden: Brill.

Thirsk, Joan (1973), 'The Fantastical Folly of Fashion: The English Stocking Knitting Industry, 1500–1700', in N. B. Harte and K. G. Ponting (eds), *Textile History and Economic History: Essays in Honour of Miss Julia de Lacy Mann*, Manchester: Manchester University Press.

Thirsk, Joan (1978), *Economic Policy and Projects: The Development of a Consumer Society in Early Modern England*, Oxford: Clarendon Press.

Thomis, Malcolm I. (1970), *The Luddites: Machine-Breaking in Regency England*, Newton Abbot: David & Charles.

Thompson, E. P. (1963), *The Making of the English Working Class*, Harmondsworth: Penguin Books.

Thomson, K. J. (2003), 'Transferring the Spinning Jenny to Barcelona: An Apprenticeship in the Technology of the Industrial Revolution', *Textile History*, 34: 21–46

Ulrich, Laurel Thatcher (2001), *Age of Homespun: Objects and Stories in the Creation of an American Myth*, New York: Vintage Books.

Vicente, Marta V. (2007), *Clothing the Spanish Empire: Families and the Calico Trade in the Atlantic World, 1700–1815*, Basingstoke: Palgrave.

Wadsworth, A. P. and Julia de Lacy Mann (1931), *The Cotton Trade and Industrial Lancashire, 1600–1780*, Manchester: Manchester University Press.

Walsh, Claire (2006), 'Shops, Shopping and the Art of Decision-Making in Eighteenth-Century England', in John Styles and Amanda Vickery (eds), *Gender, Taste, and Material Culture in Britain and North America, 1700–1830*, New Haven: Yale University Press.

Weatherill, Lorna (1988), *Consumer Behaviour and Material Culture in Britain, 1660–1760*, London: Routledge.

White, Shane and Graham White (1995), 'Slave Clothing and African-American Culture in the Eighteenth and Nineteenth Centuries', *Past and Present*, 148: 149–86.

Wigston Smith, Chloe (2007), '"Calico Madams": Servants, Consumption, and the Calico Crisis', *Eighteenth-Century Life*, 31: 29–55.

Wright, Gavin (2003), 'Slavery and American Agricultural History', *Agricultural History*, 77: 527–52.

ILLUSTRATIONS CREDITS

COLOUR PLATES

Plate 1 Courtesy of the Victoria and Albert Museum, London. IS. 94-1993.

Plate 2 Courtesy of the Victoria and Albert Museum, London. IM. 49-1919.

Plate 3 Courtesy of the Victoria and Albert Museum, London. IS. 29-1889.

Plate 4 Philadelphia Museum of Art, 1996.107.3. Gift of the Friends of the Philadelphia Museum of Art.

Plate 5 Collection American Folk Art Museum, New York. Promised gift of Ralph Esmerian. P.1.2001.292. Photo © John Bigelow Taylor, New York.

Plate 6 Collection American Folk Art Museum, New York. Promised gift of Ralph Esmerian. P1.2001.290. Photo © John Bigelow Taylor, New York.

Plate 7 Nordiska Museet, 183.511, Stockholm.

Plate 8 Rijksmuseum, Amsterdam. BK-NM-8247.

Plate 9 © National Portrait Gallery, London. NPG 1920.

Plate 10 Courtesy of the Victoria and Albert Museum, London. IS.-14-1950.

Plate 11 Courtesy of the Victoria and Albert Museum, London. T.274 & A-1967.

Plate 12 Courtesy of the Lewis Walpole Library, Yale University. Call number 784.14.2. Image ID lwlpr05402.

Plate 13 Courtesy of the Victoria and Albert Museum, London. T. 438-1882.

Plate 14 Photograph © 2011, Museum of Fine Arts, Boston. 50.3408.

Plate 15 Photograph © 2011, Museum of Fine Arts, Boston. 50.3224.

Plate 16 Rijksmuseum, Amsterdam. Inv. BK-14656.

Plate 17 Los Angeles County Museum, Los Angeles. Gift of Mrs. Henry Salvatori (M. 73.27.8). Digital Image © 2009 Museum Associates/LACMA/Art Resource, NY.

Plate 18 Courtesy of the Victoria and Albert Museum, London. CIRC. 465-1912.

Plate 19 Frans Hals Museum, Haarlem. Purchased with the support of the Rembrandt Society.

Plate 20 Courtesy of the Victoria and Albert Museum, London. T. 417-1971.

Plate 21 Clothing and Textile Collection, Department of Human Ecology, University of Alberta, Canada. 2005.18.1.

Plate 22 Photograph © 2011, Museum of Fine Arts, Boston. 64.619.

Plate 23 Rosenberg Quilt Collection, Department of Human Ecology, University of Alberta, Canada. 2006.19.154.

Plate 24 Rosenberg Quilt Collection, Department of Human Ecology, University of Alberta, Canada. 2006.19.413.

Plate 25 Clothing and Textile Collection, Department of Human Ecology, University of Alberta, Canada. 1995.14.1.

FIGURES

Fig. 2.1 Courtesy of the University of Hawai'i Press and Philippe Beaujard, 'The Indian Ocean in Eurasian and African World-Systems Before the Sixteenth Century', *Journal of World History*, 16(4) (2005): 425.

Fig. 2.2 The British Library. Add. Or. 5110. © All rights reserved, the British Library Board. Licence number: UNIALB07.

Fig. 2.3 Courtesy of the Victoria and Albert Museum, London. IS. 96-1993.

Fig. 2.4 Ashmolean Museum, Oxford. EA1990.161.

Fig. 2.5 Courtesy of the University of Hawai'i Press and Philippe Beaujard, 'The Indian Ocean in Eurasian and African World-Systems Before the Sixteenth Century', *Journal of World History*, 16(4) (2005): 428.

Fig. 2.6 Courtesy of the Victoria and Albert Museum, London. IS. 64-1972.

Fig. 2.7 Collection American Folk Art Museum, New York. Gift of Virginia Esmerian. 1995.32.2.

Fig. 3.1 Guildhall Library Print Room, 29289. City of London, London Metropolitan Archives.

Fig. 3.2 Courtesy of The Lewis Walpole Library, Yale University. Call number 807.1.13, image number lwlpr10809.

Fig. 3.3 Reproduced in E. Lipson, *The History of the Woollen and Worsted Industries* (1921, reissued Frank Cass & Co., 1965). Frontispiece.

Fig. 3.4 Courtesy of the Victoria and Albert Museum, London. T. 879-1919.

Fig. 3.5 John Johnson Collection, Trades and Professions, Box 4, No. 35. Bodleian Library, Oxford.

Fig. 4.1 Photograph © 2011, Museum of Fine Arts, Boston.

Fig. 4.2 The Metropolitan Museum of Art, New York (1997.117.10). Bequest of Lore Heinemann, in memory of her husband, Dr Rudolf J. Heinemann, 1996. Image copyright © The Metropolitan Museum of Art/Art Resource, NY.

Fig. 4.3 Michael M. Edwards, *The Growth of the British Cotton Trade, 1780–1815* (Manchester: Manchester University Press, 1968), p. 84.

Fig. 4.4 Manchester Archives and Local Studies, Manchester, UK.

Fig. 4.5 Library of Congress Prints and Photographs Division, Washington, DC. LC-USZC4-7992.

Fig. 4.6 Library of Congress Prints and Photographs Division, Washington, DC. LC-USZ62-68073.

Fig. 4.7 Library of Congress Prints and Photographs Division, Washington, DC. LC-USZ62-83675.

Fig. 4.8 Manchester Local Image Collection, Manchester Archives and Local Studies, Manchester, UK.

Fig. 5.1 Costume and Textile Department, Los Angeles County Museum of Art. M.86.134.21. Digital Image © 2009 Museum Associates/LACMA/Art Resource, NY.

Fig. 5.2 Rosenberg Quilt Collection, Department of Human Ecology, University of Alberta, Canada. 2006.19.357b.

Fig. 5.3 Rosenberg Quilt Collection, Department of Human Ecology, University of Alberta, Canada. 2006.19.282.

Fig. 5.4 Library of Congress Prints and Photographs Division, Washington, DC. LC-USZ62-53633.

Fig. 6.1 Library of Congress Prints and Photographs Division, Washington, DC. LC-USZ62-56423.

INDEX

Note: Numbers in **bold** indicate illustrations